T0329930

Gendered Lives

Gendered Lives

Gender Inequalities in Production and Reproduction

Edited by

Jacqueline Scott

Professor of Empirical Sociology, University of Cambridge, UK

Shirley Dex

Emeritus Professor of Longitudinal Social Research in Education, Centre for Longitudinal Studies, Institute of Education, University of London, UK

Anke C. Plagnol

Postdoctoral Research Fellow, University of Cambridge, UK

Edward Elgar

Cheltenham, UK • Northampton, MA, USA

Published by
Edward Elgar Publishing Limited
The Lypiatts
15 Lansdown Road
Cheltenham
Glos GL50 2JA
UK

Edward Elgar Publishing, Inc.
William Pratt House
9 Dewey Court
Northampton
Massachusetts 01060
USA

A catalogue record for this book
is available from the British Library

Library of Congress Control Number: 2012930577

ISBN 978 1 84980 626 8 (cased)

Typeset by Servis Filmsetting Ltd, Stockport, Cheshire
Printed and bound by MPG Books Group, UK

Contents

List of contributors   vii
Acknowledgements   xiv

Introduction: gender inequalities in production and reproduction   1
Jacqueline Scott, Shirley Dex, Heather Joshi and Anke C. Plagnol

PART I   GENDERED LIVES UNFOLDING ACROSS TIME

1   The childhood origins of adult socio-economic disadvantage:
    do cohort and gender matter?   23
    John Hobcraft and Wendy Sigle-Rushton

2   Changing career trajectories of women and men across time   48
    Erzsebet Bukodi, Shirley Dex and Heather Joshi

3   Halfway to gender equality in paid and unpaid work?
    Evidence from the multinational time-use study   74
    Jonathan Gershuny and Man Yee Kan

PART II   GENDER INEQUALITIES IN THE HOUSEHOLD
          AND WORKPLACE

4   Financial togetherness and autonomy within couples   97
    *Fran Bennett, Jerome De Henau, Susan Himmelweit and
    Sirin Sung*

5   Global flows and local labour markets: precarious
    employment and migrant workers in the UK   123
    Linda McDowell, Adina Batnitzky and Sarah Dyer

PART III   GENDER INEQUALITIES IN A CHANGING
           WORLD

6   Equality law and the limits of the 'business case' for addressing
    gender inequalities   153
    Colm McLaughlin and Simon Deakin

7   Work–family conflict and well-being in Northern Europe   174
    Jacqueline Scott and Anke C. Plagnol

8   Gender equality and work–family balance in a cross-national
    perspective   206
    Jane Lewis

    Index   225

Contributors

Adina Batnitzky is an Assistant Professor in the Department of Sociology at the University of San Diego (USD). Prior to coming to USD, Adina was a tenure-track assistant professor at the University of Texas at Austin in the Department of Geography and the Environment, and a faculty affiliate of the Population Research Center and the Center for Middle Eastern Studies. From 2005 to 2008, she was a Postdoctoral Research Fellow in the School of Geography at the University of Oxford. She holds a BA with honours from Barnard College, Columbia University, and an MA and a PhD in Sociology from Brown University, where she was a trainee in demography at the Population Studies Training Center. Her past and current research includes work on Arab American health disparities; women's health and household labour in Morocco; the built environment and obesity in India; and embodied labour in London's globalized service sector.

Fran Bennett is a Senior Research Fellow (half-time) at the Oxford Institute of Social Policy. She is also an independent consultant and has written extensively on social policy issues for the UK government, non-governmental organisations (NGOs) and others. With Professor Jonathan Bradshaw, she is the UK independent expert on social inclusion for the European Commission. She is joint editor of the online Social Policy Digest for the *Journal of Social Policy* and co-editor of the *Journal of Poverty and Social Justice*. She has been director of the Child Poverty Action Group; more recently, she was a policy adviser on UK and EU poverty issues for Oxfam GB. She has a particular interest in social security policy, gender issues, poverty, income distribution and participation.

Erzsebet Bukodi is University Lecturer in Quantitative Social Policy in the Department of Social Policy and Intervention at the University of Oxford. She is also a Fellow of Nuffield College, Oxford. She has a DPhil in Sociology from Corvinus University of Economics, Budapest and was a Max Weber Postdoctoral Fellow at the European University Institute, Florence. She previously worked as a research director of the National Child Development Study and the 1970 British Cohort Study in the Centre for Longitudinal Studies at the Institute of Education, University of London. She was a senior research fellow in the Department of Sociology,

Bamberg University, and was Head of Section of social stratification in the Department of Social Statistics of the Hungarian Central Statistical Office, Budapest. Her research interests involve educational inequalities, trends in intergenerational and intragenerational mobility, different aspects of life-course analysis, partnership behaviour and gender differences in the labour market.

Simon Deakin is Professor of Law at the Faculty of Law, University of Cambridge, and a Fellow of Peterhouse. He is a programme director in the Cambridge Centre for Business Research and an associate faculty member of the Judge Business School. He has a BA and a PhD in Law from the University of Cambridge. He has held visiting professorships at the European University Institute, Columbia University, and Doshisha University. He is the editor of the *Industrial Law Journal* and a member of the editorial board of the *Cambridge Journal of Economics*. He has researched widely on labour law and corporate governance issues, from the perspectives of the economics of law and empirical legal studies. His books include *The Law of the Labour Market* (2005, with Frank Wilkinson) and *Capacitas: Contract Law and the Institutional Foundations of the Market* (edited with Alain Supiot). He was elected a Fellow of the British Academy in 2005.

Jerome De Henau is a Lecturer in Economics at the Open University, Milton Keynes. He is a co-investigator on an Economic and Social Research Council (ESRC)-funded research project that aims to understand the factors that influence the entitlements of individuals to household resources. Previously, he was a research fellow at the Open University and a teaching assistant at the Université Libre de Bruxelles. He holds an MSc degree (DEA) in Management and a PhD in Management and Applied Economics from Université Libre de Bruxelles (ULB) – Solvay Business School. His main research interests involve gender, family policies, tax and benefit policies, labour and household economics. He is also a member of the International Association for Feminist Economics and of the Women's Budget Group.

Shirley Dex is Emeritus Professor of Longitudinal Social Research in Education, University of London. She has previously held posts at the Judge Business School, University of Cambridge, the Institute for Social and Economic Research at the University of Essex and the Economics Department at the University of Keele. From 1998 to 2003 she was Research Adviser to the Joseph Rowntree Foundation's Work and Family Life Programme. She has published many books and articles on women's employment and cross-national comparative research, equal opportunities, families and work, ethnic minorities and employment, flexible working arrangements in organisations, work and care and family policy. She is continuing to work in the Department for Education's Childhood Wellbeing Research Centre, based in the Institute of Education as well as being involved in research in the Centre for Longitudinal Studies.

Sarah Dyer is a Senior Teaching Fellow in the School of Geography at the University of Exeter. She is Treasurer of the Royal Geographical Society's History and Philosophy of Geography Research Group (HPGRG) and a co-ordinator of the Geography, Science and Politics Research Network. She has previously worked as a lecturer at King's College, London, and was a lecturer in Human Geography at the University of Oxford from 2006 to 2008. She is a human geographer with research interests in science and healthcare. Her current research examines the mechanisms structuring scientific labour markets in a clustered knowledge economy and the narratives of work, identity, and ethics of scientists working in such labour markets along with those who have left them. Her recent work includes research on migration to work in London's healthcare and hospitality sectors, in collaboration with Linda McDowell and Adina Batnitzky.

Jonathan Gershuny is a University Professor of Economic Sociology and a Senior Research Fellow of Nuffield College, University of Oxford. He is the Director of the ESRC-funded Centre for Time Use Research, and is a former Head of the Oxford Sociology Department. He was the Director of the Institute for Social and Economic Research at the University of Essex, and the Principal Investigator of the British Household Panel Study, and continues as Principal Investigator of the Multinational Time Use Study. He has been a Fellow of the British Academy since 2002. He won the Silver Medal of the Market Research Society in 1986. In his research he uses narrative data-sets (life and work histories, time-use diaries) to investigate interconnections among household organisation (the division of domestic labour and the distribution of leisure), labour force participation, and family formation and dissolution, with the aim of providing improved accounts of socio-economic structure and of processes of social change.

Susan Himmelweit is a Professor of Economics at the Faculty of Social Sciences, Open University. Her research is in the field of the economics of the household, the economics of caring, feminist economics and the gender implications of economic policy, and she is the Principal Investigator for the ESRC-funded project 'Gender and intra-household entitlements. A cross-national longitudinal analysis'. She is on the editorial board of *Women, Politics and Policy* and an Associate Editor of the journal

Feminist Economics of which she was joint guest editor of special issues on Lone Mothers (2004) and Children and Family Policy (2000). She is a member and past chair of the UK Women's Budget Group, a think tank monitoring and advising government on the gender aspects of social and economic policy, for whom she has helped carry out gender analysis of the UK's government's budgets and spending reviews. She was President of the International Association for Feminist Economics in 2009.

John Hobcraft is Professor of Demography and Social Policy in the Department of Social Policy and Social Work at the University of York. He plays an active role in shaping the design and analysis of prospective cohort and panel studies. This includes chairing the Consortium Board and Network of National Focal Points for the Generation and Gender Programme, being Vice-Chair of the Governing Board for Understanding Society, and chairing the Scientific Committee for the British Birth Cohort Studies. He has become a leading proponent of the inclusion of biomarkers in prospective surveys. His recent research explores the intergenerational and life-course pathways to adult social exclusion, human reproductive and partnership behaviour, and the role of gender and generations in human behaviour. Recent work has examined health outcomes, becoming a parent, resilience, and the links between depression and divorce. Currently, he is exploring pathways to educational, cognitive and behavioural performance for children using the Millennium Cohort Study. He is also working on gene–environment interactions and a pilot epigenetic study with the US Fragile Families Study.

Heather Joshi is Emeritus Professor of Economic and Developmental Demography at the Institute of Education, University of London. She was Director of the UK Millennium Cohort Study from 2000 to 2011. She was also the Director of the Centre for Longitudinal Studies from 2003 to 2010, and its Deputy Director from 1994. She is the Co-Chair of the European Child Cohort Network fostering international collaboration and comparison between cohort studies, and President of the Society for Lifecourse and Longitudinal Studies. Her own research at the intersection of economic and demographic issues has covered gender, family, the labour market, co-education, health inequalities, maternal employment and child development, migration and neighbourhood effects. She was one of the first economists to analyse the Women and Employment Survey in 1984 which opened a vein of research on women's lifetime incomes leading to the award of an OBE in 2002.

Man Yee Kan is a Research Councils UK Academic Fellow at the Department of Sociology, University of Oxford, and a Research Fellow at

St Hugh's College. Her main research project aims to investigate changes in working time patterns in Britain and France over the past four decades and the impacts of work schedules on the quality of family life. She previously held a British Academy Postdoctoral Fellowship and was a Senior Research Officer at the Institute for Social and Economic Research, University of Essex. She completed an MSc and a DPhil in Sociology at St Antony's College, Oxford. Her research interests include gender equality issues, the domestic division of labour, the interactions between the household and the labour market, working-time schedules and family time, and empirical and methodological topics in time-use research.

Jane Lewis is Professor of Social Policy at the London School of Economics and Political Science. She was previously the Barnett Professor of Social Policy at the University of Oxford. She is a Fellow of the British Academy and of the Canadian Royal Society, and a founding fellow of the Academy of Social Sciences. She has long-standing interests in gender and family policies from a comparative perspective. Over the past decade, her research focused on lone parents, marriage and cohabitation, risk and intimate relationships, and work/family balance policies in England and Western Europe. Her latest book *Work–Family Balance, Gender and Policy* (2009) examines the three main components of work–family policy packages – childcare services, flexible working patterns and leaves from work in order to care – across EU15 member states.

Linda McDowell is Professor of Human Geography at the University of Oxford and a Professorial Fellow of St John's College, where she is also the director of the Research Centre. She has held lectureships at the Open and Cambridge Universities and chairs at the London School of Economics and University College London. She is interested in the connections between economic restructuring and divisions of labour in Great Britain since 1950 and in feminist theory and methodology. She was elected to a fellowship of the British Academy in 2008. Her most recent book is *Working Bodies* (Blackwell 2009).

Colm McLaughlin is a Lecturer in Industrial Relations and Human Resources at the Smurfit School of Business, University College Dublin. He is also a Research Associate of the Centre for Business Research at the University of Cambridge. Prior to joining UCD, Colm was a research fellow at the University of Cambridge and a lecturer in Management and Employment Relations at the University of Auckland, and has held management positions in local government and the hospitality sector. He graduated from the University of Auckland (BA and MComm) and holds a PhD from the University of Cambridge (Judge Business School). His research interests include: labour market protections and low-paid work; gender equality; corporate governance and reflexive regulation; the relationship between labour market institutions and economic performance; and comparative industrial relations.

Anke C. Plagnol is a Postdoctoral Research Fellow (Leverhulme Trust Early Career Fellowship and Isaac Newton Trust) in the Faculty of Human, Social and Political Science at the University of Cambridge and a Research Fellow of Darwin College, Cambridge. She was previously a Research Associate for the ESRC-funded Research Priority Network on Gender Inequalities in Production and Reproduction (GeNet), University of Cambridge. She holds a BA in European Economic Studies from the University of Bamberg, Germany, and an MA and PhD in Economics from the University of Southern California, USA. Her research interests include female labour-force participation, subjective well-being, life-course studies and applied microeconomics.

Jacqueline Scott is Professor of Empirical Sociology at the Faculty of Human, Social and Political Science at the University of Cambridge and a Fellow of Queens' College, Cambridge. She was the Director of the ESRC Research Priority Network on Gender Inequalities in Production and Reproduction, the largest research multidisciplinary network of its kind in the UK. Her former positions include Director of the Detroit Area Study, from 1989 to 1990, and Director of the ESRC Centre on Micro-Social Change at the University of Essex from 1990 to 1994, where she was responsible for the original design and implementation of the British Household Panel Study. She was also a Guest Professor at the Zentrum für Umfragen, Methoden und Analysen (ZUMA) in Mannheim, Germany. Her research interests focus on changing family and household structures, intergenerational relations, changing gender roles, and generational shifts in attitudes and behaviour across the life course.

Wendy Sigle-Rushton is a Reader in Gender and Family Studies at the London School of Economics and Political Science where she teaches a range of courses in Gender and Social Policy and convenes an MSc programme in Gender, Policy and Inequalities. She is also an Associate at the Centre for Analysis of Social Exclusion (CASE). She has published extensively on the relationship between family structure and the well-being of children and adults in the US and other industrialised countries. Ongoing work considers the interaction of family structure and ethnic status in the production of child health outcomes in the USA and the UK. She is also interested in issues surroundings men's unpaid work and care. Recent publications include an examination of the relationship between fathers' unpaid work and divorce in the UK, and an assessment of the gendered and classed incentive effects of recent changes to Swedish family policy.

Sirin Sung is a Lecturer in Social Policy in the School of Sociology, Social Policy and Social Work at Queen's University Belfast. She was involved in various research projects at the Manchester Business School, University of Manchester. Her research there mainly focused on gender and employment issues in England; gender inequalities in different sectors, the tension between providing and accessing childcare for childcare workers, and two-tier workforces in homecare and childcare. She was also involved in an ESRC-funded research project on 'Within household inequalities and public policy' at the Department of Social Policy and Social Work at the University of Oxford. She was awarded a Leverhulme Study Abroad Fellowship in 2010 – with a research focus on 'Gender and welfare state in the UK and US: work–family balance issues'. She holds an MA and a PhD degree from the University of Nottingham. Her main research interests focus on gender and social policy, gender and employment, work–life balance policies, care workforce, gender and benefits, and East Asian welfare states.

Acknowledgements

We gratefully acknowledge support for this research from a grant by the Economic and Social Research Council (RES-225-25-1001) which funded the ESRC Research Priority Network on Gender Inequalities.

Introduction: gender inequalities in production and reproduction

Jacqueline Scott, Shirley Dex, Heather Joshi and Anke C. Plagnol

How are gendered lives changing? This book examines not only how gender inequalities in contemporary societies are changing, but also how further change towards greater gender equality might be achieved. We focus on inequalities in productive and reproductive activities, as played out over time and in specific contexts. We examine how lives and structures are changing and how policy can intervene to promote further advances towards greater equality. We explore why changes in gender inequalities are so much faster and more consistent in some spheres and social groups than in others. In particular we investigate the dynamic processes that lead to and shape inequalities between adult men and women; the different patterns of resource allocation and constraints in reproductive and productive activities; and the reciprocal influences of changing lives and structures. We also consider how the time-processes involved in individual and institutional change can differ, for example if organisational inertia causes institutions to lag behind individual change.

Gender inequality is a well-worked field. However, the research presented in this book is both innovative and timely. It moves discussion forwards from misleading static and universal accounts to dynamic and contextualised ones. We use life-course perspectives and longitudinal accounts of resources and constraints to understand more of how the lives of women and men are changing. However, we push beyond the standard analysis of life-course stages. These have been depicted as a sequence of configurations of status in different life spheres – mainly education, work, family and welfare (for example, Heinz and Marshall 2003). In such accounts, the male life-course is conceptualised primarily in terms of occupational trajectories from education, through employment and into retirement, while the female life-course is viewed as being orientated around the family, with paid occupation as a secondary activity. Thus the traditional gender role division between men's production and women's reproduction is built into much of life-course analysis, which is unhelpful if we want to examine how the gendering of lives is changing.

In this book our focus is not only on the interplays between men's and women's life courses. We also examine how institutional structures help shape gendered lives. There has been a good deal of social theory that emphasises how individuals 'do gender', that is, adopt behaviour conforming to different expectations for men and women (McDowell 1992; Sullivan 2004; West and Zimmerman 1987). What is sometimes overlooked is that while interacting individuals are 'doing gender' institutions are doing gender as well (Kruger and Levy 2001). Institutional logics not only include the labour market, the family and their linkages, but also the arrangements of costs and schedules of kindergartens and schools, of caregiving institutions for sick and older family members, and so on. These create monetary demands but also transportation needs, management and planning requirements to such an extent that Hochschild (1997) calls them producing a 'third shift' besides those of paid work and housework. Such institutional structures reflect and reinforce gendered expectations. They provide constraints and opportunities for the family and work choices of men and women. They also have a marked influence on how couples manage their finances and time.

Virtually all human societies display a gender division of labour, both between and within the spheres of paid work and unpaid activities. Very broadly, men's activities are primarily productive and women's (traditional) activities have been more concerned with reproduction, unpaid housework, and nurturing or caring activities within the family. This book confronts a puzzle. With the demise of the male breadwinner family there has been something of a paradigm shift in gender relations. But has this shift brought more or less equality?

Shifts towards gender equality have been very uneven across ethnic and social groups, age and geographical regions; and often far slower than many of the conventional theories of human capital would suggest, predicting that market forces would make gender discrimination too costly for good business. The gender 'wage gap' has proved unexpectedly stubborn and marked new inequalities between women – linked to education and class differences – are emerging. The life chances of women, men and children are increasingly polarised by educational attainment, but it is far from clear whether and under what circumstances a convergence of men's and women's education and employment experience will result in further reductions in gender inequalities.

In this book we insist that to understand the way gendered lives are changing it is necessary to take seriously the importance of time. It is also necessary to investigate the different timescales involved in how gender relationships are changing in the interlinked spheres of family, education, labour market and welfare state. As we shall see, progress on gender equality has been very uneven across these different domains, with the narrowing of the gender gap in education and employment far outstripping gender changes in the domestic sphere. Moreover, policies have varied markedly across different countries in their promotion of egalitarian arrangements for supporting parents and workers. The Swedish state has pioneered policies to encourage egalitarian parenthood, giving workers of both sexes support for combining employment and parenthood. Other countries, particularly in Southern Europe, have few such policies in place. Yet even in a country such as the UK, where the state has had a relatively hands-off stance in pushing the gender-equality agenda, there is no denying the massive changes across and within the lifetimes of women and men born in the twentieth century.

It is more than eight decades since the Equal Franchise Act of 1928 gave men and women equal voting rights in the UK. The period since then has seen great changes in the lives of women and men. Girls have become as likely as boys to receive secondary education and, eventually, to overtake them in entering higher education. Marriage has ceased to be a bar to women's employment or a prerequisite for living together or having children. Divorce has become easier, as has legal redress against domestic violence. Fertility control and childbirth have become safer. Child health has improved and housework has become less onerous. And there is opportunity for women to have paid careers in an increasing number of occupations.

Technology has transformed the tasks needed in paid and domestic work. The boundaries between them have shifted and the lines of gender demarcation have blurred. Women now work in formerly male fields – from clergy to football journalism, for example. The expectation that motherhood and employment are incompatible has been overtaken by the experience that they are increasingly combined. For all the qualifications that should be made about the limits to some of these changes – few women in top jobs, the persistence of the gender pay gap, and the sacrifices needed to combine paid work and caring roles – it is important to acknowledge there has already been great progress towards gender equality.

The UK has not been at the forefront of change in gender equality legislation and policy. In particular, compared with some other countries in Europe, the UK was relatively late in recognising that sex equality in employment was not attainable without complementary support for nurturing activities. Elder care, childcare and early education only became part of the New Labour agenda in the 1990s. Moreover, it has only been in the last couple of decades that employment legislation in the UK has begun to recognise fathers' rights to time off for parental duties. Yet changing fathers' involvement in childrearing is crucial if societies are to achieve gender equality without problematic levels of fertility decline.

In her Presidential Address to the European Society for Population Economics, Joshi (1998) argued that too many formal and informal structures have been based on a presumption of the male breadwinner model, at least in the UK. This hampers the renegotiation of family life. She suggested that we need a more 'family friendly' employment structure which ensures that there is enough time for caring activities for both men and women. Furthermore, she warned that if the issue of men's shared responsibility for their children is avoided, if child-rearing is regarded as only mothers' business, it could be a business with a bleak future. This taps into a wider debate about the conflict or compatibility of gender equality and sustaining 'replacement level' fertility. As McDonald (2000) suggests, if women are provided with opportunities nearly equivalent to those of men in education and market employment, but these opportunities are severely curtailed by having children, then, on average, women will restrict the number of children that they have to an extent where fertility rates are precariously low. He suggests that the answer for countries concerned about low fertility rates is more not less gender equity and that fertility tends to be higher in countries that provide more family-friendly working conditions.

Although women's and men's lives are changing in terms of the division of domestic and paid work, it is far from clear whether trends are leading to a situation where gender differences become irrelevant. In the UK, families with young children in the twenty-first century still predominantly have 1.5 breadwinners rather than dual full-time earning career couples. It is not obvious in which direction changes may or should continue. A norm of dual full-time earning by both parents implies a norm of full-time alternative childcare, which may not be desirable or sustainable for many families. Greater flexibility for both parents to maintain paid careers is another possibility currently being promoted by European initiatives and canvassed by a coalition government consultation (HM Government 2011). A third possibility, that would be compatible with gender equality goals, is a unisex version of the single breadwinner partnership. This outcome, however, faces considerable obstacles when the male breadwinner model is still embedded in cultural and structural conditions that favour the traditional gender role divide. Another outcome as pointed out above is that the stresses of combining employment and childbearing may lead to an increasing proportion of couples postponing or rejecting parenthood.

That low reproduction may be one adaptation to increases in women's production is also discussed in Esping-Andersen's book *The Incomplete Revolution: Adapting to Women's New Roles* (2009). An alternative adaptation could be greater sharing of domestic roles. He doubts whether it is realistic for men to substitute entirely for the decline in female domestic work without support from the state. He sees more scope for public policies that promote the reconciliation of work and motherhood, and support child development. Interestingly, Esping-Andersen does present evidence about the participation of men in housework from both Denmark and Spain, which are positioned at opposite ends of the spectrum of gender specialisation practice in Europe. This suggests that an increasing male contribution to domestic work may be 'incomplete' but it is not inconceivable. It also appears more likely where the household has help from outside (market or state) and where the woman is more educated.

However, the major respect in which the 'revolution is incomplete' for Esping-Andersen, is in its limited reach down the education and social scale. Highly educated dual-earner (full-time) couples with high incomes contribute to a widening of income inequalities, with one-earner couples, workless families and youths at the bottom of the distribution. The increased employment of women both boosts the prosperity of some dual-earner families and raises other people out of poverty. In the last decades of the twentieth century in Britain the latter, equalising, tendency was dominant (Davies and Joshi 1998), but this is under-charted territory. Esping-Andersen (2009) finds some international evidence of female earnings contributing to disequalising trends. Thus, another concern is how best to tackle increasing social inequality.

Tackling gender inequalities is intrinsically linked to addressing unacceptable social inequalities. Although it might not be clear whether gender differences will become less important in the way parenthood and employment are combined in the future, what is clear is that many unacceptable gender differences remain. The poverty among today's elderly women still bears witness to the inadequacy of the earnings and pensions over the lifetime of their generation. The poverty of lone mothers is still a major source of disadvantage for the next generation. The equalities agenda matters and so does the issue of how society rewards nurturing activities, whether caring is done by men or women, paid or unpaid.

In this book we present some of the findings from a five-year research initiative that brought together a strong team of internationally renowned researchers with the common goal of studying the changing lives and structures that govern gender inequalities in production and reproduction. From the outset, the research was devised with the view that the collective 'output' would add to more than the sum of the parts, with similar issues tackled from different theoretical and methodological orientations of different disciplines. Thus, the book, of necessity, crosses disciplinary boundaries, drawing together experts from sociology, economics, demography, human geography, social policy, management and law. Because the authors have all worked together over a five-year period and have met frequently to present and discuss their work, it has been possible to identify common themes and complementary questions.

At the outset the authors of the book were given questions which were relevant to the overarching theme of gendered lives. Although individual chapters do not necessarily address every question, most contribute to answering a good number. The ten questions are these:

1. Has the significance of gender declined over time?
2. What are the causes and consequences of the incomplete revolution in gender roles?
3. Why are gender inequalities in access to resources so resistant to change?
4. Does it make sense to focus on gendered lives, given the interplay of gender with other identities such as class, race, age and citizenship?
5. Does a focus on gender inequalities make sense, given that male and female lives are so closely interlinked?
6. What are the main drivers of change in the gendered aspects of production and reproduction?
7. What is the role that institutional structures play in helping shape gendered lives?
8. Who stands to gain or lose from the traditional gender order?
9. Is there clear evidence showing how gender equality benefits individuals and society?
10. What policy interventions might be most effective in promoting gender equality and why?

In the remaining sections of this chapter, we set out some of the necessary background information that illustrates the social changes that have been going on in the UK and in Europe more widely regarding the changes in family life, education, labour-force participation and the gender pay gap. These institutional structures help shape the interweaving life-course experiences of the women and men who are the subjects of this book. We then give a brief summary of the organisation of the book and an account of the main focus of individual chapters. In the final section, we highlight some of the unexpected findings from our research and tentatively pull together some of the overarching themes and policy recommendations concerning gendered lives.

DEMOGRAPHIC, EDUCATION AND LABOUR-FORCE CHANGE

Men and women have been caught up in an era of considerable family change that has affected the rates and timing of partnership formation and dissolution and childbirth throughout Europe (and most of the Western world). In Figure I.1 we can see for 15 European Union (EU) countries the decline in the marriage rate, the rise in the divorce rate and the rise of extramarital births. The first-marriage rate almost halved since the 1960s, the divorce rate quadrupled and more children than ever are born outside of marriage. It would be wrong to conclude that people are less likely to live in partnerships because cohabitation rates have also been on the rise. Nevertheless, the changing partnership patterns do go hand in hand with women delaying childbirth, as Figure I.2 shows. Childlessness has

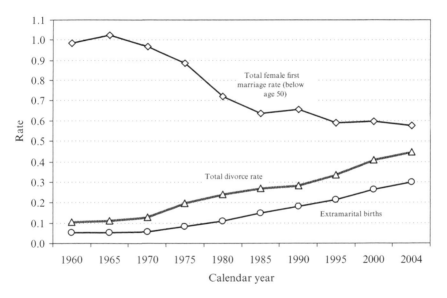

Note: Definitions. Total female first marriage rate: sum of age-specific first marriage rates (for women up to the age of 50 years) in one year of observation. The total divorce rate is similarly the sum of duration-specific proportions of married women divorcing in a given calendar year. Extramarital births show the proportion of births where the mother was not legally married.

Source: Council of Europe (2006).

Figure I.1   Total female first marriage rate (below age 50), total divorce rate, and extramarital births, 1960–2004, EU15

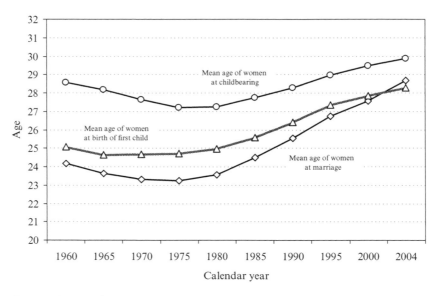

Source: Council of Europe (2006).

Figure I.2   *Mean age of women at marriage, at birth of first child and at*
              childbearing, 1960–2004, EU15

also been on the increase in recent decades. For example, Portanti and
Whitworth (2009) show that in the UK the proportion of women remaining childless has increased from an estimated 10 per cent of the 1945
cohort, to 19 per cent of women born in 1960. Their analysis also shows
that, for women born between 1956 and 1960, childless women were less
likely than mothers to be in partnerships and more likely to have higher
educational qualifications and managerial or professional occupations.
Thus, partnership and fertility trends interlink with the rapid increase of
women into higher education and employment.

In terms of changing gender roles, women's lives have undoubtedly
changed more than those of many men over the past half century or so.
In the UK, social norms of the early post-war years led women to believe
that their future would be defined by marriage and motherhood, not by
occupational careers. Yet the second half of the twentieth century saw dra-
matic increases in women's educational qualifications and employment.
It is salutary to remember that women were not permitted to become full
members of the University of Cambridge until 1947. Prior to this, women
could be admitted to study but were not entitled to take degrees. More
generally, on the eve of the Second World War women constituted less

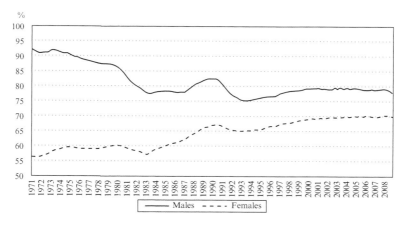

Note: Years indicate Q1 figures.

Source: Quarterly Labour Force Survey.

*Figure I.3   Percentages of men and women of working ages employed in
the UK*

than a quarter of the entire university population in England (Dyhouse
2006). At the start of the twenty-first century, the proportion of women in
tertiary education is higher than men in most countries in the Organisation
for Economic Co-operation and Development (OECD), including Britain
(Broecke and Hamed 2008).

Not surprisingly, the increase in women's educational qualifications was
accompanied by an increase in women's participation in employment (see
Figure I.3). Men by contrast, have been on a declining path in their aggregate employment rates, as restructuring and decline took place in labour
sectors that formed the traditional employers of men (see Dex 1999).
Other aggregate level changes went hand in hand with women's qualification changes. No longer were women located in a few occupational
ghettos. In Britain, there was a large growth of jobs in professional occupations, for both men and women. Also, for women but not men, there
was a rise in associate professional and technical occupations that require
vocational qualifications, such as healthcare associates (see Figures I.4a
and I.4b). There has been a decline in both men's and women's jobs in
elementary occupations, which come at the bottom of the occupational
ladder and require no more than basic education. In Figure I.5 we can see
that the more recent increase in women's employment has been concentrated overwhelmingly in two industry sectors, the public sector (education, health and public administration) and the financial services sector.

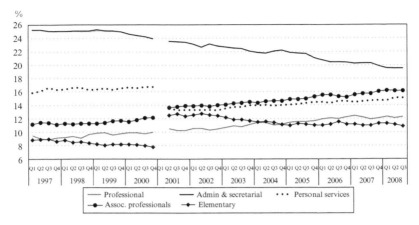

Figure I.4a   Percentage of employed women in selected occupation groups, UK

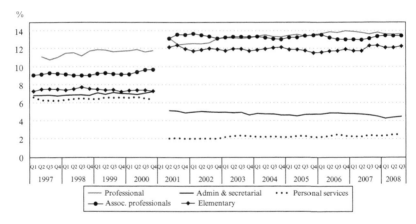

Note: The gap disjointed series in 2001 resulted from changes in the definitions of occupational categories moving from SOC90 to SOC2000.

Source: Quarterly Labour Force Survey.

Figure I.4b   Percentage of employed men in selected occupation groups, UK

Men's employment by industry (not shown) also increased in financial services over the same period, but remained at a stable level in the public sector and declined markedly in manufacturing.

One of the main gender equality indicators, the female to male hourly

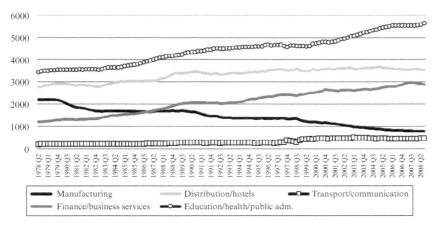

Source: Quarterly Labour Force Survey.

Figure I.5 *UK women's employment numbers in thousands, for selected industry sectors*

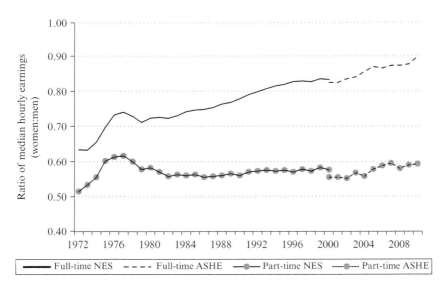

Sources: NES – New Earnings Survey; ASHE – Annual Survey of Hours and Earnings.

Figure I.6 *Ratio of women's median hourly earnings to those of male full-time employees, 1972–2010, by hours worked, UK*

wage ratio has also been improving, following an upward path for women working full-time hours (see Figure I.6). In 2010 women working full-time were earning 90 per cent of the median hourly wage of the man in full-time employment. However, when women working part-time hours are considered, the ratio has been much lower and flatter over the 1980s and 1990s, with signs of improvement only occurring since 2000 (still below 60 per cent of a man's wage in full-time work). While the wage ratio of women's to men's hourly rates of pay has improved, it has not reached levels of equality, even after controlling for other influences (Neuburger 2010). In all OECD countries the proportion of women who work part-time exceeds the proportion of men (OECD 2010). However, only the Netherlands and Switzerland have a higher proportion than the UK of women working part-time and the gender difference in the UK is particularly stark. In the UK, almost 40 per cent of women work part-time compared with less than 10 per cent of men (OECD 2010). The main reason for part-time work is that the hours and locality make it easier to combine employment and family responsibilities. The low rates of pay reflect the typically low-level occupations involved.

Even among UK graduates, the gender pay gap increases as men's and women's careers advance. According to Purcell and Elias (2008) this is mainly due to the gender division of labour in the public and private spheres. For 1995 graduates, the gender pay gap in their first job after their degree was 11 per cent and this rose to 19 per cent seven years later (in 2002–03). They note that there are many factors that help explain the gender pay gap. For example, sector and hours of work alone accounted for half of the gender differences in earnings seven years after graduating. In addition, many women made career adjustments because of family responsibilities. Undoubtedly children reap the benefits of mothers having higher education. However, it is more doubtful whether the UK economy is reaping its maximum payback for the investment in education, when so many women have few options but to rein in their careers to facilitate family demands.

THE OVERVIEW AND ORGANISATION OF *GENDERED LIVES*

The chapters are grouped in three parts. Part I examines gendered lives unfolding across time. This section contains three chapters, with Hobcraft and Sigle-Rushton (Chapter 1) examining the childhood origins of adult socio-economic disadvantage. Their focus is on whether cohort and gender matter. Using data from two British birth cohort studies – children born in

1958 and 1970 – they compare to what extent there are common predictors across gender and birth cohorts of adult socio-economic disadvantage. A striking feature of their analysis is how few gender differences they found. They do find some positive effects of structural changes for women in terms of job outcomes. However, their main conclusion warns against simplistic models of causation and they suggest that adult disadvantage is likely to involve the accumulation of a series of experiences and a variety of complex interplays of childhood circumstances. Bukodi, Dex and Joshi (Chapter 2) examine changing career trajectories of men and women across time. As well as examining gender differences, they investigate whether education and childbirth have different career implications across generations. They also look at how the various labour market conditions facing different cohorts as they enter the labour force affect the career progression of men and women. The findings suggest a shift towards greater occupational gender equality across time. It also seems that the new legislative environment in the UK helps reduce the loss of occupational status that was associated with motherhood in the past. The authors specify additional ways that policy can help reduce the occupational penalties associated with family care. Gershuny and Kan (Chapter 3) present a fascinating account of how the gender gap in paid work-time and unpaid work-time is closing slowly. Using the Multinational Time Use Study from 12 OECD countries, they see a slow but continuing trend of gender convergence in work time and in the domestic division of labour regardless of policy regime types. Policy regimes do make a difference though and the move towards gender equality has been much faster in Nordic countries than in the Southern countries of Europe. They also examine men's and women's total work hours, which show similar amounts of total work time but different gendered shares of paid and unpaid work. They conclude that, as far as gender roles are concerned, there is lagged adaption, rather than a stalled revolution.

Part II is about gender inequalities in the household and workplace. Bennett, De Henau, Himmelweit and Sung (Chapter 4) examine financial togetherness and autonomy within couples. While it has long been a policy focus to consider differences between household incomes, there has been much less concern about how that income is made up, or how it is received and by whom. Using both qualitative and quantitative data, they find that gender roles matter in what makes couples satisfied with their household income. The qualitative interviews with low to moderate income couples show that a woman's earnings were seen as less important than the man's for the household, but also more likely to be hers to spend. Thus, notions of 'togetherness' tend to favour the man's employment and relative entitlements within the household at the cost of the woman's access to household resources and overall financial autonomy. If gender roles matter in household finances, they seem to matter far less when it comes to migrants' experience of precarious employment. McDowell, Batnitzky and Dyer (Chapter 5) explore the world of waged work for both men and women migrants who have come to the UK in search of a better life. Their study examines the experiences of 37 workers who obtained basic entry-level jobs in service jobs at a hospital or hotel through an employment agency. The study suggests that national stereotypes matter in terms of job allocation. In the hotel, for example, Indian men, because of their association with colonial hospitality and service, were given more visible jobs than men of other nationalities. In the hospital, skin colour seemed a less significant axis of differentiation between migrants, perhaps because of the long association between the National Health Service and Caribbean nurses. Migrant men may have had to take on 'feminised' work such as cleaning and caring for others; but men in more traditional jobs that rely on bodily strength such as security and portering were no less at risk when it comes to job security or job conditions. The overall finding is that migrants, male and female alike, are among the most exploitable and exploited of bottom-end service sector employees, with little security and almost no labour market rights.

Part III focuses on gender inequalities in a changing world. McLaughlin and Deakin (Chapter 6) examine the equality law and the limits of the 'business case' for addressing gender inequalities in corporations in the UK. Their focus is particularly on the gender pay gap. Their findings are not encouraging. They suggest that shareholders engaged with socially responsible investment have so far proved to have very little impact in the area of employment conditions and pay. Moreover, the implementation of the section of the 2010 Equality Act, which contains mandatory reporting of gender pay gaps, has been postponed by the Conservative-Liberal coalition government. Their interviews with managers from firms in both private and public sectors that have explicitly endorsed commitment to greater gender equality were also discouraging. Few were sufficiently persuaded by the business case for equality for 'good practice' to be likely to prevail in the absence of legal compulsion.

Scott and Plagnol (Chapter 7) examine work–family conflict (WFC) and well-being in Northern Europe. Using data from the European Social Survey, they examine how both the experience of WFC and well-being are gendered in ways that reflect the gendered division of paid and unpaid work. They also explore how different policies in support of maternal employment and a more equitable divide of domestic labour may reduce or enhance men's and women's well-being. Contrary to expectations, they found that men, not women, benefited from a less traditional gender role divide in household chores. They suggest that men may be uncomfortably conscious of work getting in the way of their doing a fair share of chores at home, whereas women have long been used to doing a 'double shift'. They conclude that more attention needs to be paid to the gender division of unpaid work if we are to understand how changes in family and employment impinge on well-being. Lewis (Chapter 8) examines the policy challenges of achieving greater gender equality and work–family balance cross-nationally. Her focus is on the way in which time to care and time to work have been balanced over the past decade. In particular, she examines how part-time work and different forms of care leave (maternal, paternal and parental) influence the time available to care, and how childcare services and care by kin influence the time available for paid work. One problem for policy-makers is that the interests of family members may conflict. While it is commonly acknowledged that children need one-to-one care for their first year, it is problematic to provide that when mothers have increased their participation in paid work and fathers have not made a similar change in their contribution to unpaid work. Focusing on reducing work–family conflicts for women alone only reinforces gender inequalities, including pension inequalities in later life. However, making an adult worker family model a practical reality requires considerable policy skill, if the welfare of families is to be maximised, while the trade-offs between the interests of family members are minimised.

UNEXPECTED FINDINGS, TENTATIVE ANSWERS AND POLICY SUGGESTIONS

Gendered Lives offers many examples of unexpected findings. Here we highlight two.

The first example comes from the research that explored the early childhood origins of adult disadvantage (Chapter 1). One of the great contributions of social science has been to show the importance of early childhood in shaping subsequent life experiences, whether in health, education, relationships or socio-economic status. We know, for example, that children who display aggression in childhood are more likely to end up in disadvantaged circumstances, such as living in social housing, receiving benefits and having a low-skilled occupation. Given that women are more likely than men to be in such disadvantaged adult circumstances, it seems likely that the childhood origins would also differ by gender. Surprisingly, Hobcraft and Sigle-Rushton (Chapter 1) find few gender differences in the pathways to adult disadvantages. Thus, despite there being pronounced gender differences in both childhood experiences and adult outcomes the mechanisms that link the two are surprisingly similar for both men and women. This is important because it points away from a single or simple explanation of adult gender inequalities. Causation in human behaviour is often complex. The challenge is to take account of the complex interplays between biological (for example, hormonal) and social factors, and the experiences that accrue as a result. This points the way towards a still more nuanced approach to the measurement and analysis of the dynamics of gender inequalities than has been achieved to date.

A second unexpected finding is from the research that seeks to unpack how individuals in heterosexual couples talk about and assess their household finances (Chapter 4). In particular, the study focused on accounts of 'togetherness' and financial autonomy and how these ideas feature in the lives of couples managing their household income. It was a break-through in social science when research began to unpack the 'black box' of household finances. Policy-makers tend to show more of an interest in a household's total income than who has access to that income and how it is used. Yet we know from many studies that household income is rarely shared evenly. It seems likely that both men's and women's satisfaction with their household income would be different depending on whether they have earned the money themselves or whether it has been earned by the partner. However, that common-sense assumption is wrong. Bennett et al. (Chapter 4) find that gender roles matter in what makes couples satis-fied with their household income and, for both men and women, the job of the man matters more than the job of the woman.

Such unexpected findings contribute to the answers we can tentatively draw out from our ten questions. The first three questions asked: (1) 'Has the significance of gender declined over time?' (2) 'What are the causes and consequences of the incomplete revolution in gender roles?' and (3) 'Why are gender inequalities in access to resources so resistant to change?' These three questions interlink. There is certainly evidence of a shift across generations towards gender equality in the occupational careers of men and women, as Bukodi et al. demonstrate in Chapter 2. Education is an important part of the story of the decline in gender inequalities, but so too is the increasing instability in the career paths of men. Yet, as Gershuny and Kan illustrate in Chapter 3, gender inequities in the division of labour persist and, at best, there has been a lagged adaptation in both the slow change of institutional structures and gender-role ideologies. Moreover, in times when marital break-up is relatively common, the gender specialisa-tion in paid and unpaid work makes the woman economically vulnerable. Bennett et al. (Chapter 4) show that traditional gender role attitudes are well entrenched, at least in households with relatively limited resources. They claim that the view that the man has more entitlements, relative to the woman, to the resources and benefits from the household's collective labour is but a modern version of the notion that it is in the whole family's interest that the man eats well even when food is scarce for other family members, because all their fortunes depend on his strength as the main breadwinner. The saying 'plus ça change, plus c'est la même chose' comes to mind – the more things change, the more they stay the same. But this is too pessimistic, because as Gershuny and Kan (Chapter 3) suggest lagged adaptation does not imply a permanently stalled gender-role revolution.

Question 4, 'Does it makes sense to focus on gendered lives, given the interplay of gender with other identities such as class, race, age and citizenship?' is an important one. Yet it is not always possible or appropriate to focus on complex interactions, which the concept of 'intersectionality' implies. However, it is necessary to bear in mind that discrimination and inequalities will interact in ways that depend on the context and are specific to time and place (McCall 2005). McDowell et al. in Chapter 5 illustrate how labour market, migration patterns, national origins, gender and skin colour intersect in particular ways to construct workers who are seen as appropriate 'warm bodies' for low-level service sector jobs. However, there are always trade-offs in empirical research and by focusing on the wider picture of labour inequalities, they lose some of the up-close focus on gender differences. Whether the focus on gendered lives makes sense depends on what research question is being addressed.

The related question 5, 'Does a focus on gender inequalities make sense, given that male and female lives are so closely interlinked?' is addressed by almost all the chapters in this book. It is the way that male and female lives interlink – particularly in terms of the division of labour between the reproductive and productive spheres – that helps create and sustain gender inequalities. Question 6, 'What are the main drivers of change in the gendered aspects of production and reproduction?' relates to the changes in family life, education and employment that we have briefly illustrated in the earlier sections of this chapter. Question 7, 'What is the role that institutional structures play in helping shape gendered lives?' refers to a theme that is picked up throughout the book about the reciprocal influences that flow between changing gendered lives and institutional structures such as, family, education, employment, trade unions, welfare state and law. There is a complex set of interlinked cultural and structural changes that reflect and shape both the changes going on in individual lives and also the changes in the institutional contexts, in which gendered lives are set. Examples include the change in the social respectability of paid work for women, the demise of the male-breadwinner family, the shifting reliance of labour-market demand from brawn to brain, the rise of the knowledge economy, the increased emphasis on individualisation in everything from childcare to pensions, the decline of religious authority, the increasing fluidity of partnerships, changing incentives for the domestic division of labour, and improvements in fertility control, health and longevity.

Question 8, 'Who stands to gain or lose from the traditional gender role order?' in part refers to the conflicting interests at stake of men, women and children. The cross-national analysis of Lewis (Chapter 8) of gender equality and work–family balance unpacks some of these conflicts and the challenge they pose for policy. Question 9, 'Is there clear evidence showing how gender equality benefits individuals and society?' is addressed by McLaughlin and Deakin (Chapter 6) whose qualitative research of employers suggests that the 'business case' for addressing gender inequalities is unlikely to be fully persuasive, even in organisations committed to the diversity agenda. Scott and Plagnol (Chapter 7) look at this in the different context of work–family conflict and well-being in Northern Europe showing that a more equitable gender division of labour has beneficial effects for men as well as women.

The final question, Question 10, 'What policy interventions might be most effective in promoting gender equality and why?' is addressed by all chapters, with authors reflecting on the implications of their findings for policy. McLaughlin and Deakin (Chapter 6) emphasise that legal compulsion will be necessary if much progress is to be made on gender inequalities in pay, even among those UK organisations that emphasise corporate social responsibility. Unfortunately, the implementation of the mandatory pay section of the UK 2010 Equality Law has been put on hold in 2011, with the change in government. This is because there is a perceived conflict between gender equality and the interests of business and economic growth. Thus the question of policy intervention is not straightforward. It depends in part on the political and public will for introducing measures that would enhance gender equality. As Lewis (Chapter 8) suggests, UK policies seek to make adults become more self-provisioning, with welfare increasingly privatised as the individual's responsibility. Given this, government may be argued to have a responsibility to ensure more equal labour market participation and terms and conditions, which in turn means that fathers need to be encouraged to pick up more of the unpaid work of care.

In this introductory chapter, we have sought to set the scene for the subsequent chapters on gendered lives, by examining gender inequalities in production and reproduction. As Glucksmann (1995, p. 70) has put it: 'The economic bottom line is that if babies are not looked after they will die; if food preparation ceased people would eventually starve'. Glucksmann (1995, p. 67) has described this as the 'total social organisation of labour' (TSOL), that is 'the manner by which all labour in a particular society is divided up between and allocated to different structures, institutions and activities'. More recently (Glucksmann 2005) has extended the TSOL concept to consider the complex interconnections and shifting boundaries between work activities of all kinds, including paid and unpaid work. From this perspective, the work in the reproductive sphere provides an indispensable contribution to human flourishing and is central, not peripheral to productive activities. Folbre (2009) goes further and argues that the highly gendered and uneven responsibilities for the care of dependents undermines trust and reciprocity between men and women, old and young, rich and poor. Thus, as these authors and many of the chapter findings conclude, change in the gendering of lives is crucial for both the economic well-being and social integration of society.

REFERENCES

Broecke, S. and J. Hamed (2008), 'Gender gaps in higher education participation', Department for Innovation, Universities, and Skills Research Report 08-14, available at: http://www.bis.gov.uk/assets/biscore/corporate/migratedD/publications/D/DIUS_RR_08_14 (accessed August 2011).

Council of Europe (2006), *Recent Demographic Developments in Europe*, Strasbourg: Council of Europe Publishing.

Davies, H.B. and H.E. Joshi (1998), 'Gender and income inequality in the UK: 1968–1990: feminization of earning or of poverty?', *Journal of the Royal Statistical Society, Series A*, 33–61.

Dex, S. (ed.) (1999), *Families and the Labour Market*, London: Family Policy Studies Centre with Joseph Rowntree Foundation.

Dyhouse, C. (2006), *Students: A Gendered History*, London: Routledge.

Esping-Andersen, G. (2009), *The Incomplete Revolution: Adapting to Women's New Roles*, Cambridge: Polity.

Folbre, N. (2009), *Greed, Lust and Gender: A History of Economic Ideas*, Oxford: Oxford University Press.

Glucksmann, M. (1995), 'Why "work"? Gender and the "total social organisation of labour"', *Gender, Work and Organisation*, **2** (2), 63–75.

Glucksmann, M. (2005), 'Shifting boundaries and interconnections: Extending the "total social organisation of labour"', *Sociological Review*, **53** (s2), 19–36.

Heinz, W. and V. Marshall (eds) (2003), *Social Dynamics of the Life Course*, New York: Aldine de Gruyter.

HM Government (2011), 'Modern workplaces consultation document, May 2011', available at: http://c561635.r35.cf2.rackcdn.com/11-699-consultation-modern-workplaces.pdf (accessed September 2011).

Hochschild, A. (1997), *The Time Bind. When Work Become Home and Home Becomes Work*, New York: Metropolitan.

Joshi, H. (1998), 'The opportunity costs of childbearing: more than mothers' business', *Journal of Population Economics*, **11**, 161–83.

Kruger, H. and R. Levy (2001), 'Linking life courses, work, and the family: theorizing a not so visible nexus between women and men', *Canadian Journal of Sociology*, **26** (2), 145–66.

McCall, L. (2005), 'The complexity of intersectionality', *Signs: Journal of Women and Culture and Society*, **30**, 1771–802.

McDonald, P. (2000), 'Gender equity, social institutions and the future of fertility', *Journal of Population Research*, **17** (1), 1–16.

McDowell, L. (1992), 'Doing gender: feminism, feminists and research methods', *Transactions of the Institute of British Geographers*, **17**, 399–416.

Neuburger, J. (2010), 'Trends in the unequal pay of women and men across three British generations', PhD thesis, Institution of Education, University of London.

Organisation for Economic Co-operation and Development (OECD) (2010), 'Employment Outlook, LMF1.6 Gender differences in employment outcomes', available at: www.oecd.org/els/social/family/database (accessed August 2011).

Portanti, M. and S. Whitworth (2009), 'A comparison of the characteristics of childless women and mothers in the ONS Longitudinal Study', Population Trends No. 136, available at: http://www.statistics.gov.uk/articles/population_trends/PT136MothersAndChildlessWomenArticle.pdf (accessed August 2011).

Purcell, K. and P. Elias (2008), 'Achieving equality in the knowledge economy', in J. Scott, S. Dex and H. Joshi (eds), *Women and Employment, Changing Lives and New Challenges*, Cheltenham, UK and Northampton, MA, USA: Edward Elgar.

Sullivan, O. (2004), 'Changing gender practices with the household: a theoretical perspective', *Gender and Society*, **18** (2), 207–22.

West, C. and D. Zimmerman (1987), 'Doing gender', *Gender and Society*, **1**, 125–51.

PART I

Gendered Lives Unfolding across Time

1. The childhood origins of adult socio-economic disadvantage: do cohort and gender matter?

John Hobcraft and Wendy Sigle-Rushton

1. INTRODUCTION

In this chapter we use data from the 1958 National Child Development Study (NCDS) and the 1970 British Cohort Study (BCS70) to explore inter-cohort comparisons on childhood markers of adult socio-economic disadvantage. Exploiting the similar design and content of these two studies, we investigate, for individuals born in 1958 and in 1970 in Great Britain, whether the family and childhood antecedents of adult socio-economic disadvantage have changed over time and whether they differ for men and women. We are particularly interested in assessing how far there are common predictors across birth cohorts, and for both men and women, of adult socio-economic disadvantage. To explore this we use a regression model to test explicitly for evidence of common (or 'main') effects that apply to both men and women and to both cohorts, of cohort-specific differences in response to disadvantaged origins ('cohort' interactions), of gendered differences in response to disadvantaged origins ('gender' interactions) and of differential gender responses to childhood disadvantage across cohorts ('cohort-gender' interactions). To provide greater insight into the underlying processes involved in the pathways of experiencing disadvantage in the family of origin or during childhood, and the resulting legacies during early adulthood, we estimate models that allow us to identify the important factors that influence adult disadvantage for both men and women across time and to document which relationships have changed over time or that differ by gender.

2. LITERATURE REVIEW

Research on the life course and human development emphasises that events occurring during childhood are likely to be strongly associated with adult functioning and well-being (for example, Elder 1974, 1998). These include the child's individual attributes as well as the home environment. For example, children who experience financial difficulty in childhood often have lower educational attainment (Duncan et al. 1998; Hobcraft 2000) and lower household income or earnings in adulthood (Hobcraft 1998; McKnight 2002; Sigle-Rushton 2004). Similarly, residing in social housing in childhood is linked to a greater risk of living in social housing in adulthood (Hobcraft 1998; Lupton et al. 2009; Sigle-Rushton 2004). The social class of the family in which an individual was raised is related to the adult's own socio-economic status (Schoon et al. 2002). Also, children who experience (longer) episodes of living in a single-parent home are more likely to enter single parenthood themselves (Kiernan 1996; McLanahan 1985; McLanahan and Sandefur 1994) or to be more generally disadvantaged (Sigle-Rushton et al. 2005).

Childhood behavioural trajectories, related to contextual variables (such as neighbourhood and the home setting) and childhood stressors (such as family structure and conflict), may affect well-being in late adolescence and early adulthood (Hobcraft, 1998; Moffitt 1993; Schoon et al. 2003; Sigle-Rushton, 2004). Another related childhood attribute that is strongly associated with socio-economic success in adulthood is academic ability. Higher cognitive test scores in childhood have been found to be associated positively with subsequent educational attainment (Bynner and Joshi 2002) and level of adult earnings (McKnight 2002). Childhood test scores have also been shown to have powerful residual associations with a wide range of adult disadvantages, net of qualification levels (Hobcraft 2000), or of a wide range of late adolescent and very early adult experiences (Hobcraft 2003, 2004).

Past work has emphasised the relevance of the wider social context as well. This is an important consideration in our study which examines members of two British cohorts. The 1970 cohort was born at a time when traditional gender roles and norms were being increasingly questioned and challenged. In Britain, these changes led to increasing female employment and a narrowing of the gender gap in educational attainment (Bynner and Pan 2002). Gender remains an important source of stratification for both cohorts (Hobcraft 2003; McKnight 2002), but gains in gender equality mean that gender differences in both outcomes and their associations with childhood disadavantage may have changed over time. In addition, the two cohorts encountered different economic circumstances during their transition to adulthood. The decline of well-paid industrial jobs and greater job insecurity meant that educational achievement was more likely to be important to the socio-economic success of the younger cohort (Bynner and Parsons 2000, 2001). Members of the 1958 cohort were leaving home and entering the labour market in the mid- to late-1970s, just as much of the social housing stock was being sold at well under market value. One result of this policy was an extremely favourable housing market. In contrast, the 1970 cohort reached adulthood when housing costs were prohibitively high and stocks of social housing were less plentiful (Lupton et al. 2009).

Building upon past research on the life course and on intergenerational processes of social disadvantage, this chapter explores whether and in what way pathways to disadvantage are gendered, whether they appear to have altered or changed over time and, finally, whether or not any temporal changes themselves were gender specific. In doing so, we hope to improve our understanding of continuity and change in the life course.

3. DATA AND METHODS

Our analysis pools data from two prospective large-scale longitudinal studies of birth cohorts in Great Britain: the National Child Development Study (NCDS) and the British Cohort Study (BCS70).

The NCDS is a longitudinal study of children born in one week of 1958. A total of 17414 cohort members' mothers were originally interviewed. Follow-up NCDS interviews were conducted when the cohort members were aged 7, 11, 16, 23, 33, 42, 46 and 48. The BCS70 is a longitudinal study of children born in Great Britain in one week of 1970, with just under 18000 cohort members' mothers originally interviewed. Successive BCS70 interviews were conducted when the cohort members were aged 5, 10, 16, 26, 30, 34 and 38. The studies contain a wealth of behavioural, health, socio-economic and demographic information. Moreover, much of the information is collected using the same (or similar) questions. Because we rely only on those measures that are in both data-sets, we exclude a few control variables that we know from previous research to be important. Nonetheless the number of these variables is not large, and our pooled data-set contains a rich set of information on the cohort members' lives.

As with any prospective study, missing information is an issue. The outcome measures were taken from the fifth follow-up surveys when the NCDS cohort was age 33 and the BCS cohort was age 30. A total of 11260 members of the BCS cohort were successfully interviewed at age 30 and 11405 members of the NCDS cohort were interviewed at age 33. However, information for some outcome variables is missing. Rather than restrict our sample to those individuals with information on every outcome, we have allowed the samples to fluctuate in order to include all valid cases for each outcome. For our control variables, following Hobcraft (1998), we construct categorical summary variables that combine information collected at different childhood waves which are coded to allow for some missing information. In the main, the first three follow-up waves which cover childhood and adolescence (although age 16 is rather late in childhood and perhaps marks the beginning of the transition to adulthood, for reasons of brevity, we refer to these three waves collectively as the 'childhood waves') were used to construct many of the controls from each cohort; for NCDS at ages 7, 11 and 16 and for BCS70 at ages 5, 10 and 16. Each summary measure is then converted into several dummy variables, and only those cases with no information at all are coded as missing.

Outcome Measures

We consider four dichotomous outcomes. These indicators of disadvantage include living in social housing, being in receipt of non-universal (or means-tested) benefits, having household income that falls in the bottom quartile of the distribution (determined separately for each cohort) and having a low occupational class. Household income includes the earnings of the cohort member plus those of any co-residential partner and all other sources of income, including benefits. Occupational class refers to the current or last job and is based on the Registrar General's measure of social class (RGSC). The Registrar General's scale of Social Class and Socio-economic groups includes five major classes, ranging from 'Professionals' in class I to 'Unskilled' in class V. Class III is generally subdivided into manual (IIIb) and non-manual occupations (IIIa). Those whose jobs are classified as partly skilled or unskilled (RGSC IV or V) are identified as having a low social class occupation (Leete and Fox 1977; OPCS 1980). Table 1.1 contains descriptive statistics for these outcome variables, disaggregated by cohort and gender.

As Table 1.1 shows, the percentage of social housing tenants has remained relatively stable over time. However, in both cohorts women were more likely than men to be living in social housing in adulthood. Similarly, a greater percentage of women in both cohorts were in receipt of non-universal benefits. In addition, a higher proportion of the 1970 cohort received non-universal benefits. Despite a higher proportion of single mothers in the 1970 cohort, the gender gap in household income emerged only for members of the 1958 cohort. The percentage recorded as working (or having worked, if not employed at the time of interview) in a low social class occupation declined over time. This trend is particularly strong in the case of women and may be due to rapid increases in their educational attainment and labour force participation, combined with delayed marriage and childbearing.

*Table 1.1   Descriptive sample statistics (percentages) for all adult
outcomes and all childhood indicators, by cohort and gender**

	NCDS		BCS	
	Female	Male	Female	Male
Outcomes				
Social housing	17.04	13.54	16.80	12.14
	(5430)	(4984)	(5749)	(5388)
Receipt of non-universal benefits	14.83	9.86	19.95	12.14
	(5757)	(5568)	(5780)	(5455)
Bottom quartile household income	26.35	23.73	24.85	25.17
	(4270)	(4479)	(5195)	(4882)
Registrar General Social Class	23.59	16.30	14.44	12.92
(RGSC) IV or V	(5291)	(5265)	(5108)	(4931)

Note: *Sample sizes for each outcome vary by gender and cohort and are shown in
parentheses below the percentages.

Control Variables

Our control variables are presented in Table 1.2. Family poverty during
childhood is measured by combining two indicators: obtaining free school
lunches at age 10/11, and whether the family was in financial difficulty at
age 16. Housing tenure summarises information collected at all three childhood follow-up waves and distinguishes between social housing, private
rented accommodation and owner occupation. Social class of origin,
which is meant to reflect the parents' backgrounds and the circumstances
of the family at the time the cohort member was born, is measured using a
combination of the occupational class of the father at birth of the cohort
member and the social class of the paternal and maternal grandfathers.
We also measure the social class of the father during childhood in order to
capture the circumstances of the family in which the cohort member was
living during childhood as well as changes in family circumstances during
childhood. This measure combines information on father's social class at
each of the three childhood waves.

The figures in Table 1.2 indicate that the majority of cohort members
had no experience of living in poverty through their childhood. However,
the percentage of individuals with at least one poverty indicator is higher
for the cohort born in 1970 (18.9 per cent of women and 17.2 per cent of
men have at least one poverty indicator suggesting their family experienced poverty) than for the cohort born in 1958 (14.5 per cent of women
and 13.5 per cent of men). As previous research has demonstrated the

Table 1.2   Descriptive sample statistics (percentages) for all childhood indicators, by cohort and gender

	NCDS		BCS	
	Female	Male	Female	Male
Childhood indicators (additional information about how the indicator was constructed)				
Poverty (constructed using two poverty indicators: financial difficulties at age 16 and free school meals at age 10/11)				
Not poor, no missing information	53.04	53.23	59.79	57.82
Not poor, some missing information	26.18	26.90	18.19	21.17
Mixed evidence (1 indicator suggests poverty, the other does not)	8.33	7.81	13.24	11.96
Poor, some missing information	3.69	3.59	3.23	2.89
Poor, no missing information	2.43	2.10	2.42	2.32
Both missing	6.33	6.37	3.14	3.85
Housing tenure (constructed using measures of housing tenure collected at ages 5/7; 10/11 and 16)				
2–3 waves in social housing	34.25	33.32	22.21	22.01
1 wave in social housing	10.64	10.19	11.86	10.61
0 wave social housing, 0–1 waves as an owner-occupier	15.33	15.14	12.70	13.90
2–3 waves as an owner-occupier	37.66	39.17	49.81	49.60
All missing	2.12	2.18	3.42	3.89
Social class of origin (constructed using information on the occupational class of three male relatives collected over two waves: birth-father, age 5-maternal and paternal grandfathers)				
2–3 manual relatives (RGSC social class IV or V)	15.02	13.93	10.67	10.81
1 manual relative	32.28	32.47	26.58	26.52
0 manual relatives, 0–1 non-manual relatives	34.56	34.89	38.47	37.33
2–3 non-manual (RGSC I–IIIa)	14.78	15.07	16.38	17.13
All missing	3.36	3.64	7.90	8.22

Table 1.2   (continued)

	NCDS		BCS	
	Female	Male	Female	Male
Father's social class (constructed using information on the occupational class of the father figure at ages 5/7; 10/11 and 16)				
2–3 waves manual	14.52	13.84	7.51	6.87
1 wave manual	15.30	15.77	13.51	13.64
0 manual and 0–1 waves non-manual	40.47	39.46	42.85	43.35
2–3 waves non-manual	25.16	26.42	27.98	28.29
All missing	4.55	4.51	8.15	7.85
Family status (constructed using information on resident mother-figure and father-figure at ages 5/7; 10/11 and 16 and reasons for family structure change)				
All natural, no missing information	49.94	49.86	40.42	37.97
All natural, some missing information	32.88	34.23	35.83	40.32
No father at birth	3.26	2.71	2.81	2.23
Ever in foster care	1.93	2.21	3.43	3.07
Parental divorce/separation, no remarriage	4.04	3.59	6.94	6.90
Other one parent, no remarriage (lived with a lone parent for some other reason – death or missing information on cause of family transition)	3.91	3.78	3.05	2.59
Parental divorce, remarriage	1.86	1.84	5.16	4.57
Other one parent, remarriage	1.52	1.21	1.00	0.49
All missing	0.66	0.57	1.35	1.86
Parental interest in school (teachers' reports collected at age 10/11)				
Both parents very interested	24.02	23.72	25.80	26.31
One parent is very interested	14.24	13.40	16.66	14.65
Neither parent is very interested	25.45	25.81	22.20	22.68
One parent has low interest	6.12	6.23	2.88	3.40
Both parents have low interest	7.36	8.90	3.05	3.34
Both missing	22.80	21.94	29.41	29.62
Child behaviour (based on Rutter Scale, mothers' reports of the behaviour at ages 5/7; 10/11 and 16)				
Aggression subscale				
Very high (high score in 2–3 waves)	3.76	6.12	3.30	6.54

Table 1.2   (continued)

		NCDS		BCS	
		Female	Male	Female	Male
High	(high score in 1 wave)	12.17	17.41	10.39	15.10
Low	(no high scores, no more than 1 low score)	36.33	39.96	32.46	34.20
Very low	(low scores in 2–3 waves)	45.53	34.07	49.69	39.48
All missing		2.21	2.44	4.16	4.67
Anxiety subscale					
Very high		6.98	7.03	6.28	5.35
High		23.06	22.78	17.60	15.03
Low		40.83	39.14	33.29	35.88
Very low		26.92	28.61	38.78	38.92
All missing		2.21	2.44	4.04	4.82
Restlessness subscale					
Very high		4.79	6.46	2.50	3.76
High		13.23	17.05	9.01	12.73
Low		34.61	36.82	37.40	39.48
Very low		45.16	37.23	47.03	39.21
All missing		2.21	2.44	4.06	4.82
Child cognitive test scores (summary of quartile rank of the cohort member's performance on two cognitive tests applied at ages 5/7; 10/11 and 16)					
Very low	(bottom quartile scores in 2–3 waves)	15.74	16.95	9.82	9.19
Low	(bottom quartile scores in 1 wave)	15.92	16.43	22.30	22.52
Middle	(no bottom quartile scores, 0–1 top quartile)	48.84	43.40	48.65	47.66
High	(2–3 top quartile scores)	18.00	21.60	12.27	12.44
All missing		1.50	1.62	6.96	8.20
Sample size for childhood indicators		5799	5606	5794	5476

percentage of children observed living in social housing at some point during childhood has declined substantially over time (Lupton et al. 2009). Well over 40 per cent of the 1958 cohort were observed living in social housing at least once during childhood. For members of the 1970 cohort, the figure is about one-third. Both social class measures indicate that fathers and grandfathers were of higher occupational class for members of the 1970 cohort. The differential is particularly pronounced for Father's Social Class. Between 14 and 15 per cent of cohort members born in 1958 had fathers who worked in a manual class at 2 or 3 childhood waves. For members of the 1970 cohort, this figure fell to between 7 and 8 per cent.

The family structure variables summarise information collected at all three childhood waves (for more detail refer to Hobcraft 1998 and Sigle-Rushton 2004). As previous research has established, members of the 1970 cohort were about twice as likely as members of the 1958 cohort to experience a parental divorce (Sigle-Rushton et al. 2005).

At the second childhood follow-up surveys (though at all three childhood waves in the NCDS), teachers were asked to indicate the level of parental interest in the cohort member's school activities. From the age 10 and 11 waves of the BCS70 and NCDS, respectively, we combine reports of the mothers' and fathers' interest into one summary measure. Following Hobcraft (1998; see also Elander and Rutter 1996), we use questions from the Rutter behavioural scale to construct three measures of the cohort member's behaviour or temperament: aggression, anxiety and restlessness. At each of the childhood waves, the parent is asked to agree or disagree with a range of statements about the child's behaviour. For each subscale, the parental responses are added together with high scores reflecting more behavioural difficulties and, based on terciles of the distribution, the cohort members' scores are coded as high, moderate, low or missing. The categorical variables for each of the first three follow-up waves are combined to form a single summary variable for each behavioural measure. The academic test scores variable summarises performance on age-appropriate tests at each of the three childhood waves. Different tests were administered to each cohort so the measures are not entirely comparable (Sigle-Rushton 2004), but they provide a summary of academic performance at roughly the same ages. Each score was standardised and then the two were added together. The total was then divided into quartiles; the top quartile was coded as high performance, the bottom quartile was coded as low performance. Each of the three age-specific performance measures was then combined to form a summary variable.

As the figures in Table 1.2 demonstrate, in both cohorts boys were more likely to be ever or consistently described as aggressive or restless. Gender differences in anxiety are less marked. Members of the 1970 cohort were less likely to be ever or consistently described as restless. Boys and girls with at least one high restlessness score comprised around 23.5 and 18.0 per cent of the NCDS sample respectively; the equivalent figures for the BCS70 cohort are 16.5 and 11.5 per cent. In both cohorts, girls are more likely than boys to have one or both parents reported as being very interested in their education (38.3 per cent versus 37.1 per cent in the 1958 cohort and 42.5 versus 41.0 per cent in the 1970 cohort). Interestingly, we do not see a significant gender difference in having two to three top quartile academic test scores in the 1970 cohort, a finding that was present in the NCDS. Girls in the younger BCS70 cohort appear to have closed that gender gap.

Analytic Strategy

For estimation purposes, we followed Hobcraft (1998) and coded each of the summary variables, except the family type variable, into a series of 'hierarchical' dummies. The missing category was first identified and, for the remaining cases, the most advantaged group formed the reference category. The first dummy set all categories other than the reference category equal to one. For example, in the case of housing tenure, those individuals observed living in owner-occupied housing at least twice form the reference category and all other non-missing categories were coded 1. The second dummy picked out those cases with slightly more evidence of disadvantage. For housing tenure, this variable was coded 1 for those individuals observed living in social housing at least once. A final dummy variable was set to equal 1 only for those with the clearest evidence of disadvantage. Following the housing tenure example, this final dummy identified those with at least two observations in social housing during childhood.

Since family type cannot be readily ordered from least to most disadvantaged, for estimation purposes the summary variable was coded into dummies that are best described as partially hierarchical. The missing category and the first four categories (both natural parents throughout; both natural parents but partial information; no father present at birth; and ever in care) were all coded as straightforward indicator variables. However, the remaining categories were coded hierarchically. The first hierarchical dummy variable was set equal to one if the respondent ever experienced a family disruption (due to divorce or widowhood). The next variables selected from among this group those who experienced a divorce or separation, those who experienced a parental remarriage and, finally, those with evidence of both a parental divorce and a remarriage. Coding all of the summary childhood antecedent variables into hierarchical or partially hierarchical dummies created 45 dummies to capture the main effects.

Unlike standard dummies which simply compare a distinct category to a distinct reference group, we used hierarchical dummies and step-wise regression analysis to identify significant thresholds of disadvantage in relation to a given outcome. With standard coding, if a dummy variable is dropped, it becomes part of the reference category. In our specification, if a dummy variable is dropped it becomes part of the previous category in the hierarchy. It only becomes part of the reference group if all intervening dummies are dropped as well. This approach allows us to identify where categories in Table 1.1 can be combined with adjacent categories. For example, if we enter all of the hierarchical dummies for housing tenure into a model and only the second hierarchical dummy variable is retained, we identify two significant categories. Because the first dummy is dropped, the reference category 'grows' to include cohort members in the next most advantaged category. Continuing with the example of social housing, the reference category would include those with any observation in owner-occupation. Because the second dummy variable is retained and the third dummy is dropped, cohort members who ever lived in social housing form one group which is significantly different from the reference group of owner-occupiers but not significantly different from each other. In contrast, if the first and the third hierarchical dummies are retained, we have evidence for three significant categories including the reference group. Those with less evidence of home ownership differ significantly from the reference category (those most advantaged cohort members who were observed living in owner-occupation in two to three waves) and those with the most evidence of disadvantage (two to three waves in social housing) differ significantly from the middle group.

Because we are interested in identifying both cohort and gender differences, we created three sets of interaction terms. Each of the 45 main effect dummy variables was interacted with the female dummy variable so that we could test for any gender differences in childhood associations with adult disadvantage. In order to identify cohort effects, a cohort dummy variable (BCS70=1) was interacted with all of the main effect dummy variables. Finally, a female-BCS70 dummy variable was interacted with each of the main effect dummies so that we could test whether or not any gender differences have changed over time. These interactions added another 135 (45 × 3) variables for possible inclusion in our models. Estimating and interpreting models with such a large number of parameters is fraught with difficulties. Consequently, we used step-wise regressions to identify those models with the most highly significant parameters. However, with 183 potential parameters (45 main effects, 135 interactions, a constant, a female dummy and, for all outcomes except income, a cohort dummy), some of which are highly correlated, we were concerned that some important variables might be erroneously eliminated from the final models. For this reason, we decided to first narrow down the 183 variables to a smaller set of strong candidates. This subset of variables was then entered into final step-wise regression models, the results of which are presented in Table 1.3.

Gendered lives

Table 1.3   Odds ratios for childhood antecedents from backwards stepwise logistic models for four outcomes, including interactions by cohort, gender, and gender × cohort (p < 0.001)

Childhood characteristics	Adult outcomes			
	Social housing	Benefits	Low household income	Low social class
BCS70			N/A[c]	0.807
Female		1.750		
Poverty				
Any evidence (mixed evidence; poor, some missing; poor, no missing)	1.359	1.545	1.302	1.244
Stronger evidence (poor, some missing; poor, no missing)	1.417			
Housing				
All but the most advantaged (0 social housing, 0–1 wave owner; 1 wave social housing; 2–3 waves social housing)	1.459	1.000[a]	1.000[a]	1.000[a]
Any evidence of disadvantage (1 wave social housing; 2–3 waves social housing)	1.753	1.378	1.284	1.279
Social class of father				
All but the most advantaged (0 manual, 0–1 wave non-manual; 1 wave manual; 2–3 waves manual)	1.473	1.269	1.000[a]	1.330
Any evidence of disadvantage: (1 wave manual; 2–3 waves manual)	1.188		1.000[a]	1.310
All missing	1.582			1.559
Family type				
Born to a single parent	1.600	1.526		
Ever in care	1.508	1.678	1.449	
Parental interest in school				
All but the most advantaged (one parent is very interested; neither parent is very interested; one parent has low interest; both parents have low interest)	1.493	1.000[a]	1.000[a]	1.323

Table 1.3   (continued)

Childhood characteristics	Adult outcomes			
	Social housing	Benefits	Low household income	Low social class
Any evidence of disadvantage (one parent has low interest; both parents have low interest)	1.608	1.490	1.297	1.289
Both missing	1.669	1.357		1.353
Child behaviour				
Aggression				
All but the most advantaged (low; high; very high)	1.326	1.384	1.164	1.158
Child restlessness				
Any evidence of disadvantage (high; very high)	1.348	1.224	1.193	1.242
All behaviour scores missing[b]	2.583	2.296		
Academic test scores				
All but the most advantaged (middle; low; very low)	1.765	1.575	1.784	2.246
Any evidence of disadvantage (low; very low)	1.613	1.624	1.618	1.813
Strongest evidence of disadvantage (very low)	1.317	1.291	1.243	1.465
Missing test scores in all three waves	2.520	2.411	2.521	3.731
Interactions				
By cohort (× BCS70)				
Housing: all but the most advantaged (0 social housing, 0–1 wave owner; 1 wave social housing; 2–3 waves social housing)	1.000[a]	1.421		
Housing: any evidence of disadvantage (1 wave social housing; 2–3 waves social housing)	1.336			
Parental interest in education: all but the most advantaged (one parent is very interested; neither parent is very interested; one parent has low interest; both parents have low interest)		1.313		
Social class of origin: Any evidence of disadvantage (1 manual relative; 2–3 manual relatives)				1.346

Table 1.3 (continued)

Childhood characteristics	Adult outcomes			
	Social housing	Benefits	Low household income	Low social class
Social class of father: all but the most advantaged (0 manual, 0–1 wave non-manual; 1 wave manual; 2–3 waves manual)			1.367	
Social class of father: all missing			1.503	
Academic test scores: all but the most advantaged (middle, low, very low)			0.769	
By sex (× female)				
Social class of origin: all but the most advantaged (0 manual, 0–1 wave non-manual; 1 wave manual; 2–3 waves manual)	1.513			1.807
Family type: any disruption (parental divorce/separation, no remarriage, other lone parent, no remarriage; parental divorce, remarriage; other lone parent, remarriage)		1.314		
Parental interest in education: missing			1.194	
By cohort and gender (× BCS × female)				
Housing: all but the most advantaged (0 social housing, 0–1 wave owner; 1 wave social housing; 2–3 waves social housing)				1.381
Social class of origin: all but the most advantaged (0 manual, 0–1 wave non-manual; 1 wave manual; 2–3 waves manual)				0.528
Df	21	18	14	19
Likelihood ratio chi square	2865	1804	1065	2000
N	21 551	22 560	18 826	20 595

Notes:
a. Not significantly different from the reference category (not retained in the model for this outcome) and therefore subsumed into the reference category.
b. Because children with missing information on one set of behavioural scores are also likely to be missing them for them for all subscales, we constructed just one missing variable for all three summary variables.
c. The main cohort effect was not included in this model because the outcome was measured using cohort-specific quartiles.

Our strategy for reducing the number of candidate variables took place in several stages. In the first stage, we ran a series of 'blocked' step-wise models. For these and all of our step-wise models estimated in this chapter we employed a strict significance threshold of 0.001 and permitted re-entry of eliminated variables. In stage 1, we identified a subset of likely covariates by applying a four stage approach. For each outcome, we first estimated a backward step-wise logistic model with all of the main effects entered as covariates. Next, we ran a model which included all of the main effects retained from the first model as well as the gender interactions. In this model, the main effects were not eligible for elimination but the interaction terms were. Third, we ran a model that included all of the main effects and gender interactions retained from the first two models as well as the cohort interactions. As with the second model, only the cohort interactions were eligible for elimination. Fourth, we ran a model that included the gender and cohort effects, again locking in the previously retained variables. The retained variables from each of these four models comprised our subset of likely covariates.

In the second stage of the analysis, we re-ran the second, third and fourth models from stage 1, but this time we allowed any previously retained elements to be eliminated. Any additional covariates that were retained were added to our subset of likely covariates.

In the third stage, we again ran a series of blocked models, the first of which included the set of likely covariates which were locked in and could not be eliminated as well as the main terms that were not retained in previous models. Similar to the first stage of the analysis, three additional step-wise models were run with the gender interaction, the cohort interaction and the gender-cohort interaction terms that were not included in the set of likely covariates added (in that order). In each model, the set of likely covariates was locked in as well as any additional retained variables from the previous steps.

Finally, any additional terms retained in either forward or backward step-wise models that included all 183 potential correlates at once were added to the subset of likely covariates. These variables were then entered into one backwards step-wise model for each outcome and the results of these constituted our final model. Our approach allowed for gender or cohort effects (which are interaction terms in a statistical sense) of a precursor to be retained where 'main' effects were not included. Although there is some debate in the literature about whether it is appropriate to estimate models that include interaction terms without also including the corresponding main effects, we are interested in identifying those situations where there are differential responses for one group, but not a general response for all groups. For example, socialisation patterns and gender norms may mean there is a link between some background factors and an adult outcome for women but not men. Such results are substantively interesting and the search for such differential effects of cohort and gender are a primary purpose of our analysis. However, when this is the case, the results should be interpreted carefully. The size and significance of the parameter may differ relative to models where the insignificant main effects (or effect) are included as additional covariates.

4. RESULTS

Results from the complete fitted models are shown in Table 1.3. The estimated parameters for all the models are presented and discussed as odds ratios (OR) – the proportional change in the odds of an event occurring due to a change from zero to one of the corresponding control variable. When an odds ratio exceeds one, there is a positive association between the control variable and the outcome, and when an odds ratio is less than one, there is a negative association between the control variable and the outcome. We begin by looking at those childhood antecedents that show a strong net association with disadvantage on all four of the socio-economic outcomes. Such associations have been termed 'pervasive' (across many adult outcomes, for example, Hobcraft 1998, 2004), but these results also suggest that the associations are 'persistent' over time and gender.

Pervasive Antecedents

Most striking, and consistent with earlier findings (Hobcraft 1998, 2000, 2003, 2004; Sigle-Rushton 2004), was the 'clean sweep' for academic test scores: all four ('main effect') measures were significant in all four models and the odds ratios were typically among the highest we observed. However, for this covariate we found evidence of only one differential response by cohort, and none by gender: academic test scores are strongly associated with early adult socio-economic disadvantage in a clear and consistent way, regardless of cohort or gender. A bottom quartile test score at any one of the three childhood waves (compared with having two or three high quartile scores, the reference category in all four models because all hierarchical dummies are retained) raised the odds of disadvantage to 2.89:1 [1.78*1.62] for low household income, to 2.56:1 [1.58*1.62] for benefit receipt, to 2.85:1 [1.77*1.61] for living in social housing and to 4.07:1 [2.25*1.81] for being in a low skill manual occupation. Two or three low quartile test scores raised these odds ratios further, to 3.58:1, 3.30:1, 3.76:1, and 5.99:1, respectively.

The effect of test scores on low household income also varied by cohort. For those with fewer than two high quartile scores, the odds of having low household income in adulthood was reduced for the 1970 cohort. Why test scores would affect household income differentially across cohorts for low income, but not the other outcomes, is not immediately obvious, and may have something to do with differential missing values for this particular outcome. It may also be due to our decision to exclude a main cohort effect in the income regressions, a matter we return to below. A small group who had all test scores missing (4.5 per cent) were also substantially disadvantaged in adulthood. Some of this group may have been of such low ability that they could not take the tests, but most were probably missing in each of the childhood waves for some other reason (this can be inferred from the odds ratios for these groups being intermediate between the odds ratios for the fewer than two high quartile group and the any low quartile group).

Five other childhood antecedents showed a clear relationship with all four adult socio-economic outcomes considered here: any evidence of poverty during childhood (mixed evidence; poor, missing information; poor, complete information); having lived in social housing at any of the three childhood waves; having either (or both) parent(s) reported as showing little or no interest in the cohort member's education at the middle childhood wave; having low, high or very high (reference category – very low) aggression scores over the three childhood waves; and having high or very high (reference category – low and very low) restlessness scores over the three childhood waves. These pervasive associations, which are discussed in more detail in the following paragraphs, cover nearly two-thirds (36 out of 57) of the 'main effect' childhood antecedent indicators included in the models and comprise half of all the parameters retained (72).

Any evidence of childhood poverty was associated (net of all other childhood antecedents retained in the models) with an increased risk of living in social housing (OR 1.36:1), having a low adult household income (OR 1.30:1) as an adult, being in receipt of benefits (OR 1.55:1), and being in a low-skilled occupation (OR 1.24:1). More extensive experience of poverty during childhood further increased the chances of living in social housing when an adult (OR 1.93:1).

Members of either cohort who were not observed to be living in owner-occupation at two or more childhood waves – in other words, all but the most advantaged – were somewhat more likely to be living in social housing as adults (OR 1.46:1). If they had been observed living in social housing at any wave, they were much more likely still to be living in social housing as adults: for members of the 1958 cohort, the odds ratio for those with any evidence of disadvantage rises to 2.56:1, and for the 1970 cohort to 3.42:1. We thus see indications of the probable impact of the shift to owner-occupation for parents of the two cohorts, which meant that those who lived in social housing as children among the 1970 cohort were more selected for disadvantage (Lupton et al. 2009). There is an increased risk of adult benefit receipt for the 1970 cohort members who did not live in owner-occupied housing at two or more childhood waves (OR 1.42:1). In addition, adult benefit receipt is more likely amongst members of both cohorts with any evidence of disadvantage (those observed in social housing at least once during the three childhood waves: NCDS OR 1.38; BCS OR 1.96). The relationship with low social class in adulthood is slightly more complex as the effect varies by cohort and gender. Amongst BCS females, all but the most advantaged had an increased chance of being unskilled in adulthood (OR 1.38:1), as did those in both cohorts with any evidence of having lived in social housing (NCDS, male BCS OR 1.28; female BCS OR 1.43). However, the relationship was much simpler in the case of low household income. The relevant risk measure (OR 1.28:1) for any evidence of living in social housing during childhood was equivalent across cohort and gender.

A teacher's report of either parent showing little or no interest in the cohort member's schooling at age 10 or 11 (any evidence of disadvantage) was associated with all four of our adult socio-economic outcomes. For low household income this was the only effect (OR 1.30:1), although women whose reports were missing also showed a small excess risk of low adult household income. For this measure, all but the most advantaged children were more likely to be living in social housing (OR 1.49:1) and to be in low-skill occupations (OR 1.32:1) in early adulthood. For those with some evidence of disadvantage (if either parent was reported as showing little or no interest in the cohort member's schooling) this relationship was reinforced to raise the odds ratios of living in social housing as an adult to 2.40:1 and to 1.70:1 for being in a low-skilled occupation. Lastly, all but the most advantaged 1970-born cohort members were more likely to be in receipt of benefits (OR 1.31:1). If either parent was reported as showing little or no interest in their schooling (any evidence of disadvantage), the risk of benefit receipt as a young adult increased: to an odds ratio of 1.49:1 for the 1958 cohort members and to 1.95:1 for the 1970 cohort. Missing information on parental interest in schooling was fairly pervasively associated with adult socio-economic disadvantage. The only exception was low household income for men. The incidence of missing information for this measure was higher than for any other childhood antecedent because it was based on information collected in a single sweep of data collection.

Variables identifying cohort members with fewer than two low aggression scores (all but the most advantaged children who have two or three low scores) and with any evidence of high restlessness were both pervasively and persistently associated with all four adult measures of adult socio-economic disadvantage. Conversely, no measure of childhood anxiety reached sufficient statistical significance to gain entry into any of the final models. The combination of fewer than two reports of low aggression and any report of high restlessness gave odds ratios of 1.79:1 for living in social housing when an adult, 1.68:1 for being in receipt of benefits, 1.38:1 for having low household income, and 1.44:1 for being in a low-skilled occupational class. Lastly, we note that having all childhood behaviour scores missing (3.2 per cent of the sample) was associated with considerable excess risk of living in social housing (OR 2.58:1) and receiving benefits (OR 2.30:1) in early adulthood.

Gender and Cohort Interactions

A striking feature of our analyses is that we found little evidence of significant differentials in the parameter estimates by gender (only five in total across the four outcomes), by cohort (only eight in total), or by the combination of gender and cohort (only two for social class). Moreover, only the model for benefit receipt retained an undifferentiated (main) gender effect: in both cohorts women had an excess risk over men of receiving benefits in early adulthood (OR 1.75:1). However, this was reinforced for those women who had experienced any form of family disruption during childhood (OR 2.30:1). The differential consequences of early demographic behaviour for men and women are likely to be implicated here. The consequences of early and out-of-partnership childbearing and of partnership breakdown resulting in lone motherhood are well documented as are their links to later disadvantage (for example, for the 1958 cohort Cherlin et al. 1995; Hobcraft 2003; Hobcraft and Kiernan 2001; Kiernan 1992, 1995, 1997, 2002; Kiernan and Cherlin 1999; and for the 1970 cohort, Kiernan 2004). Moreover, this interpretation and the additional link to family disruption during childhood fit with the evidence on intergenerational links in family disruption.

The observed gender effect on living in social housing as an adult is captured by an apparent pathway through social class of origin. Those from the most advantaged backgrounds (that is, those with two or three reports that the father at birth and grandfathers were in non-manual occupations) were less likely to live in social housing in adulthood. However, this pathway seems less compelling than those discussed so far.

Turning to cohort differences in adult outcomes, we see that any evidence of having lived in social housing during childhood was differentially associated with living in social housing as an adult for members of the 1970 cohort. This probably reflects the greater level of disadvantage among social housing tenants in this cohort (Lupton et al. 2009). At the same time, it is somewhat surprising that we found three cohort differences for the outcome household income in the lowest quartile. Since this was defined to have fixed proportions for each cohort, we opted not to include a BCS70 main effect in the income model. The significant interactions may be due to our decision to leave out a main cohort effect. Moreover, there was also a relatively small and not especially interpretable gendered differentiated response associated with the measures of parental interest both being missing, which arose particularly for those who were not interviewed at the middle childhood wave.

The final interactions were associated with being in a low-skilled occupational class in early adulthood. The mediation of gender and cohort differentials on social class in adulthood through parental and grandparental social class is reassuring, in view of the vast literature on intergenerational occupational mobility (for example, Erikson and Goldthorpe 1993). Effectively, what we found is that women in the 1958 cohort who were from families where fewer than two male relatives (among the grandfathers and the father at the time of birth) were in non-manual occupations – that is, all but the most advantaged – were considerably more likely to be in low-skilled occupations when they reached adulthood. This seems to capture some structural change, particularly the moves toward greater gender equality in educational achievement and in subsequent employment opportunities and towards delayed marriage and childbearing for the women in the 1970 cohort. Conversely, women in the 1958 cohort seem to have been less affected than those in the 1970 cohort by housing tenure in childhood. However, the effect is weakened somewhat by an overall reduction in the odds of being in low-skill occupations for all 1970 cohort members.

All other gender and cohort differentials in our outcomes were mostly mediated through the childhood antecedents. This is suggestive, though not conclusive evidence, that structural changes between the cohorts have not played a key role. Because our models retain few 'black-box' cohort or gender effects, it also suggests that our models successfully captured mediating childhood antecedents involved in the genesis of cohort or gender differences.

5.   CONCLUSION

In this chapter, we found consistent and pervasive linkages of adult outcomes to childhood test scores (especially), parental housing tenure, living in poverty during childhood, parental interest in schooling and to being a child who displayed aggressive and restless behaviour. Although the persistence and strength of these relationships have been identified in previous research (Hobcraft 1998; Sigle-Rushton 2004), there has been little attempt thus far to test rigorously for evidence of gender differentials or change over time in the size and significance of these associations. It is worth stressing that most of the linkages are common for both birth cohorts and for men and women. Although we applaud efforts to address issues of intersectionality by estimating models that take into account differences between social groups, researchers need to be aware that this degree of regularity is often missed when similar analyses are done separately by gender or by cohort without testing for evidence of statistically significant differences across groups (Sigle-Rushton 2008). The key lesson to emerge from our application here is that there is a great deal of common structure. The responsiveness for most of the childhood antecedents measured does not differ very much, if at all, by gender or cohort. The strength and consistency of the findings does perhaps suggest that some of the linkages and pathways are real and not artefacts of unobserved heterogeneity or unmeasured variables, although we cannot rule out earlier mediating pathways (through genetic inheritance or early childhood experiences and parenting) or subsequent mediating linkages, particularly during the transition from adolescence to adulthood.

Of the consistent relationships we identified across the four adult outcomes, the most salient interactions were retained for measures of parental housing tenure. Although not consistently retained across the four outcomes we consider, these relationships merit further exploration and explanation. Indeed, researchers have only recently begun to focus their attention on the meaning and role of social housing in the production of disadvantage (Lupton et al. 2009). Given recent government evaluations of social housing (Hills 2007) and proposals to change the housing benefits system, a better understanding of the role of housing tenure in the production and intergenerational transmission of disadvantage is clearly warranted. The cohort studies that we analyse in this chapter offer a rich source of information that can shed light on the stratifying effects of childhood housing tenure and how they differ by gender (and across other social groups) as well as over time. Our findings suggest that the increased odds of being a social housing tenant among children who grew up in social housing have strengthened for children born in 1970 relative to 1958. Moreover children whose parents were not consistently identified as owner-occupiers were more likely to be in receipt of benefits in their early thirties. Like the results for social housing, the odds of benefit receipt for these children were larger for the 1970 cohort than for the 1958 cohort. Finally, women with all but the best housing circumstances were more likely to have a low occupational class as adults if they were born in 1970 rather than in 1958. These findings suggest that children of social tenants (or who did not grow up with parents who are long-term owner-occupiers) have become increasingly vulnerable to socio-economic disadvantage in adulthood. Further research is needed to understand and explain women's greater sensitivity to housing disadvantage. The relative risk and the subsequent gendered effects of early parenthood might be one pathway to explore (Hobcraft 2003; Lupton et al. 2009).

Among the remaining pervasive antecedents, there is less evidence of differential responsiveness by cohort and/or gender. No interactions were retained for poverty, aggression or restlessness. Although evidence of associations of adult outcomes with childhood academic test scores was particularly strong, the only differential response we identified was a significant cohort interaction with low household income. And as we discussed above, this may be due, in part, to our decision to exclude a main cohort indicator in these models. The only other exception was parental interest in education. The protective effects on being in receipt of benefits in adulthood, of having parents that teachers perceive as most strongly interested in their children's education appeared to have strengthened for the 1970 cohort. Girls with missing information on their parents' educational interest were more likely to have low household income. The former relationship, when put alongside the evidence of social class background, suggests that parents' cultural capital may have become increasingly important as the labour market became less industrial and more knowledge based. Among the 1970 cohort, children whose parents did not or could not help them negotiate the educational system and the changing labour market may have struggled more than their counterparts born in 1958.

The pervasive linkages and significant interactions point to areas where additional research could perhaps provide useful information on the genesis of gender differences in the outcomes we consider. However, explanations of the patterns we identified in this chapter should not be pursued without acknowledging that real progress in understanding pathways to disadvantage has to involve multiple well-measured factors and a study of the pathways and interlinkages through life, rather than trying to rely merely on a single cause. Causation in human behaviour is relatively unlikely to arise from any single manipulable variable, and much more likely to involve the accumulation of a series of experiences and a variety of complex interplays over the life course.

REFERENCES

Bynner, J. and H. Joshi (2002), 'Equality and opportunity in education: evidence from the 1958 and 1970 birth cohort studies', *Oxford Review of Education*, **28** (4), 405–25.

Bynner, J. and H. Pan (2002), 'Understanding transition', in J. Bynner, P. Elias, A. McKnight, H. Pan and G. Pierre (eds), *Young People's Changing Routes to Independence*, York: Joseph Rowntree Foundation, pp. 27–36.

Bynner, J. and S. Parsons (2000), 'Marginalization and value shifts under the changing economic circumstances surrounding the transition to work: a comparison of cohorts born in 1958 and 1970', *Journal of Youth Studies*, **3** (3), 237–49.

Bynner, J. and S. Parsons (2001), 'Qualifications, basic skills and accelerating social exclusion', *Journal of Education and Work*, **14** (3), 279–91.

Cherlin, A., K.E. Kiernan and P.L. Chase-Lansdale (1995), 'Parental divorce in childhood and demographic outcomes in young adulthood', *Demography*, **32** (3), 299–318.

Duncan, G.J., W.J. Yeung, J. Brooks-Gunn and J.R. Smith (1998), 'How much does childhood poverty affect the life chances of children?', *American Sociological Review*, **63**, 406–23.

Elander, J. and M. Rutter (1996), 'Use and development of the Rutter parents' and teachers' scales', *International Journal of Methods in Psychiatric Research*, **6**, 63–78.

Elder, G.H. Jr (1974), *Children of the Great Depression: Social Change in Live Experience*, Chicago, IL: University of Chicago Press.

Elder, G.H. Jr (1998), 'The life course as developmental theory', *Child Development*, **69** (1), 1–12.

Erikson, R. and J.H. Goldthorpe (1993), *The Constant Flux: A Study of Class Mobility in Industrial Societies*, Oxford: Clarendon Press.

Hills, J. (2007), *Ends & Means: The Future Roles of Social Housing in England*, CASEreport 34, London: ESRC Research Centre for the Analysis of Social Exclusion.

Hobcraft, J. (1998), *Intergenerational and Life-Course Transmission of Social Exclusion: Influences of Child Poverty, Family Disruption, and Contact with the Police*, CASEpaper 15, London: London School of Economics, ESRC Centre for the Analysis of Social Exclusion.

Hobcraft, J. (2000), *The Roles of Schooling and Educational Qualifications in the Emergence of Adult Social Exclusion*, CASEpaper 43, London: London School of Economics, ESRC Centre for the Analysis of Social Exclusion.

Hobcraft, J. (2003), *Continuity and Change in Pathways to Young Adult Disadvantages: Results from a British Birth Cohort*, CASEpaper 66, London: London School of Economics, ESRC Centre for the Analysis of Social Exclusion.

Hobcraft, J. (2004), 'Parental, childhood and early adult legacies in the emergence of adult social exclusion: evidence on what matters from a British cohort', in P. L. Chase-Lansdale, K. Kiernan and R.J. Friedman (eds), *Human Development across Lives and Generations: The Potential for Change*, Cambridge: Cambridge University Press, pp. 63–92.

Hobcraft, J. and K. Kiernan (2001), 'Childhood poverty, early motherhood and adult social exclusion', *British Journal of Sociology*, **52** (3), 495–517.

Kiernan, K.E. (1992), 'The impact of family disruption in childhood on transitions made in young adult life', *Population Studies*, **46** (2), 213–34.

Kiernan, K.E. (1995), 'Transition to parenthood: young mothers, young fathers: associated factors and later life experiences', *LSE-STICERD Discussion Paper 113*, London: LSE.

Kiernan, K.E. (1996), 'Lone-motherhood, employment and outcomes for children', *International Journal of Law, Policy and the Family*, **13** (3), 233–49.

Kiernan, K.E. (1997), 'Becoming a young parent: a longitudinal study of associated factors', *British Journal of Sociology*, **48** (3), 406–28.

Kiernan, K.E. (2002), 'Disadvantage and demography – chicken and egg?', in J. Hills, J. LeGrand and D. Piachaud (eds), *Understanding Social Exclusion*, Oxford: Oxford University Press, pp. 84–96.

Kiernan, K. (2004), 'Cohabitation and divorce across nations and generations', in P.L. Chase-Lansdale, K. Kiernan and R.J. Friedman (eds), *Human Development across Lives and Generations: The Potential for Change*, Cambridge: Cambridge University Press, pp. 139–70.

Kiernan, K. and A. Cherlin (1999), 'Parental divorce and partnership dissolution in adulthood: evidence from a British cohort study', *Population Studies*, **53** (2), 39–48.

Leete, R. and J. Fox (1977), 'Registrar General's social classes: origins and users', *Population Trends*, **8**, 1–7.

Lupton, R., R. Tunstall, W. Sigle-Rushton, P. Obolenskaya, R. Sabates, E. Meschi, D. Kneale and E. Salter (2009), *Growing up in Social Housing in Britain: A Profile of Four Generations from 1946 to the Present Day*, London: Tenant Services Authority.

McKnight, A. (2002), 'From childhood poverty to labour market disadvantage', in J. Bynner, P. Elias, A. McKnight, H. Pan and G. Pierre (eds), *Young People's Changing Routes to Independence*, York: Joseph Rowntree Foundation, pp. 49–66.

McLanahan, S. (1985), 'Family structure and the reproduction of poverty', *American Journal of Sociology*, **90**, 873–901.

McLanahan, S. and G. Sandefur (1994), *Growing up with a Single Parent: What Hurts, What Helps*, London: Harvard University Press.

Moffitt, T.E. (1993), 'Adolescence-limited and life-course-persistent anti-social behavior: a developmental taxonomy', *Psychological Review*, **100**, 674–701.

Office of Population Censuses and Surveys (OPCS) (1980), *Standard Classification of Occupations (SOC)*, London: Her Majesty's Stationery Office.

Schoon, I., J. Bynner, H. Joshi, S. Parsons, R.D. Wiggins and A. Sacker (2002), 'The influence of context, timing, and duration of risk experiences for the passage from childhood to midadulthood', *Child Development*, **73** (5), 1486–504.

Schoon, I., A. Sacker and M. Bartley (2003), 'Socio-economic adversity and psychosocial adjustment: a developmental-contextual perspective', *Social Science and Medicine*, **57**, 1001–15.

Sigle-Rushton, W. (2004), *Intergenerational and Life-Course Transmission of Social Exclusion in the 1970 British Cohort Study*, CASEpaper 78, London: London School of Economics, ESRC Centre for the Analysis of Social Exclusion.

Sigle-Rushton, W. (2008), 'Looking for difference?' in W. Østreng (ed.), *Complexity: Interdisciplinary Communications*, Oslo: Centre for Advanced Study at the Norwegian Academy of Science and Letters.

Sigle-Rushton, W., J.N. Hobcraft and K.E. Kiernan (2005), 'Parental disruption and subsequent disadvantage: a cross-cohort comparison', *Demography*, **42** (3), 427–46.

2. Changing career trajectories of women and men across time

Erzsebet Bukodi, Shirley Dex and Heather Joshi

INTRODUCTION

As we know from cross-sectional snapshots and their time trends, women's and men's labour market behaviours have grown closer together as women have participated increasingly in paid work. From the mid-twentieth century onwards, women have increasingly moved out of the private sphere of the home, into the public sphere previously occupied mainly by men assisted by their large increases in educational qualifications (see Scott et al., Introduction, this volume). Over the same period, men's employment participation rates have declined, largely linked to sectoral changes and the decline of occupations in the manufacturing sector. What is less well documented is the extent to which women's or men's career trajectories have changed, and whether these also have grown closer over time. Career trajectories are the longitudinal and more dynamic elements of working lives that this book is concerned with. It is important to examine them to see whether men and women are still on gendered pathways as they go through their working lives, a task that is implicitly a comparison across generations and across time.

There are a number of reasons why we should be interested in the changing career trajectories of women and men. Charting such longitudinal careers over time across generations will help to answer policy-related questions about whether women and men have grown more equal following the 1970s, in which decade sex discrimination and unequal pay for equal work were made illegal. We hope to document how far we have come. We also need to understand how and why the changes have occurred, as well as whether and why gender equality in labour market experiences has not been fully achieved. Childbirth was a pivotal point in the gendering of women's labour market experiences in the past. It interrupted many women's careers (Dex 1984), led to a loss of occupational status (Dex 1987) and to lower earnings trajectories (Joshi et al. 1996). The career and pay effects were sometimes linked to combining motherhood with working part-time hours in new service sector jobs. However, the introduction of Statutory Maternity Leave for women in 1975 also secured their entitlements to jobs with the same employer after childbirth. Over time, eligibility has been extended to an increasing proportion of women. This suggests we should see less evidence of women experiencing downward occupational mobility after childbirth, in successive generations of mothers. It is important to investigate whether this Achilles' heel for women's careers in earlier generations continues to be a major disruption.

Setting out to document gendered occupational careers across generations is possible because of Britain's tradition of rich longitudinal data collection, in the form of the British birth cohorts' lives. These data-sets have been accumulating evidence on large representative samples of men and women born in 1946, 1958 and 1970 (see Ferri et al. 2003). Now spanning nearly a half century of working life trajectories, these lives, from one cohort to the next, are a lens on societal change and diverse individual pathways within it. However, while these are very rich data, we should not underestimate the complexity of unravelling the components of social change. These components include legislation and policy, the extent of educational opportunities, macroeconomic factors such as the sectoral balance of employment and business cycle fluctuations, employers' practices as well as individuals' aspirations and preferences. Men and women live out their lives in the context of these multiple influences. Increasing educational opportunities for women and the wave of new legislation in the 1970s have had a greater chance to influence cohorts of women born in 1970 than those born in 1958 or 1946. At the macro level there have been substantial changes in employment through the decline of the manufacturing sector, reducing men's full-time job opportunities. There have been parallel rises in service sector and public sector employment which have offered many new and often part-time job opportunities mainly to women (see Figures I.4a, I.4b and I.5 in the Introduction to this volume). Conditions at labour market entry have varied substantially for the different birth cohorts (see Figure 2.1) and these variations may have affected women's and men's careers differently. At the micro level, demand for labour varies and changes across occupations and sectors (see Figures I.4a, I.4b and I.5 in the Introduction to this volume), but employers also determine whether and how equal opportunities are practised in the workplace. This can be, for example, through selection, recruitment and promotion practices and the extent of flexible or family-friendly working arrangements (see Dex and Forth 2009). In addition, any particular cohort will bring their aspirations and preferences to face a different set of opportunities and constraints. Women of

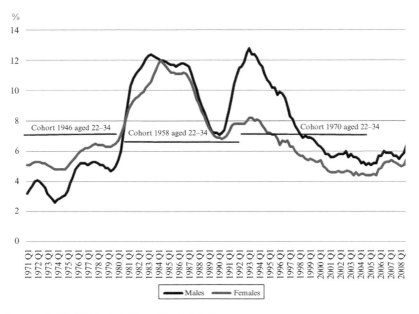

Source: ONS, Quarterly Labour Force Survey.

Figure 2.1   ILO unemployment rates in the UK

more recent cohorts are likely to have higher aspirations than past generations due to increased levels of qualifications. Men preferring jobs in skilled
manual craft trades have had to adjust their aspirations downwards across
successive cohorts as jobs in the manufacturing sector shrunk (see Figure
I.4b in the Introduction to this volume, or Dex 1999, table 3.1).

This chapter is a study of gender equality at the dynamic level of
individuals' lives, showing that the gendering of lives has changed
across recent generations and against the background of initiatives
promoting gender equality, varying labour market conditions, sectoral
and weekly hours changes, and changes in men's and women's aspirations and preferences. Our aim is to address the following research
questions:

1.   How have men's and women's occupational trajectories, and the
     differences between them, changed over time?
2.   Has women's increased education made a difference to the influ-
     ence of education on the careers of women or men across different
     generations?

3. Has the disruption to careers associated with childbirth seen in earlier generations of mothers been ameliorated by staying with the same employer across childbirth which the introduction of Statutory Maternity Leave facilitated?

4. Have the labour market conditions faced by different birth cohorts at their entry into the labour market influenced their career progress? Have women and men been affected in the same ways and to the same extent by variations in labour market conditions over their early careers? Has this affected the extent of or movement towards gender equality across cohorts?

In the remainder of this chapter, we first describe the birth cohort data. Then we chart a series of narratives around the analyses we have carried out on three generations of working lives. These are some of the broad conclusions of a more detailed set of analyses, too extensive to present in full in this chapter, but to which the interested reader is referred. We conclude that there has been some convergence in men's and women's working life trajectories and career progression in more recent cohorts. These are consistent with equal opportunities legislation which improved the career chances of women relative to men. For instance, Statutory Maternity Leave and more flexible working arrangements allow mothers in more recent generations to combine paid work and childcare more easily. However, working part-time after childbirth still risks the loss of occupational status and pay for women, especially when combined with a change of employer. This overall picture is complicated by within-gender variations and subject to the influence of business cycle fluctuations which have left their mark on particular cohorts' lives, as well as on the extent of gender differences in career progression.

THE BIRTH COHORTS' LIVES AND THEIR CONTEXT

The three principal data-sets used in this study are all cohort studies following the life course of all children born in Britain in a particular week. The Medical Research Council National Survey of Health and Development (NSHD) started in 1946, the National Child Development Study (NCDS) in 1958, and the British Cohort Study (BCS70) in 1970. The data available for our analyses included 19 data collection 'sweeps' up to age 63 (NSHD), the NCDS's eight sweeps up to age 50 and the BCS70's seven sweeps up to age 38. The 1958 and 1970 cohorts originally contained around 17 000 children, but the 1946 cohort follow-up sample is significantly smaller, at around 5000 children. These data-sets include recalled information on each job men and women held since leaving full-time education. Our analyses focused particularly on trajectories of occupations and earnings, but there are many other explanatory variables available to understand the reasons associated with occupational attainment and career progression across gender groups. As with all longitudinal studies, the problem of missing data in the form of attrition and item non-response arises. However, studies of attrition and non-response are encouraging and suggest that no major biases are being created (Hawkes and Plewis 2006; Nathan 1999; Wadsworth et al. 2005). Further details about the job and occupational histories can be found in Bukodi and Neuburger (2009) and Ward (2007).[1]

The employment and fertility histories of the 1946 and 1958 cohorts provide benchmark career profiles, as necessary background for an examination of the effects of the changing policy environment in the late twentieth and early twenty-first centuries which have had more impact on the later cohorts. Against this background, the evolving Millennium Cohort Study (MCS) of children born across the UK in 2000–01 can also provide evidence on how the careers of recent generations of mothers (and fathers) are evolving in children's early years (Sweep 1 data in 2001 at 9 months; Sweep 2 data in 2004 at age 3; Sweep 3 data in 2006 at age 5). The parents of MCS children were born between the 1960s and 1980s, many of them around 1970, but a substantial minority of mothers come from a generation born after the 1970 BCS cohort.

While the three cohorts (1946, 1958 and 1970) were growing up, the legal and policy landscape changed in a number of ways. When the equality legislation of the 1970s was being enacted, the members of the 1946 cohort were aged 24 to 33, of the 1958 cohort aged 12 to 21 and the 1970 cohort members were only just born. Over the next 35 years, up to around 2005, further legislation was passed to strengthen sex discrimination legislation, extend women's rights, expand eligibility for statutory maternity leave, and to introduce parental leave and paid paternity leave to give fathers a right to time off work around childbirth. After the Labour government's accession to power in 1997, there were a large number of new initiatives aimed at enabling parents to combine work and family life more easily. The National Minimum Wage was introduced in 1999 in Britain, improving wage rates at the lowest end of the distribution, including many part-time wage rates. The European Union (EU) Part-time Work Directive, enacted in law in the UK in 2000, required that employees working part-time be given the same rights as full-time employees. Childcare provision increased markedly in the 1990s and into the 2000s, boosted by the National Child Care Strategy of 1998 and programmes such as Sure Start. This allowed

Table 2.1   *Labour market conditions at the point of leaving school for three cohorts*

Left school at	Unemployment rate when leaving school:					
	Cohort 1946		Cohort 1958		Cohort 1970	
	Year	Rate (%)	Year	Rate (%)	Year	Rate (%)
Age 15	1961	2.0	1974	3.0	1986	11.8
Age 18	1964	1.8	1976	5.8	1989	8.6
Age 21	1967	2.5	1979	4.2	1991	10.4

Source: ONS historical series.

Britain to catch up somewhat with other European countries with regards to childcare places, especially for 3 to 4-year-olds. During the 1990s and into the twenty-first century, employers also took initiatives to improve the retention of female employees by offering more flexibility and incentives to returning mothers (Dex and Smith 2002). It is worth remembering that the 1946 cohort members were 51 years old in 1997 at the start of this new wave of post-1997 policies, while the 1958 cohort were 39 and the 1970 cohort were 27 years old. The 1970 cohort, and the parents of the Millennium children were best placed to take advantage of the new opportunities for combining employment and parenthood. This set of changes would lead us to expect that gender inequality would be greater in earlier than in more recent cohorts. We might also expect that as opportunities for women expanded, women's preferences and aspirations would change to reflect the wider range of available occupations. Also, women might be expected to (gradually) stop believing that 'a woman's place is in the home' and consider it the norm to combine employment, full- or part-time, and motherhood. Fathers, on the other hand, might be expected to start considering that they too could combine employment and active involvement in childcare.

Yet another important variation in experiences across cohorts relates to the labour market conditions that were operating in Britain since the 1970s. As Table 2.1 displays, national unemployment rates were very low when the 1946 cohort typically entered the labour market; rates were higher when the 1958 cohort entered but considerably higher when the 1970 cohort faced finding a first job after leaving full-time education. These labour market conditions may lead us to expect that the most recent 1970s-born cohort, facing the worst conditions at entry, would do least well at entry into the labour market, while the 1946 cohort would be expected to exhibit the best performance. But what happened in the early careers of these cohorts may also be instructive (see Figure 2.1). The 1958 cohort faced severely deteriorating labour market conditions over the whole of their twenties. However, the 1970 cohort, while facing difficult entry conditions, experienced improving conditions in their early careers. Later in this chapter, we return to comment on how these conditions affected career entry and development.

CREATING A VERTICAL OCCUPATIONAL SCALE

As we are interested in career progression, we first needed to devise a vertical ranking of occupations, after first coding all the occupations in individuals' work histories based on a common coding frame. The official 1990 Standard Occupational Coding (SOC90) (ONS, [1990] 2010) was the only coding frame that could be applied across all available sweeps of data from these three birth cohorts. This provided 77 occupational codes. The ranking of occupations is a challenge in itself as different criteria and different subsets of data can be used to devise the ranking. In our analyses, we used two main rankings, one based on average hourly pay (see also Nickell 1982), and one based on status as devised by Chan and Goldthorpe (2004, 2007). However, we only have space to report on the first type of ranking in this chapter, the one based on hourly earnings.[2]

This occupational earnings scale is an updated, extended version of that constructed by Nickell (1982). Data from the New Earnings Survey 2002 on the average hourly earnings of full-time employees by occupation were matched with each of the 77 minor occupational groups in the SOC90 classification. These occupation scores were further converted into percentile distributions ranging from 1 to 100, to facilitate comparisons with other scales. All of the occupations in an individual's occupational history were then given the appropriate score using these percentiles.

FIRST OCCUPATIONS

We now examine individuals' careers focusing on occupational earnings and starting out at their first entry into the labour market. An examination of the ranked scores of occupations men and women entered after leaving full-time education shows some gender and cohort differences. Women's average occupational scores at their entry to the labour market, in all three cohorts, was mostly substantially lower, by approximately 15 points on average, than men's average scores within the same cohort. Average entry-level occupational scores increased, not surprisingly, as educational qualifications at entry increased.

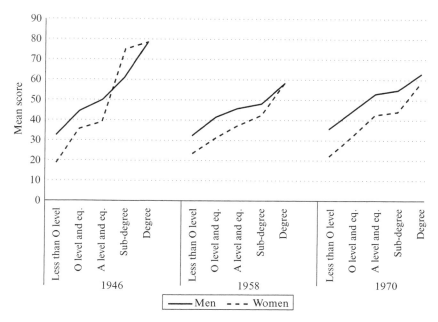

Figure 2.2   Mean occupational earnings score in first job by cohort and gender

Wider cohort differences were also visible (Figure 2.2). Average entry-level occupational scores of women born in 1946 were mostly lower compared with those born in 1970. However, average levels of entry occupations were considerably higher in 1946 than in the later cohorts, at higher education levels. Worsening labour market conditions at the point of entry for the 1958 and 1970 cohorts compared with the 1946 cohort may have led us to expect better outcomes for the 1946 cohort entrants, but this only applies in the case of the most highly educated women. However, we also need to recognise the more selective nature of the 1946 cohort, particularly, but not solely, for the women who entered the labour market, as there was likely a greater sorting of those with high ability into higher educational attainment in this cohort. The expansion of higher education over time would also be expected to lead to lower occupational scores for later cohorts compared to the 1946 cohort of highly educated women.

The gap between men's and women's entry occupational scores also widened as labour market conditions at entry worsened. However, one finding emerged from the 1946 cohort's entry experiences which was unexpected. Women with qualifications at entry between A level and degree

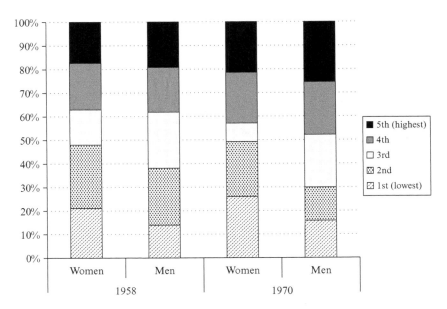

Figure 2.3   Quintile distributions of first occupational earnings scores for men and women by cohort

had a higher average occupational score at entry than men born in the same year and women of later cohorts. Labour market conditions were very favourable for their employment. Nonetheless, this probably reflects the fact that these women were predominantly holders of the highly feminised teaching and nursing qualifications which for later cohorts were reclassified to be equivalent to degree-level qualifications in the National Vocational Qualifications (NVQ)[3] framework as NVQ4. Highly educated women born in 1946 may also have come from more advantaged backgrounds, and have been more highly motivated.

It is also instructive to see the distribution, as well as the mean occupational scores, for first occupations (Figure 2.3). We can see that women born in 1970 did progressively better than those born in 1958 at the top end of the occupational distribution. A greater proportion of those born in 1970 entered the top occupations, reflecting their higher educational qualifications. However, men also improved their position at the top between these two cohorts and retained their lead over women. Higher proportions of both women and men were in occupations at the bottom of the hierarchy in the 1970 compared with the 1958 cohort, although the men's proportions were not statistically significantly different. This probably reflects the worsening entry conditions when the 1970 cohort were leaving full-time education, than was the case for those born in 1958. In this respect, women at the bottom of the occupational hierarchy seemed to suffer more than men when economic and labour market conditions were poor. Women continued to enter occupations that had lower wages than men. For women there was a marked squeezing of the middle group, implying a polarisation in first occupations not seen among men. There was some evidence of a gradually polarising occupational structure over time and across cohorts where a growing proportion of workers can be seen in both 'top' and 'bottom' occupations. Notable in the 'bottom' occupations were many female-dominated low-level service and sales occupations.

CAREER PROGRESSION OVER THE LIFE COURSE

Career progression over the early career years, based on hourly earnings-based rankings of occupations, are shown in Figure 2.4a for men and in Figure 2.4b for women. Overall, we can see that there were relatively small differences by cohort in the average occupational attainment in men's

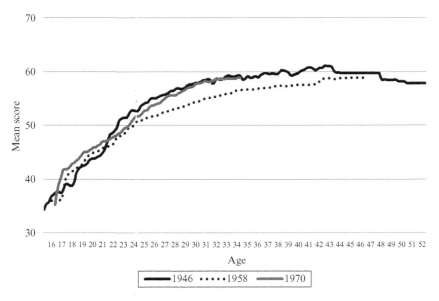

Figure 2.4a   Men's mean occupational earnings scores across age by cohort

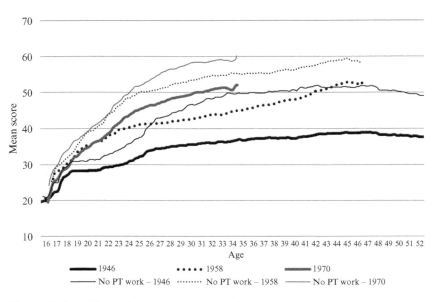

Figure 2.4b   *Women's mean occupational earnings scores across age by*
                 cohort

early to mid careers. The 1958 cohort of men reached lower mean levels of
occupational attainment than the earlier 1946 and the later 1970 cohorts
of men. Their experience of severely deteriorating labour market conditions is likely to be the main reason that the 1958 cohort stands out from
the others. This point has been noted in other studies (Gregg 2001). There
were much larger cohort differences in women's occupational progression
across these early years. In the 1958 cohort, women's career progression
improved compared to the 1946 cohort's profile, and the 1970 cohort
improved compared with the 1958 cohort.

Men tended to reach higher levels of occupational attainment than
women in each cohort (Figures 2.4a and 2.4b). Figure 2.4b includes
the mean trajectories for women in each cohort who had never worked
part-time over their career (from labour market entry to age 34 for
the 1970 cohort, age 46 for the 1958 cohort and age 53 for the 1946
cohort). It can be seen that women who did not work part-time reached
career levels much closer to men's. In the 1970 cohort we scarcely see
any differences between men and women who never worked in part-time
jobs.

The determinants of career progression were also analysed and
some common predictors emerged for both men and women, although

varying in importance (Bukodi 2009). Education was found to be the single most important determinant of occupational attainment for both men and women from all three cohorts. However, education was more important for women's than it was for men's occupational attainment, but its influence did not change across cohorts. There have been debates about the role of education in occupational attainment. One view suggested that with modernisation education has become increasingly important for individuals' occupational attainment (Hendrickx and Ganzeboom 1998). An alternative view suggested that the relative importance of education in influencing occupational attainment has weakened or stayed the same over time (Blossfeld et al. 2006, 2008). Our analyses suggested that education has remained important at a relatively stable level.

Having a father in a managerial or professional occupation was a more important influence on men's than on women's career progression. In addition, family background was even more important for men in the early working years of the 1958 cohort when labour market conditions were extremely difficult. This was especially the case for the more highly educated who were developing their early careers in the labour market context of the severe recession of the early 1980s.

The upward and downward occupational mobility of men and women in our three birth cohorts is revealing. A set of five classifications were devised from the varying experiences over the early career period – the time between leaving full-time education up to age 34 in all cohorts. Individuals could be making upward moves only (steadily upwards), downward moves only (steadily downwards), both upward and downward moves but end up in a lower occupation (unstable downwards) or higher occupation (unstable upwards) by age 34 than earlier. Lastly, individuals could make both upward and downward moves but end up at the occupational level they started from (stable counter mobile). There are differences in mobility across cohorts and some smaller differences by gender (Figure 2.5). If anything, women with only full-time jobs did slightly better than men in the same cohort with regards to having steadily upwards career experiences, although they did less well than men at having unstable upwards early career profiles. Women born in 1946 were more likely to have steadily downwards careers than those born in 1958. This career trajectory was less frequent again in the 1970 cohort than in the 1958 cohort of women, such that by then a lower percentage of women than men had this steadily downwards experience. Men in each of the three cohorts were more likely than women of the same cohort to experience unstable downwards careers. The stable or counter-mobile career was more evident among women who never worked part-time than among men in each cohort. Women who had

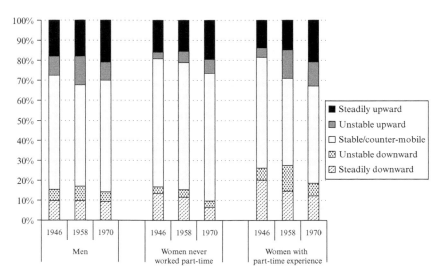

Figure 2.5   Classification of women's and men's occupational earnings
histories up to age 34 by cohort

some part-time work experience over their early career were likely to have
had far more of the steadily downward and unstable downwards and less
of the steadily upward occupational trajectories than women without any
part-time work experience and than men in the same cohort. We should
note that members of the 1958 cohort, and men to a greater extent than
women, experienced the most unstable occupational careers of these three
cohorts, a large part of which was due to the worsening macroeconomic
conditions over their early careers.

There are a number of points worth noting about these experiences.
Men of all three cohorts had considerable amounts of downward occupational mobility over their early careers. While it has been common to
bemoan women's loss of occupational status and point out the inefficiency
for the economy, less attention has been drawn to men's experience and
loss of occupational status. We suspect this is largely because there has
been relatively little investigation of men's occupational trajectories in
the past. There is also evidence, for the most recent birth cohort, of some
movement towards greater gender equality in the extent of these various
occupational career trajectories, but mainly where women avoided part-
time employment spells. This convergence has its origins in some improvements for women alongside some deterioration for men in their career
progression.

STARTING OUT IN A LOW PAID OCCUPATION

In order to understand the mechanisms which underpin gender gaps in occupational career attainment over time, we carried out further analysis of how the first entry job affected later occupational attainment. We found an effect on subsequent wage-based occupational attainment from entering the labour market via one of the lowest ranked occupations (see Bukodi and Dex 2010).[4] However, an overwhelming majority of men who entered the labour market via low-quality jobs not only got out of these positions with a relatively high probability but also managed to maintain their more advantaged occupational position over their early employment careers. For many men, therefore, employment at entry in the lowest level of the occupational hierarchy was a stepping stone rather than a trap, and may indicate a period of investment in human capital or a period of 'experiment' in order to find the most suitable career path and a good match of the individual to their job. Women were also able to progress upwards out of an entry job in one of the lowest level occupations, even at a fairly similar rate to men with the same level of qualifications. However, women's improved occupational position was more transient. They were much more likely than men to experience downward mobility, in most cases back to their initial low occupational level, over their relatively early employment histories. Also, where women moved up the occupational scale, a significant proportion of these shifts were quite 'short-distance', to the second worst level of the hierarchy at most. Men were more likely to make bigger jumps up the scale. For women, therefore, starting their employment career in the lowest level of the occupational hierarchy was more of a 'trap' rather than a 'stepping stone' as it was for men.

Gender differences in our comparison of the implications of a bad entry job and subsequent career chances changed over time, between those born in 1958 and 1970. The detrimental effects of starting a career in the lowest occupational quintile appeared to be more pronounced for women of the 1970 than of the 1958 cohort. As noted above, women born in 1970 had higher proportions than those born in 1958 with jobs at the bottom of the occupational scale. But the mobility chances out of these positions were clearly lower for the 1970 born women than for those born in 1958. This suggests that an increasing polarisation of women's employment and occupational structure occurred and intensified in the 1990s coupled with growing uncertainties about labour market conditions. These led to lower probabilities for career advancement out of the lowest occupational positions for women.

WOMEN'S CAREERS AFTER CHILDBIRTH

Women of earlier twentieth-century generations tended to stop work, often from full-time jobs, to have children, or even at the point of getting married. Men of successive generations have not exhibited changes in their careers that are specifically linked to childbirth so they are not the focus of this discussion. When mothers started to return to paid work in larger numbers, after the mid-twentieth century, they often took up part-time jobs at the point of re-entry. Part-time jobs since the 1950s were typically low paid and low skilled, and concentrated in a few occupations and sectors. Thus, this transition from full-time to part-time work after childbirth involved a downward occupational move for many mothers. By the twenty-first century, 6 million women in Britain were working part-time hours,[5] representing around two-fifths of the female workforce, and even more women have worked part-time at some point in their career (Connolly and Gregory 2008). The proportion is even higher when mothers are considered. In 2006, a third of female part-time employees were working in one of only five low-ranking occupational groups: namely, as sales assistants, cleaners, care assistants, general clerks, and educational assistants (Connolly and Gregory 2008).

The introduction of Statutory Maternity Leave and its extended eligibility would be expected to improve the status of mothers' occupations after childbirth if they stayed with the same employer. However, there is yet no absolute right to switch from full-time to part-time hours – since 2003 the employer has the duty to give mothers' requests to work part-time serious consideration (see also Lewis, Chapter 8 in this volume) – and many mothers therefore leave their employment. Despite the lack of statutory right, we would expect to see less occupational downgrading after childbirth across successive generations of mothers.

For women, a move into part-time work following a first birth has been associated with downward occupational mobility (Connolly and Gregory 2008; Dex et al. 2008). Studies of women's employment up to the 1980s, based on the Women and Employment Survey (WES), documented the extensive amount of downward occupational mobility experienced by women at this point in their lifecycle (Dex 1987; Joshi and Hinde 1993; Joshi and Newell 1987). The likelihood of a downward occupational move after a birth decreased for women who became mothers in the 1980s and 1990s, compared to earlier quasi cohort generations,[6] but a substantial minority is still affected (Dex et al. 2008). In fact, among first-time mothers born in 1958, taking a part-time job made it more likely, compared with earlier generations, that they would suffer occupational downgrading. Moving from full-time hours in one of the top occupations to part-time

Table 2.2   Proportion of women who experienced downward mobility on occupational earnings scale around first childbirth

Job before first childbirth	Job after first childbirth	% downwardly mobile	
		1958	1970
Full-time	Part-time	43	29
Part-time	Full-time	18	15
Part-time	Part-time	22	9
Full-time	Full-time	17	5
Total		31	14

hours was even more damaging to women's occupational status (Dex and Bukodi 2010).[7] However, moving from full-time hours to part-time hours in a female-dominated occupation did protect 1958-born women from experiencing any further occupational downgrading.

For more recent generations, things seem to have improved compared with those born in 1958. Whereas 31 per cent of first-time mothers born in 1958 experienced downward occupational mobility on their first return to work, the equivalent percentage for mothers born in 1970 was 14 per cent (Table 2.2). However, we should also note that life-course occupational mobility decreased between these two cohorts for both genders, independently of transitions between full-time and part-time work. For first-time Millennium cohort mothers who had returned to work by nine months after the birth, 11 per cent had experienced downward occupational mobility despite many having decided to work part-time – as discussed below. This indicates that the extensive occupational downgrading from taking up a part-time job after childbirth suffered by earlier generations has been declining across successive generations of mothers.

In both cohorts, switching from full-time to part-time employment after childbirth involved more occupational moves than was the case for transitions from a part-time to full-time job or from staying in a full-time or a part-time job (Table 2.2). In the 1970 cohort, mothers staying in part-time or full-time employment after returning to the labour market (in many cases staying in the same job with the same employer) tended to experience much less downward mobility than their counterparts in the 1958 cohort. In other words, in the 1970 cohort, staying in the same job (in many cases with the same employer) endowed a kind of protection from occupational downgrading.

However, this decline in downward occupational mobility after childbirth has not occurred mainly as a result of fewer new mothers choosing to work part-time hours after childbirth, although rates of part-time work after childbirth have fluctuated. Of first-time mothers born in 1958, 66 per cent of those returning to employment worked part-time hours (34 per cent full-time hours). The equivalent figures for mothers born in 1970 was 57 per cent of those returning worked part-time hours (43 per cent full-time). However, among first time mothers having a baby around the Millennium, the figure was up again with 68 per cent of such returning mothers working part-time (32 per cent full time). We need to remember that the Millennium mothers are not a new birth cohort and not, therefore, strictly comparable with mothers born in 1958 or 1970. Nonetheless, it does suggest that part-time work after childbirth has become more attractive for mothers of the Millennium cohort than it was for those women of the 1970 generation who became mothers in the 1990s. Thus the various initiatives to improve the status of part-time work from the end of the 1990s onwards may well be in the early stages of bearing some fruit. The gradually improving occupational profile of part-time work in the cross-section is consistent with this view (see Appendix Tables A2.1 and A2.2 using different occupational classification schemes; see also ONS (2000, 2010)).

PART-TIME PAY PENALTY

Part-time work has also been associated with lower hourly rates of pay than full-time employment and is usually concentrated in lower ranking occupations. Earlier studies found that a pay gap for women employed in full- and part-time jobs remained after controlling for other important differences (Ermisch and Wright 1993; Joshi and Paci 1998; Manning and Petrongolo 2008). Estimates of the gap ranged from 2 to 8.5 per cent lower. Occupational segregation of full-time and part-time jobs was also important in explaining the part-time pay gap (Manning and Petrongolo 2008), as was occupational downgrading when moving from full-time into part-time work (Connolly and Gregory 2009; Manning and Petrongolo 2008). The combined effects of moving into a part-time job and changing occupation were found in these studies to predict an immediate earnings drop of around a third, followed by a permanently lower earnings trajectory. However, as mentioned earlier in this chapter, the picture is not necessarily static and there have been a number of attempts to improve the status and rewards of part-time jobs. In principle, these regulations should be improving the pay and conditions for more recent cohorts of mothers in part-time work.

We examined the recent effects on pay of mothers in the Millennium Cohort Study who reduced their working hours after having a first baby around the Millennium, all since the introduction of the Part-time Workers Regulations and the National Minimum Wage (Neuburger et al. 2010). These new mothers represent a diverse group of women of different ages, different levels of education, different ethnic backgrounds and different family and employment circumstances from all four countries in the UK. The raw part-time to full-time wage gap for these mothers showed a part-time pay penalty of approximately 13 per cent nine months after the birth, rising to 18 per cent at three years and 24 per cent by five years. The difference in average hourly pay for full-time and part-time employees, after controlling for a range of individual characteristics, was reduced substantially at each survey and was insignificantly different at nine months after the birth. At age 3 the gap was 12 per cent and at age 5, 20 per cent. However, the best estimates, from those who stayed with their employer after childbirth and for the next five years suggested that working part-time compared with full-time did not have a significant pay penalty five years after the birth.

The results suggest, therefore, that mothers who reduced their hours of work after childbirth, but who remained with the same employer, were more likely to sustain their relative levels of pay during the five years after the birth. This result, about the protective effects of staying with the same employer, is consistent with those from earlier analyses of part-time pay by Manning and Petrongolo (2008) and Connolly and Gregory (2009). This benefit for women having babies in the twenty-first century has undoubtedly arisen mainly from the ability to take up statutory maternity leave, with its right to return to the same job with the same employer after childbirth. Alongside a decline in the pay penalty associated with part-time work, for careers interrupted only by maternity leave, the quality of part-time jobs has also risen, with higher percentages of such jobs in the top part of the occupational hierarchy. However, the distribution of part-time jobs is still weighted more to the bottom end of the occupational hierarchy than is the case for full-time jobs.

CONCLUSIONS

Our analysis of individuals' occupational trajectories found evidence of a shift across generations towards gender equality. By the 1970-born cohort, men and women were experiencing very similar career trajectories, but mainly if women avoided working part-time. Avoiding part-time employment also helped to reduce the amount of downward occupational mobility that women experienced. However, rather than being a case of onwards and upwards for women's careers, there are still pitfalls. Fluctuations in labour market and economic conditions, for example, can divert women or men from their career trajectories. Comparing cohorts, therefore, also means comparing careers formed in different labour market conditions rarely considered in other studies. This creates a complex story of movements towards equality. Variations across cohorts were partly due to the very different labour market conditions in which our three cohorts were developing their occupational careers. Varying labour market conditions may be responsible for Blossfeld et al.'s (2006) finding of a growing unpredictability in the transition from education to employment. The convergence of men's and women's career trajectories has partly been achieved through a mixture of improvements in women's occupational earnings and status and men experiencing considerable instability in their career paths, including more downward occupational mobility than might have been expected. We also found that women's education was important in improving their career progression, more important than for men, but education was equally important across cohorts.

Women born in later cohorts have reached professional and associate professional occupations in larger numbers. The penalties in occupational downgrading and associated lower pay for taking part-time employment after childbirth seemed to be worse in earlier generations than in later cohorts. Even the 1970 cohort of women had less stable careers if they had their children relatively early and took up part-time jobs after childbirth. And these part-time jobs were still more likely than full-time jobs to be in a more restricted set of occupations paying low wages. However, the latest generations of mothers having babies in the twenty-first century appear to be benefiting from the new legislative environment which has provided greater protection and equality of conditions for part-timers and greater flexibility for parents. Mothers in top jobs now have a much reduced chance of losing their occupational status after childbirth if they decide to work part-time hours. Staying with the same employer means that the risk of downward mobility is reduced to zero, but a pay penalty might still be a risk for those who continue longer in part-time work, or prolong their absence from the labour market.

WHERE TO NEXT? THE POLICY RESPONSE

As this project was starting, the recommendations of the Kingsmill Review (Kingsmill 2001) were still being discussed about how to implement policies and practices for gender equality in workplaces. Kingsmill recommended that public and private sector organisations should make mandatory annual reports on women's employment and pay and conduct pay reviews (see also McLaughlin and Deakin, Chapter 6 in this volume). It was suggested that the Investors in People (IIP) award should include these as criteria for awards. It was also argued that the government should carry out a number of tasks: monitor compliance on the mandatory reporting; consider whether new legislation was required if compliance was low; require its contractors to show they undertake pay reviews and evaluations; pay its own senior staff according to job objectives; and investigate further the part-time pay gap. Some of these recommendations were carried forward into a further official panel's review of UK gender equality: the Women and Work Commission (2006). This Commission's report listed 40 recommendations which built upon the Kingsmill recommendations for pay, but went much further and wider in their reach. Some of these recommendations have been put into the 2010 Equality Act. However, in other cases there is still a debate about how to legislate or implement changes argued to be needed. There is still a heavy focus in Britain on public sector changes as the potential route to lever changes in private sector organisations. Moves towards gender equality have taken place within public sector organisations but probably to a lesser extent in the private sector, making this strategy debatable.

At the European level, the 2006–10 EU gender equality agenda expressed in the *Roadmap for Equality* (European Commission, 2006) set targets for women's employment (Lisbon target to reach 60 per cent employed by 2010), older (55–64) women's employment (Lisbon target to reach 50 per cent by 2010) in all EU countries and childcare for two age groups to be extended. The women's employment target has not been difficult to reach for countries like Britain, and the older women's employment target was almost reached by 2008. The 2010 targets for childcare provision set by the 2002 Barcelona summit are more challenging; this is to provide childcare for at least 90 per cent of children between age 3 and mandatory school age and for at least 33 per cent of children under 3 years. In addition, many indicators including men's and women's unemployment rates, working hours, the unadjusted hourly pay gap, the extent of precarious contracts (temporary, fixed term), levels of education, occupational segregation by gender, gender differences in positions of responsibility and in the risk of poverty (social security, pensions) are being more closely monitored. The EU's strategic focus for the period from 2010 to 2015 (European Commission, 2011) gives a strengthened role to gender mainstreaming where gender differences are to be a central consideration in all decision-making. This is to be supplemented by special measures which will focus on the pay gap, the glass ceiling, female entrepreneurship and the provision of affordable high-quality childcare.

Our analysis showed that there is a need for more high-quality part-time jobs, which would decrease occupational downgrading after childbirth and at other stages of the life cycle. Part-time jobs would probably also be upgraded if more prime-aged men were willing to work part-time, especially in occupations and sectors that currently employ mainly men. This might be achieved by giving all employees the right to work part-time or reduced hours, not just employees with caring responsibilities for young children. This might further assist the creation of higher-quality part-time jobs and address the remaining pay penalty attributable to the occupations that part-time jobs are still, despite some improvement, concentrated in.

The Women and Work Commission recommendations would, if fully implemented, certainly be likely to have an impact on the remaining labour market gender inequalities. It is important that private sector, not just public sector organisations take these goals fully on board. A change in preferences might also enhance gender equality in the labour market. Currently, some women clearly prefer occupations that may have higher status, but are certainly not equal in terms of pay to occupations held mainly by men. Changing preferences is a more elusive goal, although, in practice, preferences and attitudes of men and women have changed enormously over the past half century.

NOTES

1. Members of the 1946 cohort have never been asked to recall the dates of every job they have held. Instead, through ten surveys conducted at ages 16, 17, 19, 20, 25, 26, 31, 36, 43 and 53, they have been asked to recall up to four job changes between that survey and the previous one, with their start and end dates and sufficient details about the job to allow for occupation codes to be attached. This information was used to construct occupational histories for cohort members (for more details see Bukodi and Neuburger 2009). The timing of job changes in all cohorts was recorded to the nearest month. Data collected also recorded whether cohort members were employed full-time or part-time in each of their jobs. Detailed information was also collected over successive interviews to provide educational histories for each respondent.
2. Readers should note that conclusions about the changes and extent of gender equality across cohorts differ to some extent depending on which criterion is used to rank occupations. The details and our longer discussion of rankings and their implications can be found in Bukodi et al. (2010).
3. For details about the NVQ levels see http://www.direct.gov.uk/en/EducationAnd Learning/Qualifications Explained/DG_10039029 (accessed 1 November 2010).
4. The same results were found when using the occupational scale based on status.
5. The standard definition of part-time work in Britain is jobs with basic working hours of less than or equal to 30 hours a week. Survey evidence suggests that this definition corresponds closely, in the majority of occupations, to individuals' own self-defined hours status (Manning and Petrongolo 2008).
6. The quasi birth cohorts were defined by age groups in the WES cross-sectional data – who had a full retrospective employment history.

7. The probability of downgrading on moving from full-time to part-time hours was 50 per cent for 1958-born women as a whole, 70 per cent for 1958-born women in top occupations and even worse for high-flying women employed in male-dominated or integrated occupations, where there were few if any part-time opportunities (Dex and Bukodi 2010).

REFERENCES

Blossfeld, H.-P., M. Mills and F. Bernardi (eds) (2006), *Globalization, Uncertainty and Men's Careers*, Cheltenham, UK and Northampton, MA, USA: Edward Elgar.

Blossfeld, H.-P., S. Buchholz, E. Bukodi and K. Kurz (eds) (2008), *Young Workers, Globalization and the Labor Market*, Cheltenham, UK and Northampton, MA, USA: Edward Elgar.

Bukodi, E. (2009), 'Education, first occupation and later occupational attainment: cross cohort changes among men and women in Britain', *GeNet Working Paper*, 2009-35, University of Cambridge.

Bukodi, E. and S. Dex (2010), 'Bad start: is there a way up? Gender differences in the effect of initial occupation on early career mobility in Britain', *European Sociological Review 2009*, **26** (4), 431–46, available at: doi: 10.1093/esr/jcp030.

Bukodi, E. and J. Neuburger (2009), *Data Note: Occupational Histories in NSHD*, London: MRC Unit for Lifelong Health and Aging, University College London.

Bukodi, E., S. Dex and J.H. Goldthorpe (2010), 'The conceptualisation and measurement of occupational hierarchies: a review, a proposal and some illustrative analyses', *Quality & Quantity*, **45** (3), 623–39.

Chan, T.-W. and J.H. Goldthorpe (2004), 'Is there a status order in contemporary British society? Evidence from the occupational structure of friendship', *European Sociological Review*, **20**, 383–401.

Chan, T.-W. and J.H. Goldthorpe (2007), 'Class and status: the conceptual distinction and its empirical reference', *American Sociological Review*, **72**, 512–32.

Connolly, S. and M. Gregory (2008), 'Moving down: women's part-time work and occupational change in Britain', *The Economic Journal*, **118** (526), F52–F76.

Connolly, S. and M. Gregory (2009), 'The part-time pay penalty: earnings trajectories of British women', *Oxford Economic Papers*, **61** (Supplement 1), i76–i97.

Dex, S. (1984), *Women's Work Histories: An Analysis of the Women and Employment Survey*, Department of Employment Research Paper No. 46, p. 129.

Dex, S. (1987), *Women's Occupational Mobility*, Basingstoke: Macmillan.

Dex, S. (ed.) (1999), *Families and the Labour Market*, London: Family Policy Studies Centre with Joseph Rowntree Foundation.

Dex, S. and E. Bukodi (2010), 'The effects of part-time work on women's occupational mobility: evidence from the 1958 Birth Cohort Study', *GeNet Working Paper*, 2010-37, University of Cambridge.

Dex, S. and J. Forth (2009), 'Equality and diversity' in W. Brown, A. Bryson K. Whitfield and J. Forth (eds), *A Quarter Century of Employee Relations in Britain*, Cambridge: Cambridge University Press, pp. 230–55.

Dex, S. and C. Smith (2002), *The Nature and Patterns of Family-Friendly*

Employment Policies in Britain, Bristol: Policy Press and Joseph Rowntree Foundation.

Dex, S., K. Ward and H. Joshi (2008), 'Changes in women's occupations and occupational mobility over 25 years', in J. Scott, S. Dex and H. Joshi (eds), *Women and Employment: Changing Lives and New Challenges*, Cheltenham, UK and Northampton, MA, USA: Edward Elgar, pp. 54–80.

Ermisch, J.F. and R.E. Wright (1993), 'Wage offers and full-time and part-time employment by British women', *The Journal of Human Resources*, **28** (1), 111–33.

European Commission (2006), *Roadmap for Equality between Women and Men*, EU. COM (2006) 92 final, Brussels: EU.

European Commission (2011), *Strategy for Equality between Women and Men 2010–2015*, COM (2010) 491 final, SEC (2010) 1079 and SEC (2010) 1080, Luxembourg: EU.

Ferri, E., J. Bynner and M. Wadsworth (eds) (2003), *Changing Britain, Changing Lives: Three Generations at the Turn of the Century*, London: Institute of Education.

Gregg, P. (2001), 'The impact of youth unemployment on adult unemployment in the NCDS', *The Economic Journal*, **111** (475), F626–F653.

Hawkes, D. and I. Plewis (2006), 'Modelling non-response in the National Child Development Study', *Journal of the Royal Statistical Society*, Series A, **169**, 479–91.

Hendrickx, J. and H.B.G. Ganzeboom (1998), 'Occupational status attainment in the Netherlands, 1920–1990: a multinomial logistic analysis', *European Sociological Review*, **14**, 384–403.

Joshi, H. and P. Paci (1998), *Unequal Pay for Women and Men: Evidence from the British Birth Cohort Studies*, Cambridge, MA: MIT Press, with Gerald Makepeace and Jane Waldfogel.

Joshi, H.E., H.B. Davies and H. Land (1996), *The Tale of Mrs Typical*, Occasional Paper 21, London: Family Policy Studies Centre.

Joshi, H.E. and P.R.A. Hinde (1993), 'Employment after childbearing: cohort study evidence', *European Sociological Review*, **9**, 203–27.

Joshi, H.E. and M.-L. Newell (1987), 'Job downgrading after childbearing', in M. Uncles (ed.), *London Papers in Regional Science 18, Longitudinal Data Analysis: Methods and Applications*, London: Pion, pp. 89-102.

Kingsmill, D. (2001), *Report into Women's Employment and Pay*, London: Women and Equality Unit.

Manning, A. and B. Petrongolo (2008), 'The part-time penalty for women in Britain', *The Economic Journal*, **118** (526), F28–F51.

Nathan, G. (1999), *A Review of Sample Attrition and Representativeness in Three Longitudinal Surveys*, London: Governmental Statistical Service Methodology Series, 13.

Neuburger, J., H. Joshi and S. Dex (2010), 'Part-time working and pay amongst Millennium Cohort Study mothers', *GeNet Working Paper*, 2010-38, University of Cambridge.

Nickell, S. (1982), 'The determinants of occupational success in Britain', *Review of Economic Studies*, **49**, 43–53.

Office of National Statistics (ONS) (2000), *Standard Occupational Classification 2000, Volume 1*, London: The Stationery Office.

Office of National Statistics (ONS) ([1990] 2010), *Standard Occupational*

Classification (SOC 1990) Volume 1, Newport: Office of National Statistics. Reprint available from 1990 publication.

Wadsworth, M., D. Kuh, M. Richards and R. Hardy (2005), 'Cohort profile: the 1946 National Birth Cohort', MRC National Survey of Health and Development, *International Journal of Epidemiology*, **35**, 49–54.

Ward, K. (2007), 'NCDS5-6 data note: programming employment histories in NCDS4, 5 and 6', Centre for Longitudinal Studies, Institute of Education, London, available at: http://www.cls.ioe.ac.uk/library.asp?section=0001000100 0600060009&orderby=title+desc (accessed 8 December 2011).

Women and Work Commission (2006), *Shaping a Fairer Future*, London: Women and Equality Unit, Department of Trade and Industry.

APPENDIX

Table A2.1   *Distribution of full and part-time jobs by SOC2000 major occupational categories, 2009 compared with 2002*

SOC2000	2009 (Q2) Women employed part-time %	2009 (Q2) All employed women %	2002 (Q2) Women employed part-time %	2002 (Q2) All employed women %
Managers and senior officials	5	12	4	10
Professionals	8	13	6	11
Associate professionals and technical	12	16	10	14
Administrative and secretarial	20	19	21	23
Skilled trades	2	2	2	2
Personal services	18	16	16	13
Sales and customer services	16	11	19	12
Process, plant and machine operatives	1	2	2	3
Elementary occupations	18	11	21	12
Total %	100	100	100	100
N thousands	5690	13405	5171	12810

Notes:
Not seasonally adjusted.
Details of SOC 2000 categories can be found in ONS (2000).

Sources: Labour Force Survey, as reported in National Statistics website for 2009, and *Labour Market Trends*, **110** (11), November 2002, pp. 615 and S22.

Table A2.2   Distribution of full and part-time jobs by SOC90 major occupational categories, 1992 compared with 2000

SOC90	1992–93 Women employed part-time %	1992–93 All employed women %	2000 Women employed part-time %	2000 All employed women %
Managers and administrators	5	11	5	12
Professionals	5	9	6	10
Associate professionals and technical	8	10	9	12
Clerical and secretarial	21	26	21	25
Craft and related	2	3	1	2
Personal and protective services	20	15	22	17
Sales	18	12	19	12
Plant and machine operators	3	4	2	4
Other occupations	18	10	14	8
Total %	100	100	100	100
N thousands	4604	10617	5144	11916

Note: Not seasonally adjusted.

Sources: Labour Force Survey, as reported in National Statistics website for 2009, and *Employment Gazette*, **101** (11), 489 for 1992–93 figures.

3. Halfway to gender equality in paid and unpaid work? Evidence from the multinational time-use study[1]

Jonathan Gershuny and Man Yee Kan

INTRODUCTION

Our daily activity patterns are closely related to the organisation of the economic systems in our societies. Over the past four decades, there have been significant changes in the economic structure and the labour market in Organisation for Economic Co-operation and Development (OECD) countries: most notably, the growth of the service sector and the rise in women's labour force participation. Such changes have brought some convergence in working time patterns among different countries. For example, time use research has shown that paid work time in the UK, the USA and most industrial countries has decreased for both male and female workers (Gershuny 2000; Harkness 2008; Robinson and Godbey 1997). As for unpaid domestic work, there has been a slight fall for women over the same period, especially for those in employment, and a moderate but continual increase in men's participation. However, women on average are still responsible for the major share of unpaid work (Gershuny 2000; Gershuny and Sullivan 2003; Harkness 2008; Sullivan 2000).

These studies suggest that the gender gap in paid work time and unpaid work time is closing slowly. Nevertheless, recent research has indicated that there is continuing gender segregation in domestic work. Kan and Gershuny (2009a, 2009b) analysed longitudinal data of the British Household Panel Survey to investigate the changes in the domestic division of labour over the life course. They found that women undertake the bulk of both core housework (for example, cleaning, washing and cooking) and less routine types of domestic work (for example, childcare, shopping and gardening). In contrast, men spend little time on core housework and concentrate their domestic work time mainly on the less routine types of chores.

Is the gender divide in work-time allocation really closing? This study first aims to chart changes in men's and women's paid and unpaid work time over the past four decades, using large-scale, nationally representative time diary data from 12 OECD countries. We are interested in finding out whether there are significant differences in the trends in paid and unpaid work time among countries with different styles of public policies in developed countries. More specifically, we examine the extent to which gender equality in work time is achieved in different countries. Countries are grouped into policy regimes according to levels of social equality and state intervention in welfare provision (see for example, Esping-Andersen 1990, 1999; Gauthier 1996; Goodin et al. 1999; Hook 2006, 2010; Lewis 1993; O'Connor et al. 1999; Sainsbury 1999). We consider three regime categories based on this literature: (1) the liberal market (anglophone) regimes, (2) the social democratic regimes, and (3) the social capitalist (or the conservative/corporatist) regimes. The literature suggests there is another main type – namely, southern European traditional regimes. We do not have sufficient countries to include this fourth type in our discussion, having only Italy as the one representative. So we have included Italy among the social capitalist regimes. We recognise, as documented in Hook (2010), that there are variations in welfare policies within each type of regime.

In the second part of this chapter, we are centrally concerned with the phenomenon of near-equality of total (paid plus unpaid) work between men and women in the rich countries of the first world. This phenomenon is well established in the time-use literature since the first cross-national comparative studies of the 1960s (Szalai 1972), and has been recently named 'isowork' (Burda et al. 2007). We first describe separately the historical trends in the paid and unpaid work time of men and women from the 12 countries over the past four decades. We then focus on the total of work time and reconsider the implications of gender segregation in unpaid work in the context of 'isowork'. We will consider, on the basis of our findings, *whether* and, if so, *when and how* gender equality in the distribution of work time is likely to be achieved.

DATA AND MEASURES

The data come from the Multinational Time Use Study (MTUS), a harmonised database of a collection of time-use diary surveys from a number of countries.[2] The original data come from large nationally representative samples collected, by various national statistical authorities and academic research groups, from the 1960s to the 2000s. The database currently contains more than 50 surveys from over 20 countries recording more than 600 000 diary days. There are some variations in the design of the diaries (for example, in the extent to which simultaneous activities and information about where and with whom the activities took place were recorded, although each of these aspects was covered to some degree by almost all of the component studies). In the MTUS, these surveys are harmonised to a common format, with an identical set of activities and sociodemographic variables. Since a major aim of this chapter is to analyse trends in work time, we have selected the 12 countries represented in the MTUS where data of at least two different periods are available. The countries selected are Australia, Canada, the UK and the USA (which represent liberal welfare regimes), France, Germany, Italy and the Netherlands (which are examples of social capitalist regimes) and Denmark, Finland, Norway and Sweden (which represent social democratic regimes). The selected countries include 437 374 diary cases[3] from 44 surveys. Table 3.1 presents the sample sizes and the periods when the surveys were conducted.

Our sample for analysis includes all individuals at working age (20–59) irrespective of their employment and marital statuses. We follow Walker and Woods (1976) and Hawrylyshn (1977) to define 'work' as including all those activities that someone might commission a 'third party' to carry out for pay without losing the main sorts of direct utility derived from that activity.[4] We employ a broad definition of employment including job-search activities as well as time spent in education and training for work among people of working age (between 20 and 59), when calculating paid work time. We include education and training time in this total because trends in paid work time are very sensitive to changes in the proportion of people in higher education. This view might also be justified in so far as time spent on education and training is an important investment in future employment opportunities.

FINDINGS

Trends in Paid Work Time

Table 3.2 presents changes in men's paid work time over time in these 12 countries. We can see that paid work time was at its maximum in the 1960s when the mean values were over 400 minutes per day in the UK, the USA, France, Germany and Denmark (the only countries for which data are available). From the 1970s until the late 1980s or the early 1990s, in most of the liberal regimes (that is, the UK, the USA and Australia), men's paid work time had dropped gradually to around 400 minutes a

Table 3.1   Survey periods and sample sizes of time use surveys (exact years of studies in parentheses)

	1961–69	1970–76	1976–84	1985–89	1990–94	1995–99	2000–04
Liberal welfare regimes:							
Australia		1491		3181	13494	14017	
		(1974)		(1987)	(1992)	(1997)	
Canada		2138	2659	9618	8936	10726	
		(1971–72)	(1981)	(1986)	(1992)	(1998)	
UK	9292	20293		9088		1905	20980
	(1961)	(1974)		(1987)		(1995)	(2000–01)
USA	1987	6682		4935	8702	1151	18751
	(1965–66)	(1975–76)		(1985)	(1992–94)	(1998–99)	(2003)
Social capitalist regimes:							
France	2893	4634				15318	
	(1966)	(1975)				(1998–99)	
Germany	3687				25778		32892
	(1965)				(1991–92)		(2000–01)
Italy				37769			51206
				(1989)			(1996)
Netherlands		1292	2727	3263	3158	3227	1639
		(1975)	(1980)	(1985)	(1990)	(1995)	(2000)
Social democratic regimes:							
Denmark	4017			3220			
	(1964)			(1987)			
Finland			11899	15184		10040	
			(1979)	(1987–88)		(1996)	
Norway		6516	6068		6129		
		(1971–72)	(1980–81)		(1990–91)		
Sweden					7065		7727
					(1990–91)		(2000–01)

Source: Multinational Time Use Study, http://www.timeuse.org/mtus.

day. Canada is an exception where the mean paid work time (365 minutes a day) was relatively lower compared to other countries in the 1970s; thereafter, it experienced only a minor drop to 332 minutes. We have fewer years of observations in other types of regimes. In general, all other countries, including Denmark, Germany, Norway and Finland, had a moderate decrease in paid work time from the 1960s until the early 1990s. Nonetheless, in the Netherlands paid work time remained rather stable at around 300 minutes per day for the period from 1970 through to the early 1990s.

Differences in trends in men's paid work time among the regimes are found mainly in the period from the early 1990s to the early 2000s. In

Table 3.2   Trends in men's paid work time (minutes per day)

	1961–69	1970–75	1976–84	1985–89	1990–94	1995–99	2000–04
Liberal welfare regimes:							
Australia		405		381	350	358	
Canada		365	332	351	354	363	
UK	434	396		327		313	333
USA	441	398		364	350	337	359
Social capitalist regimes:							
France	436	377				324	
Germany	420				353		311
Italy				337			358
Netherlands		305	293	292	317	328	344
Social democratic regimes:							
Denmark	407			358			
Finland			333	316		297	
Norway		368	332		326		315
Sweden					362		311

Source: Multinational Time Use Study.

social democratic countries, paid work time continued to fall to around 310 minutes per day in the early 2000s. Men's paid work time in these countries had also been the shortest since the late 1990s. In the liberal regimes and in the Netherlands, paid work time had increased slightly between the early 1990s and the early 2000s.

Table 3.3 shows the paid work time trends for women in the 12 countries. Women's time spent on paid work was shorter than men's and was particularly affected by their employment rate and part-time work rate. Overall, in the countries for which data were available for the period before 1970, the average paid work time of women in all the countries had increased steadily and significantly until the early 2000s. An upward trend can be observed in all the three typologies of regimes. In liberal regimes, for example, women's paid work time in Canada increased steadily from 161 minutes per day in the early 1970s to 238 minutes in the late 1990s. In the UK, the figures rose from 138 minutes in the 1960s to 202 minutes in the early 2000s. France, the Netherlands (social capitalist regimes) and Norway (a social democratic regime) also showed a similar upward trend. One major factor explaining the growth in women's paid work time is the development of post-industrial service economies with the service sector disproportionately employing women's labour.

Nevertheless, in contrast to men's, women's paid work time did not

Table 3.3   *Trends in women's paid work time (minutes per day)*

	1961–69	1970–75	1976–84	1985–89	1990–94	1995–99	2000–04
Liberal welfare regimes:							
Australia		150		189	170	186	
Canada		161	195	199	221	238	
UK	138	155		153		179	202
USA	176	180		218	255	275	247
Social capitalist regimes:							
France	167	184				203	
Germany	172				186		169
Italy				138			172
Netherlands		69	79	92	115	131	157
Social democratic regimes:							
Denmark	114			232			
Finland			242	231		213	
Norway		131	167		198		195
Sweden					249		226

Source: Multinational Time Use Study.

seem to vary substantially according to regime type in the late 1990s or the early 2000s. Although in all countries women's participation in paid work has increased, women on average worked fewer hours for pay than men, and in a number of these countries a higher percentage of women than men were legally classified as part-time workers. Women's part-time work rates related to a very complex array of polices regarding welfare and tax systems. Therefore they do not vary distinctively according to the current categories of policy regimes (for example, women's part-time work rate in the early 2000s was relatively high in the UK, the Netherlands and Norway – representing each of the three major regime types in this sample).

In Sweden (between 1990 and 2000) and Finland (between 1979 and 1996), women's paid work time showed a modest decrease, in contrast to the general rising trend in other countries during this period. However, women's paid work time in these two countries was already relatively longer than in other countries between 1979 and 2000. Overall, we find more variation in men's paid work time trends than women's among the policy regime typologies. Generally speaking, men's paid work time has decreased gradually since the 1960s. But in liberal and social capitalist regimes, this trend has been reversed since the late 1990s. In contrast,

Table 3.4   Trends in men's unpaid work time (minutes per day)

	1961–69	1970–75	1976–84	1985–89	1990–94	1995–99	2000–04
Liberal welfare regimes:							
Australia		105		125	150	147	
Canada		127	146	128	144	156	
UK	90	91		133		137	148
USA	105	132		147	140	190	173
Social capitalist regimes:							
France	114	114				157	
Germany	102				155		155
Italy				69			97
Netherlands		118	127	136	125	136	133
Social democratic regimes:							
Denmark	64			131			
Finland			126	145		150	
Norway		125	138		155		173
Sweden					171		142

Source: Multinational Time Use Study.

women's paid work time has increased steadily since the 1960s and the 1970s in most of the countries regardless of policy regime type.

Trends in Unpaid Work Time

The trends in unpaid work time to a certain extent mirror those in paid work time. As can be seen in Table 3.4, men's unpaid work time generally displayed an upward trend over the past four decades. In liberal policy regimes, men's unpaid work time increased from 90 to 148 minutes per day from the 1960s to the early 2000s in the UK, and from 105 to 173 minutes in the USA in the same period. Similar increases are observed in the four social capitalist countries, although in Germany and the Netherlands, men's unpaid work time remained stable in the most recent periods. In addition, men's unpaid work time was substantially shorter in Italy than in other countries between the 1960s and the early 2000s. The social democratic regimes had a similar increase in men's unpaid work time, with Sweden being an exception, where the number of unpaid work minutes per day declined from 171 to 142 minutes per day between 1990 and 2000. However, men's unpaid work time in Sweden was the highest among the countries in the early 1990s.

Table 3.5   Trends in women's unpaid work time (minutes per day)

	1961–69	1970–75	1976–84	1985–89	1990–94	1995–99	2000–04
Liberal welfare regimes:							
Australia		362		309	318	308	
Canada		341	291	276	276	272	
UK	369	304		320		274	280
USA	361	320		277	238	283	272
Social capitalist regimes:							
France	425	368				302	
Germany	392				323		292
Italy				375			341
Netherlands		356	363	349	308	288	278
Social democratic regimes:							
Denmark	320			234			
Finland			259	251		255	
Norway		367	305		279		276
Sweden					289		205

Source: Multinational Time Use Study.

Women's amount of unpaid work time was significantly higher than men's in all of the periods and countries observed (Table 3.5). In contrast to men's unpaid work time trends, women's displayed a gradual decline over the past four decades. In the 1960s, it was over 360 minutes in the UK and the USA and 425 minutes in France. In the early 1970s, women's daily unpaid work time in these three countries had already dropped substantially to 304, 320 and 368 minutes respectively, reflecting the effect of rapid economic development on women's time in paid work. In all 12 countries, women's unpaid work time dropped steadily from the early 1970s to the early 1990s. In the early 1990s, women in the US spent 238 minutes per day on unpaid work compared with around 300 minutes spent by women in other countries. Women's unpaid work time fell substantially to around 280 minutes between the 1990s and early 2000s in most countries. Before the 1990s, women's unpaid work time did not appear to vary significantly according to policy regime types. Since the early 1990s, Scandinavian countries had the shortest average unpaid work time for women: the figures were 255 for Finland (1996), 276 for Norway (2000s) and 205 minutes per day for Sweden (the early 2000s). In the UK and the USA, women's unpaid work time did not decrease significantly from the 1990s to the early 2000s. Italian women's

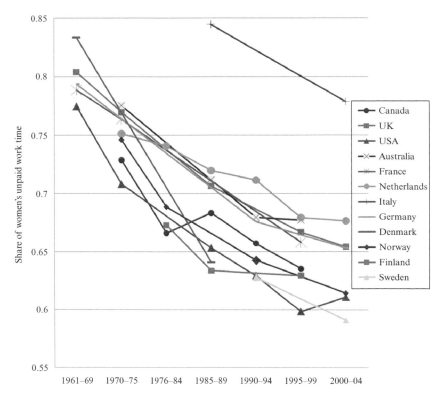

Figure 3.1   Trends in women's share of unpaid work time

unpaid work time was very high both in the late 1980s and the early 2000s; we speculate that this is representative of the other countries of Southern Europe for which we do not have trend data – certainly the more recent Italian totals here correspond reasonably well to the recent single years of time diary information for Spain and Slovenia discussed in Kan et al. (2011).

Trends in the Gender Division of Labour

What are the implications of these trends for gender equality in the division of unpaid labour? Figure 3.1 illustrates the changes in the share of unpaid work undertaken by women (defined as women's mean unpaid work time divided by the sum of women's and men's mean unpaid work time in each year) over the decades. Despite variations in the trends of paid work and unpaid work time among countries from different policy regimes, we see overall a substantial decrease of about 20 percentage points in women's share of unpaid work over the past four decades. Women's share of unpaid work time was about 80 per cent in the UK, the USA, France, Germany and Denmark in the 1960s. It declined to around 75 per cent in the early 1970s; the figures were about the same in countries where the earliest observations were available from this period onwards (Australia, Canada, the Netherlands and Norway). From the late 1980s onwards, women's share of unpaid work time was generally below 70 per cent – the single exception being Italy, where the figure was 84 per cent in the 1980s, falling to 78 per cent in the early 2000s. Also, since the 1980s women's shares were considerably lower for countries from the social democratic regime than for other countries (64 per cent in Denmark and 60 per cent in Norway in the early 1990s and 58 per cent in Finland in the late 1990s). In liberal market regime countries women's share of unpaid work continued to fall through the 1990s, so that by the early 2000s, they were just over 63 per cent in the UK and 65 per cent in the USA. By the early 2000s, countries from the social capitalist (corporatist) policy regime showed the highest share of women's unpaid labour (over 65 per cent in the Netherlands, Germany and Italy), presumably to be explained by the emphasis on traditional family roles underlying policy design and implementation in these countries.

Figure 3.1 provides a record of remarkable social change, which mirrors in reverse the much more frequently documented entry of women into the paid workforce.

Gender Segregation within Unpaid Work[5]

Unpaid work time may be divided into three categories: core domestic work (including daily routine types of housework such as cleaning, doing the laundry and cooking), caring for family members (including care for children and adults) and other non-core domestic unpaid work (including shopping, gardening and household repairs). Comparing the distribution of unpaid work time among these three categories, we can see clear patterns of gender segregation: although women spent much more time on unpaid work than men, they concentrated their time mainly on core domestic work and caring for others, while men spent the largest proportion of their time on non-core domestic work. For example, in the UK in 1961, women spent nearly 80 per cent of their unpaid work time on core domestic work while men spent 25 per cent of their much smaller total on this class of domestic work. The gender segregation within unpaid work is shown to be gradually diminishing (Figures 3.2–3.4), a finding consistent with previous results from smaller

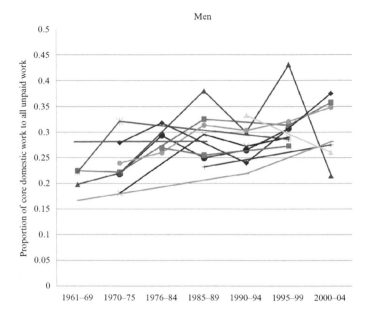

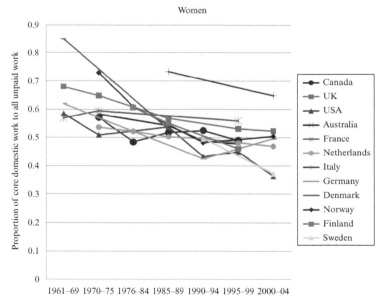

*Figure 3.2   Trends in proportion of core domestic work time to all unpaid
            work time*

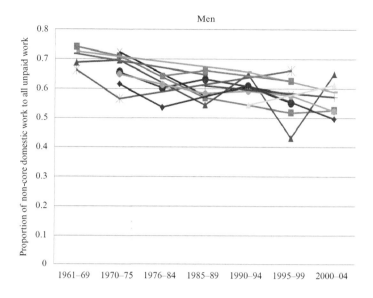

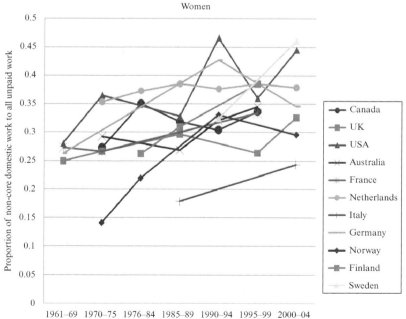

Figure 3.3   Trends in proportion of non-core domestic work time to all unpaid work time

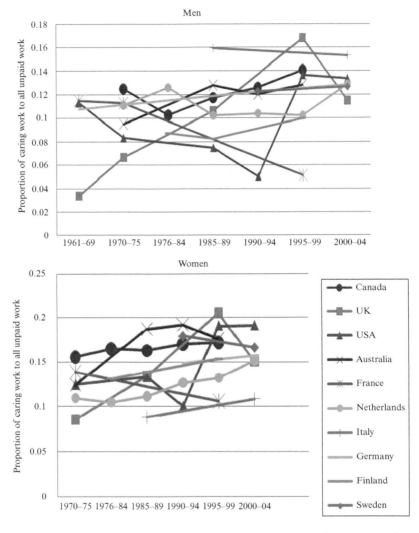

*Figure 3.4   Trends in proportion of caring work time to all unpaid work
time*

groups of countries and shorter time spans (for example, Robinson and
Godbey 1997; Sullivan 2000).

   The absolute decline in the proportion of unpaid work undertaken by
women over the years is mainly due to a reduction in women's core domestic work time. Women's average time on core domestic work was very

high in the 1960s (between 210 and 250 minutes per day in the countries where data were recorded). This was due mainly to their much shorter hours (Table 3.3) compared with men's much longer hours in employment (Table 3.2). Women's core domestic work time dropped rapidly to between 120 and 180 minutes in the late 1980s, except in Italy where the time was significantly longer (275 minutes per day). In the same period, men's core domestic work time increased gradually from around 20 minutes to about 40 minutes in most of the countries where records were available. From the late 1980s to the early 2000s, women's core domestic work continued to fall and men's increased slightly, both at a slower rate than in earlier periods.

The time spent on caring for family members has shown a somewhat different pattern of change. Women's contribution to care time is in absolute terms about 2.5 times that of men. Again, taking the UK in 2000–01 as an example, women's average time spent on caring for others was 42 minutes a day, compared with men's 17 minutes. But in contrast to core domestic work, women's time spent on caring work fluctuated and increased to some extent over the past four decades. Men spent relatively little time on caring work (about 20 minutes per day in the early 2000s), despite some increases since the 1960s.

There is also a clear gender divide in the case of non-core domestic work which continues to dominate men's as well as a minority of women's unpaid work time. Figure 3.3 shows a converging trend with non-core unpaid work constituting a diminishing proportion of men's work and an increasing proportion of women's. But this convergence process, like those in the other two unpaid work categories, is incomplete; work remains substantially segregated *within* the unpaid category, just as it does *between* the paid and unpaid categories.

Trends in Total Work Time (Isowork)

We now consider unpaid and paid work together. Figure 3.5 presents the share of women's total work time (defined as women's total work time divided by the sum of men's and women's total work time) over the previous four decades. As we can see, the figures for all countries fluctuated only slightly either side of or across the 50 per cent level in all the years of observation. In other words, men and women on average had more or less the same percentage of households' total work time. In fact, only in the Italian data did women do substantially above 50 per cent of the total work. If both paid work and unpaid work were considered to be of same value and were assumed to require the same amount of effort, then it might be thought that men and women are equal in terms of sharing total household work time.

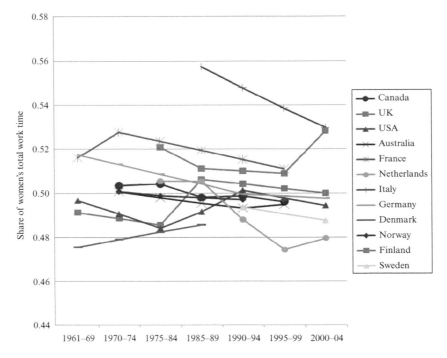

Figure 3.5   Trends in women's share of all work time

However, unpaid work and paid work have *dissimilar consequences* in modern societies. Participation in labour market work is one of the key means and the most direct route to the accumulation of human capital, which is critically important in the determination of life chances. Paid work also provides not just income but access to social networks, insurance and pension schemes, and monetary credit – all of which may improve the worker's bargaining power within the family.

We see that there has been gender convergence in paid and unpaid work time in the countries from all three types of welfare regimes. Nevertheless, a significant gender gap in the balance of unpaid work time and paid work time remained in the early 2000s. In previous decades, there has been an increasing gap between men's and women's economically salient human capital through the course of marriage, which results from women's generally shorter hours of paid work and frequent partial disengagement from the labour market after childbirth. The continued gender inequality in rates of accumulation of various sorts of fixed and embodied capital has major negative implications for women's life chances, which we further discuss in the final section.

SUMMARY AND IMPLICATIONS

We have charted changes in the division of paid and unpaid work time between men and women over the past four decades, using high-quality nationally representative time-diary data from 12 OECD countries. Our results suggest that there are more similarities than variations in work time trends among countries of different types of public policy regimes. The long-term historical decrease in men's paid work time has slightly reversed both in liberal regimes and in social capitalist regimes such as the UK, the USA and the Netherlands since the 1990s. Irrespective of policy regime category, women's time in paid work has been on the rise and their time spent on unpaid work has been declining. Since the 1990s, however, the social democratic regimes have exhibited shorter women's unpaid work time than other countries, and indeed all the main differences in work time trends are found between social democratic, on the one hand, and all the other regime types on the other.

Women's unpaid work time exhibits more variation among the three types of welfare regimes. The main difference in trends occurs between the social capitalist regimes and the other two types. While women's share of unpaid work has been declining in all 12 countries, countries from the social capitalist regime (for example, Germany), where traditional family functions and the male breadwinner family model are often maintained through policy implementation, have shown a substantially higher level of unpaid work time in the early 2000s than all other countries. In addition, countries with a social democratic regime (for example, Denmark, Sweden and Norway), where social equality is considered to be a major goal of social and public policies, have shown a relatively faster declining trend in women's unpaid work time since the 1990s. The divergence among regimes since the 1960s, apparent in Figure 3.1 and modelled formally in Kan et al. (2011) suggests that public and welfare policies are associated significantly with the gender division of labour.

Despite these regime variations, we still see a slow but continuing trend of gender convergence in work time and in the domestic division of labour regardless of policy regime types. Will this trend continue? If we were to project the curves in Figure 3.1 to continue as far forward into the future as the evidence discussed here extends into the past, we have some grounds for believing that gender equality in the division of paid and unpaid work time may *eventually* be achieved.

The slow convergence of patterns of work time change may suggest a 'lagged adaptation' in the division of labour between men and women (Gershuny et al. 1994). According to this view, market forces drive men and women to devote more time to labour market work, while ideas of fairness in the distribution of overall work burden encourage a less unequal division of domestic labour between them. Hence gender ideologies with regard to the domestic division of labour established in childhood (in historical eras when women were less committed to paid work) are challenged by observations and experiences of gender roles during adulthood. This may lead in turn to partial adaptation in ideologies and behaviours, so that the gender gap in the domestic division of labour is to some degree further closed. The outcome is a compromise between the strongly gendered inherited work ideology, and the ungendered requirements of household equity.

This speculation is consistent with the finding that more gender inequalities are found in core domestic work and caring for others, which are traditionally more associated with femininity than are other forms of domestic work. The clash between realities and ideologies may lead parents to transmit more gender egalitarian ideologies to their children, so that the gender gap in the division of labour will be further closed in the next generation. If this optimistic view holds, the first decade of the new millennium is perhaps the mid-point of a process of gender equalisation which was visible from the 1960s in the countries we are considering.

Nevertheless, traditional gender ideologies remain strong, which hinders the effect of social policies (Dex 2010). Furthermore, the decline in women's share of unpaid work time over the decades is due largely to a reduction in women's time on core domestic work, rather than a significant increase in men's unpaid work time. These changes are likely to have been brought about by the concurrent increase in the demand for women's participation in the labour market, and the diffusion of modern domestic technologies that increase efficiency in housework (Gershuny 1983, 2004),[6] rather than by a rapid transformation of gender ideologies. In short, despite equality in educational access and in legal requirements for equality of treatment in the workplace, women still take a primary role in domestic work.

There is evidence that the continuing effects of gendered domestic work ideologies may operate dynamically throughout the life course (Kan and Gershuny 2009a). It may be rational for members of couples to specialise in paid and unpaid work in direct proportion to their paid work earning power. Once an even slightly traditionally gendered work distribution (that is, men doing more paid work, women more unpaid) has emerged, perhaps subsequent to the birth of a first child, the woman accumulates human capital at a slower rate than the man, further increasing the pressure for gendered specialisation. Moreover, some research suggests that couples where the female partner has a significantly higher level of earnings than her male partner may still resort to a traditional form of domestic division of labour (for example, Brines 1994; Bittman et al. 2003).[7]

The development of dispersed work-time schedules characteristic of post-industrial economies may also not be entirely favourable to the process of gender equality in work. For example, the growth of the service sector has made atypical work schedules (shift work, long hours, part-time and fragmented hours) more common. Kan and Lesnard (2009), analysing week-long diaries in the UK and France, report that women are still far more likely than men to work on a part-time basis, and men are more prone than women to have long work hours over the week. The gendered pattern of work schedules has reinforced traditional forms of domestic division of labour, particularly for core domestic work. Such work has to be undertaken on a routine basis and does not fit well with men's long work-week schedules. The gender segregation in work schedules and in domestic work demonstrates that there are still hurdles to gender equality in work.

The fossil relics of previous historical employment patterns, in the form of gender ideologies that do not support equality for all work time, inappropriate institutional arrangements (for example, sparse and costly childcare provision, asymmetrical parental leave arrangements) and outmoded temporal organisation (short duration of childcare with services provided only from 9 a.m. to 5 p.m.) are barriers to gender equality in work time. The differences in historical trends across the regime types apparent from Figure 3.1 and formally modelled in Kan et al. (2011) tell us that public regulation and subsidies can positively influence the rate of change. Whereas most countries started from similar positions in the 1970s, there was a faster decline of gender segregation in paid work and unpaid work in Nordic countries, and the slowest decline in southern countries. Lagged adaptation does not necessarily imply a permanently stalled revolution.

This chapter has presented descriptive statistics about the trends in the gender division of paid and unpaid work. The findings suggest important causal impacts of the gender division of labour on gender equality in life chances, which need to be verified in further research. The 'isowork' phenomenon (similar amounts of total work time, differing shares) documented here points to a distinct issue: gender differentials in life chances driven by the unequal division of domestic labour. Persistent traditional gender ideologies and traditional work practices interact with another, largely independently caused, recent social trend experienced throughout the developed world. In previous eras, where marriages mostly persisted until the death of one partner, differences between men's and women's paid and unpaid work balances at least gave rise to similar long-term consequences for men and women in terms of their own household's overall access to monetary resources. However, the household dynamics leading to gender specialisation are coupled now with a high rate of marital breakup, which is associated with gendered differences in life-course prospects for financial well-being. When a husband who specialised in paid work leaves the marriage, he takes with him his relatively enhanced human capital. In contrast, a wife who specialised in unpaid work is most likely left not just with the baby but also with her human capital – and hence her future economic prospects – relatively diminished by her previous disproportionately heavy responsibility for unpaid work.

NOTES

1. This work was supported by the Economic and Social Research Council through the grant for Developing the Centre for Time Use Research (award number: RES-060-25-0037) and the British Academy through the Postdoctoral Fellowship Scheme. Direct correspondence to: Man Yee Kan, Department of Sociology, Manor Road Building, Oxford, OX1 3UQ, UK. Email: man-yee.kan@sociology.ox.ac.uk.
2. The database is prepared by the Centre for Time Use Research at the University of Oxford. More information is available at http://www.timeuse.org/mtus.
3. In the analysis presented here, based on a slightly earlier release of the MTUS, the Netherlands cases alone consist of aggregated seven-day diaries. In the most recent release, all the diary cases, including those from the Netherlands, are based on single days. Day weights and population weights are used in the analyses to ensure that the findings are representative of the week and the population. The data-set also includes anonymised identifiers allowing researchers to control for individual effects in those survey samples that contain more than one diary day per respondent.
4. We recognise that this criterion leads to a somewhat problematic distinction between unpaid work and consumption and other non-work time. Some aspects of shopping, cooking, caring and routine maintenance may be viewed by their participants as leisure activities. And paid employment may also be enjoyed for itself. The time-use study collected by Young and Willmott for their 1974 'Symmetrical Family' study shows that more than one-third of all work-time is viewed as something other than pure work – and conversely more than a quarter of all leisure is seen as pure leisure (Gershuny 2010, app. table A1).
5. We do not include figures for Denmark in 1964 in Figures 3.3 and 3.4 because the data coding for this survey does not allow us to separate caring from other non-core domestic work.
6. Based on cross-sectional evidence, Bittman et al. (2004) argue that modern domestic equipment increases women's domestic work time. Such a view is faulty because households which can afford to purchase modern domestic equipment are likely have a higher demand for housework than other households. Using longitudinal data, Gershuny (2004) shows that housework time is reduced after households are equipped with modern domestic appliances.

7. Kan and Gershuny (2009b), using longitudinal evidence of human capital and unpaid work dynamics, cast some doubt on the analyses in previous studies. They criticise the use of current labour market earnings as a measure of bargaining power in previous studies for neglecting the *potential* earnings of home carers.

REFERENCES

Bittman, M., P. England, N. Folbre, L. Sayer and G. Matheson (2003), 'When does gender trump money? Bargaining and time in household work', *American Journal of Sociology*, **109**, 186–214.

Bittman, M., J.M. Rice and J. Wajcman (2004), 'Appliances and their impact: the ownership of domestic technology and time spent on household work', *British Journal of Sociology*, **55**, 401–42.

Brines, J. (1994), 'Economic dependency, gender and the division of domestic labour at home', *American Journal of Sociology*, **100**, 652–88.

Burda, M., D.S. Hamermesh and P. Weil (2007), 'Total work, gender and social norms', in *IZA Discussion paper No. 2705*, Bonn: IZA.

Dex, S. (2010), 'Policy interventions to equalize men's and women's time spent in unpaid work: are they possible and realistic?', in J. Treas and S. Drobnic (eds), *Dividing the Domestic: Men, Women and Household Work in Cross-National Perspective*, Stanford, CA: Stanford University Press, pp. 79–104.

Esping-Andersen, G. (1990), *The Three Worlds of Welfare Capitalism*, Cambridge: Polity Press.

Esping-Andersen, G. (1999), *Social Foundations of Post-Industrial Economies*, Oxford: Oxford University Press.

Gauthier, A.H. (1996), *The State and the Family: A Comparative Analysis of Family Policies in Industrialized Countries*, New York: Oxford University Press.

Gershuny, J. (1983), *Social Innovation and the Division of Labour*, Oxford: Oxford University Press.

Gershuny, J. (2000), *Changing Times: Work and Leisure in Postindustrial Society*, Oxford: Oxford University Press.

Gershuny, J. (2004), 'Domestic equipment does not increase domestic work: a response to Bittman, Rice and Wajcman', *British Journal of Sociology*, **55**, 425–31.

Gershuny, J. (2010), 'Time, utility and national product', *Oxford University Department of Sociology Working Papers*.

Gershuny, J., M. Godwin and S. Jones (1994), 'The domestic labour revolution: a process of lagged adaptation', in M. Anderson, F. Bechhofer and J. Gershuny (eds), *The Social and Political Economy of the Household*, Oxford: Oxford University Press, pp. 151–97.

Gershuny, J. and O. Sullivan (2003), 'Time use, gender, and public policy regimes', *Social Politics*, **10**, 205–28.

Goodin, R.E., B. Headey, R. Muffels and H. Driven (1999), *The Real Worlds of Welfare Capitalism*, Cambridge: Cambridge University Press.

Harkness, S. (2008), 'The household division of labour: changes in families allocation of paid and unpaid work', in J. Scott, S. Dex and H. Joshi (eds), *Changing Patterns of Women's Employment Over 25 Years*, Cheltenham, UK and Northampton, MA, USA: Edward Elgar, pp. 234–67.

Hawrylyshn, O. (1977), 'Towards a definition of non-market activities', *Review of Income and Wealth*, **23**, 79–96.

Hook, J.L. (2006), 'Care in context: men's unpaid work in 20 countries, 1965–2003', *American Sociological Review*, **71** (4), 639–60.

Hook, J. (2010), 'Gender inequality in the welfare states: sex segregation in housework, 1965–2003', *American Journal of Sociology*, **115**, 1480–523.

Kan, M.Y. and J. Gershuny (2009a), 'Gender and time use over the life-course', in M. Brynin and E. John (eds), *Changing Relationships*, New York: Routledge, pp. 146–60.

Kan, M.Y. and J. Gershuny (2009b), 'Gender segregation and bargaining in domestic labour: evidence from longitudinal time use data', in R. Crompton and J. Scott (eds), *Gender Inequalities in the 21st Century*, Cheltenham, UK and Northampton, MA, USA: Edward Elgar, pp. 153–73.

Kan, M.Y. and L. Lesnard (2009), 'Comparing working week schedules in France 1998–99 and UK 2000–01', paper presented at the 31st International Association for Time-Use Research Conference, 23–25 September, Lüneburg, Leuphana University.

Kan, M.Y., O. Sullivan and J.I. Gershuny (2011), 'Gender convergence in domestic work: discerning the effects of interactional and institutional barriers from large-scale data', *Sociology*, **45** (2), 234–51.

Lewis, J. (1993), *Women and Social Policies in Europe: Work, Family and the State*, Aldershot, UK and Brookfield, VT, USA: Edward Elgar.

O'Connor, J.S., A.S. Orloff and S. Shaver (1999), *States, Markets, Families*, Cambridge: Cambridge University Press.

Robinson, J.P. and G. Godbey (1997), *Time for Life: The Surprising Ways Americans Use their Time*, University Park, PA: Pennsylvania States University Press.

Sainsbury, D. (1999), *Gender and Welfare State Regimes*, Oxford: Oxford University Press.

Sullivan, O. (2000), 'The division of domestic labour: twenty years of change?', *Sociology*, **34**, 437–56.

Szalai, A. (ed.) (1972), *The Use of Time: Daily Activities of Urban and Suburban Populations in Twelve Countries*, The Hague: Mouton.

Walker, K.E. and M.E. Woods (1976), *Time Use: A Measure of Household Production of Family Goods and Services*, Washington, DC: Center for the Family of the American Home Economics Association.

PART II

Gender Inequalities in the Household and
Workplace

4. Financial togetherness and autonomy within couples

Fran Bennett, Jerome De Henau,
Susan Himmelweit and Sirin Sung

1. INTRODUCTION

Whether togetherness or autonomy should be valued (more) within couples has been a long-standing topic of debate within feminism. Feminists have generally argued for women's financial autonomy – for women to be free from financial dependence on men in general and their male partner in particular (see, for example, London Women's Liberation Campaign for Legal and Financial Independence and Rights of Women 1979). However, there has also been recognition that individual independence can be a false ideal derived from a masculinist myth that is neither achievable nor desirable. Togetherness, in the sense of sharing resources within households, can be valued by household members for its practical advantages; these include economies of scale, and/or its ideological appeal to the household as a collective unit, especially when resources are limited (Daly and Leonard 2002).

This chapter examines the implications of the concepts of togetherness and financial autonomy for gender equality, drawing on findings from both qualitative and quantitative research. The qualitative research explored the two concepts in individual interviews with men and women in low- to moderate-income couples. The quantitative research used the British Household Panel Survey to analyse the factors affecting the differing assessments of their household income by men and women in couples across the range of incomes. The findings support the argument that an honest recognition of interdependence (or togetherness) is essential when analysing women's financial autonomy.

Policy-makers tend to show more interest in a household's[1] total current income level than in how that income is made up, or in how it is received or by whom. This may be particularly the case in the UK, despite the introduction of independent taxation in 1990. This is because of the UK welfare state's traditional reliance on means-tested benefits, and more recently also on tax credits. The reliance on tax credits looks likely to be consolidated in the 2010 coalition government's plans for welfare reform based on a means-tested 'universal [*sic*] credit'. Clearly adults who share a household *are* likely to share resources of various kinds, including income. If they are partners, they are presumably committed, to a greater or lesser extent, to each other in a form of togetherness. Yet we also know from earlier research that individuals may feel more entitled to spend money that they earn themselves as wages (or receive as some kinds of individual benefits) (Goode et al. 1998). As Robeyns (2003, p.65) argues: 'even if household income were shared completely, it is problematic to assume that it does not matter in a well-being assessment whether a person has earned this money herself, or obtained it from her partner'. In addition, research evidence has demonstrated that money is more likely to be spent on children if it is directed via 'the purse' rather than 'the wallet' – in other words, if it is given to the woman rather than to the man (for example, see Goode et al. 1998; Lundberg et al. 1997 – but see also Hotchkiss 2005). It is already recognised by policy-makers in some instances that it matters who receives household income. For example, in paying child benefit to mothers by default, and insisting that child tax credit be paid to the 'main carer', the UK government implicitly recognises that factors other than its level may make household income more or less effective in contributing to the well-being of children. International evidence has over many years shown that there is good reason for this: that how and by whom a household's financial resources are received affects what they can achieve (Adato et al. 2000; Dwyer and Bruce 1988; Haddad 1999). How money is managed within the household has also been shown to have an independent effect on inequalities of power between men and women (Vogler 1998).

Given these findings, focusing only on the total level of current household income is not likely to be the best way to maximise the effectiveness of policies. Instead, recognising how behaviour with respect to finances within couples may be gendered should make policy more effective in achieving its goals. In addition, if policy-makers want to further gender equality in its own right, the impact of within-household gender inequalities on access to resources and on the life chances that they facilitate should clearly be of central concern.

This chapter draws on research findings from one of the projects within the Gender Equality Network, which investigated such within household inequalities in relation to public policy. The aim of the project was to understand the impact of policies in a way which takes account of gender relations inside the household. These insights were also used to analyse the effects of policy changes in the UK, in particular those that relate to individual incomes and labour market participation. To do this necessitated some exploration of the concepts of 'togetherness' and 'financial autonomy' within couples, and the (potentially gendered) factors that influence individuals' access to household resources.

In this chapter, we report on our analysis of the concepts of financial autonomy and togetherness, using two different methods. The next section outlines the concepts and common focus of the two methods and the samples used. The following section uses the qualitative results of interviews with low- to moderate- income couples to explore the concepts of financial autonomy and togetherness. Then we present the quantitative analysis to identify the factors that affect togetherness and autonomy in a sample of couples. These couples are representative of the full range of household incomes in Britain. In the final section, we draw these findings together to reflect on their implications.

2. THE CONCEPTS AND FOCUS

Both parts of the research project reported here explored how individuals in heterosexual couples talk about and assess their household finances.[2] This chapter focuses on the complex interrelationships between ideas of 'togetherness' and '(financial) autonomy' as they feature in the lives of couples managing their household incomes.

Togetherness is a broad concept. Notions of jointness, mutuality, sharing and interdependence are all treated as synonymous with togetherness in our analysis. Togetherness stands for the extent to which members of a couple view their finances as joint to be spent for mutual benefit, rather than viewing the source of income as giving individuals claims to resources in the sense of determining how they should be spent. In economic theory, togetherness is close to the standard 'unitary' approach that models household decisions as though they were made by individuals with a single given set of preferences, influenced only by the level of household income, not by its source (see, for example, Browning et al. 2006).

Financial autonomy could be seen as the opposite of togetherness. However, we will see that togetherness and autonomy may not be mutually exclusive. They can coexist in one household, not least because of the difference between discourse and practice. We view financial autonomy in terms of economic independence, privacy and/or agency in money matters. Economic independence means (in this case) not having to depend on a partner's resources to meet one's needs. This has been a key concern for feminist campaigners, as noted above. Financial autonomy can also be understood as the absence of control or surveillance by one's partner (Bjornberg and Kollind 2005), including enjoying privacy in one's financial affairs. Financial autonomy as agency can suggest being able to take decisions or actions related to household income on behalf of the household as a whole. It can also mean having legitimate access to (command over) income to pursue one's own individual plans and purposes.

3. THE SAMPLES

The samples used in this research are both drawn from the British Household Panel Survey (BHPS).[3] For the qualitative analysis, 60 semi-structured interviews with men and women in low- to moderate-income heterosexual couples in England, Wales and Scotland were carried out in 2006 (Sung and Bennett 2007). The interviews mainly covered finances and money management issues. These couples had been selected from a discontinued sample added to the BHPS to boost its coverage of low-income households.[4] These 30 couples were largely of working age (with a few having one partner of pension age), and all had reared children at some point. They were selected on the basis of being on means-tested benefits and/or tax credits at the time of interview and/or having been so in the past. They were also all white British couples, although this was not deliberate. In most couples, the woman as well as the man had a job; but the majority of the women worked part-time. In three couples only the woman was employed, and in five couples only the man; in a few cases, neither partner had a job. Almost all the couples were married, with only one cohabiting. The interviews were carried out individually in order to explore the perceptions and views of men and women; in some couples, it turned out that men and women differed in their factual knowledge about the household finances.

The sample for the quantitative analysis includes all heterosexual couples in the BHPS, between 1996 and 2005, for whom there were at least two years of observations, where both members were of working age and not students, with or without children, but not living with others besides their financially dependent children.[5] Such couples remained in the sample so long as they stayed together. This left us with a selection of 2311 couples, giving 11 781 observations over an average five-year period per couple. Fixed effects linear regression analysis was used to identify the factors affecting individual access to household resources over time.

4. EXPLORING TOGETHERNESS AND FINANCIAL AUTONOMY THROUGH QUALITATIVE RESEARCH

The part of our research using qualitative methods allowed us to explore the nature of togetherness, and the possibility of and/or desire for financial autonomy and agency, in a sample of low- to moderate-income couples. For couples on low or moderate incomes, it could be argued that jointness in handling money is often a practical necessity. The qualitative interviews carried out with women and men in such couples indeed revealed a clear loyalty to sharing finances, often as an expression of trust and mutuality in their relationships. But underlying this was a more complex picture, with women more aware than men of tensions between togetherness and individual interests, and the importance of money in their own right.

Togetherness

There has been a series of studies of the use and management of money by low-income families in the UK (see, for example, Goode et al. 1998), as well as elsewhere. It can be argued that for low-income families drivers to togetherness in terms of dealing with household finances are particularly strong. Individual use of income without agreement may jeopardise the tight control and budgeting which are necessary to make ends meet.

Togetherness was certainly a major theme of the interviewees' responses (see also Daly and Leonard 2002). In addition to the need to pool money to maximise flexibility, our couples had often brought up children together, and many had lived together for a long time. A common phrase was that their money was 'all in one pot'; other descriptions included 'no yours and mine', and their relationship as a couple in relation to money management was described by several as a 'partnership' or 'team'. Many couples explained their decision to open a joint account in terms of trust and sharing, although some talked about practical reasons instead or in addition.

However, it would be misleading to take the existence of a joint account as an indicator by itself of togetherness in finances, as there was a spectrum in terms of sharing across couples with separate and joint accounts. Sonnenberg (2008) has argued that 'all in one pot' can be a figure of speech, which can cover a variety of money management practices. More generally, she has argued that in research interviews such as these, men and women are managing their identity as members of couples (or 'doing couple' – Stocks et al. 2007), as well as describing their management of money. Nonetheless, jointness, mutuality, interdependence or togetherness were described as being of great importance by many of our interviewees, both men and women.

Financial Autonomy

Despite the strength of this togetherness, however, it was also found that (financial) autonomy was valued, in particular by women. Autonomy was sometimes achieved, albeit in a limited way. We did not discuss the term 'autonomy' itself with our interviewees. Instead, for this we draw on evidence about women's and men's views on 'making a contribution'; what they thought about 'money in your own right' (which could be seen as including ownership and entitlement); how much they valued privacy in their financial affairs; and how they saw agency in relation to household income, as well as access to income for personal projects. A few women talked about the need to achieve economic independence for practical reasons (in case anything happened to their partners, or in one case if they needed to leave the marriage). But for many women, the aspiration for at least a degree of financial autonomy seemed to be a matter of self-esteem, and not just a practical issue in case of misfortune striking.

'Making a contribution' and 'money in your own right'

Men tended to link their own economic contribution with family survival. However, several women recognised that their contribution was not essential, but argued that it still felt important to them, as in the case of this respondent: 'Moneywise my wage is very important to me. I need to be bringing in something to contribute . . . It is emotionally very important to me' (11, female).[6] Some men and women seemed to identify 'money in your own right' with personal spending, and saw it as irrelevant to themselves because they were living on social security benefits. There was also some resistance to the idea of individual ownership of benefits, perhaps because these were often seen as just providing the basics of life, with only any money surplus to this viewed as being at the disposal of individuals. But the receipt of benefits for disability and/or caring did seem to provide some women with a measure of agency, or 'voice' (having a say), within the couple.

Some men could not understand the concept of 'money in your own right'. Others found the idea antithetical to the concept of togetherness, and so resisted it: 'I'm not a person that would say "right, I need my own money, money to myself" – I don't see the point. I'd prefer to put it into the house for everybody to benefit than just be selfish' (26, male). Some men saw it solely in terms of their pocket money – which several received regularly from their partners, especially in those couples in which the woman was not in paid work (for example, 4 and 8). It often seemed to be the woman's role to control individual financial autonomy, via their day-to-day handling of the household budget as part of managing togetherness (Bennett et al. 2010).

Women were more likely to acknowledge openly the tension between autonomy and togetherness, and to see 'money in your own right' as important. Several female respondents associated it with independence: 'I think you need to be . . . have a little bit of independence in whatever you do' (27, female). For the women, 'independence' appeared to refer to their individual economic independence from family or partner. For some men, 'independence' seemed to be seen as the family doing well financially. (As we discuss below, some women identified 'money in their own right' as money that they could decide what to do with.) However, for the people we interviewed, individual or family independence in either of these senses was difficult to achieve in practice; the women did not usually have well-paid jobs (if they had them at all), and the couples were living on low to moderate incomes rather than doing well financially.

Privacy
Our interviews did not reveal any couples with completely separate finances, and the degree of jointness or separateness in financial matters did not necessarily match the existence of joint and individual bank accounts (see Ashby and Burgoyne 2008; Lewis 2001). But the women in our sample were more likely to have individual accounts than the men, and those who did were more concerned about their privacy and independence. Some men saw individual accounts as undermining togetherness, and as symbolising selfishness. However, for women, keeping an individual account could also represent an attempt to control the spending behaviour of their partner.

Privacy can also be associated with control, in the sense of individuals being able to take financial decisions which affect the family as a whole without consultation. There were several examples of this in our sample, especially in cases in which the man was self-employed (for example, 7). In one case, for example, the man had taken out a secured loan on the house without consulting his wife, despite the fact that her salary paid the mortgage (16). However, when men appeared to be sensitive to their partner's privacy, this could be ambiguous. It could result in greater financial autonomy for the woman. But it could also convey the sense that her income was of secondary importance to the family's well-being (20 and 22) – and indeed may have resulted from this.

Agency in relation to household income

Rake and Jayatilaka (2002) found that for women a sense of entitlement to income earned or received directly tended to be accompanied by more control over how that money was spent, thereby linking economic independence or ownership with agency. Bjornberg and Kollind (2005), on the other hand, argue that women may try to compensate for the loss of what they call 'economic self-governance' (due to the effect of child-rearing on their incomes) with the acquisition of some control over the joint pool of household income. Certainly some women in our sample who had previously run households on their own (for example, 5 and 9) had appreciated the feeling of control that this brought. This led them subsequently to seek to retain some freedom of manoeuvre within the couple.

It has been noted that women are especially likely to manage the household budget on a day-to-day basis in low-income families (Sung and Bennett 2007). This may be more of a burden than a source of power (for example, Goode et al. 1998). The traditional ways of arranging this management role in such families can free women from the need to keep asking their partner for money (at least in cases in which the amount is sufficient) – for example, by the man handing over his wage packet to the woman, or giving her a specific sum for housekeeping. For some women, not having to ask for money was very important (for example, 11), although it was not as much of an issue for men. Several women in our sample had deliberately decided either to start to manage the household's money themselves (24) or to hand over management to the man (9). Spending patterns were generally gendered; as one of our male respondents described the spending responsibilities in his family: 'I'm bills, she's food etc' (17). As Vogler et al. (2008) noted in relation to working-class couples, this has the potential advantage that each partner has some autonomy within their own spending area.

Access to income to pursue personal projects

Most men and women said that they did not have to justify their personal spending to their partner, although women were more likely to say that they saw only their own money as theirs to spend. One female respondent from a couple without a joint account noted: 'Only mine, I wouldn't dare to dream of spending his. No – not unless he offered it to me' (27).

This begs the question of whether women have access to income to pursue their *own* projects, because whether spending is defined as personal or collective is key (Vogler et al. 2008). Goode et al. (1998), for example, found that among their samples of families with young children on benefits both men and women tended to see women's spending on the household and children as their 'personal' spending.

It appeared in our sample that men's identity was more likely to be bound up with the money coming into the household (making a contribution). For women, their identity was more related to the money going out (spending). In particular, instead of thinking about the source of income when discussing 'money in your own right', as men often did, some women connected it with money one could choose how to spend. For these women, this often meant money that they used to save or to buy things for others – whereas more individual men seemed to have a degree of personal financial autonomy to spend on gadgets or hobbies for themselves (for example, 24, 13, 29, 7, 26).

Peter (2003), cited in Lewis and Giullari (2005), argues that concern for others should be taken seriously as an expression of autonomy. Similarly, Cornwall (2007, p.164), in her reconsideration of female solidarity and autonomy, emphasises 'the very real implications of social connectedness for any account of agency'. Given the emphasis placed on togetherness by the women as well as the men in our sample, we have tried to take these concerns seriously in this analysis. We highlight the value which they gave to it. But we found that for many of the women, the exercise of agency could only take place within a situation of unequal gender roles and very limited resources. Partly because of this, 'togetherness' sometimes appeared to result in an isolated nuclear family, with few external contacts.

Authors' Reflections On Findings

A strong theme of money in common, and mutuality, emerges from our interviews. But 'togetherness' may not result in equal sharing of resources. In addition, it could be used in different ways – to reduce or increase inequalities within the household. One partner might use togetherness to safeguard resources for the family as a whole. Another might use it to justify the sharing of debts acquired before marriage with the other person. When combined with a gendered division of labour, and a preference for solely family-based care, 'togetherness' can act to intensify the inequalities of living in a gendered society. These findings are similar to those reported below from the quantitative research about the implications of joint labour market decisions that also often reinforce gender inequalities.

Many men seemed to see little to disturb their vision of togetherness. Alternatively, they saw ideas about financial autonomy as a threat. Many of the women were more aware of the inevitable tensions between jointness and independence. Women tended to manage togetherness in terms of money in practice. They also often had aspirations towards some financial independence, or at least a degree of autonomy expressed as agency and/ or privacy.

But it is of course more difficult to achieve such independence or autonomy when budgets are tight, as they were in these low- to moderate-income families. As we have seen, it may be especially difficult for women to exercise agency in such circumstances. Money has to be used for shared needs for the household economy to be viable. As noted above, applications for means-tested benefits and tax credits in the UK involve joint assessment of resources for male/female couples living together, regardless of whether they have decided to pool their incomes. Increasingly these are also joint claims. The 'private' nature of family life in our sample, in particular as regards bringing up children, may limit the achievement of autonomy, especially for women. In addition, attempts to achieve a degree of financial autonomy may result in a lower standard of living for women who wish to have some independence without drawing on their partners' resources.

5. QUANTITATIVE ANALYSIS OF THE FACTORS INFLUENCING 'TOGETHERNESS' AND 'AUTONOMY'

The qualitative research with members of low- to moderate-income couples suggested that men and women who shared a household could assess that same household's financial situation quite differently. In the quantitative analysis, we explored the explanatory factors behind these different financial assessments across a wider sample of British couples representative of all income levels. We were interested in identifying the factors influencing individuals' ability to make use of household financial resources. This was reflected in the economic independence and agency aspects of financial autonomy in the qualitative analysis.[7] Our approach is close to that of Amartya Sen (1990). Sen's notion of individual entitlements – the legitimate access to resources that gives rise to an individual's set of opportunities – is close to our notion of financial autonomy as the ability to make use of financial resources. The literature on household bargaining and money management suggests that this ability can vary considerably for individuals within the same household (Bennett et al. 2010; Browning et al. 2006; Friedberg and Webb 2006; Lundberg and Pollak 1996).

We hypothesised that the ability to make use of financial resources depends, first, on the household's overall financial position and, second, on individual members' relative entitlements to that household's income.

Sen makes the point that members of a household will often have a shared view of a household's collective best interests. However, structural factors, internal and external to the household, may mean that pursuing these interests legitimates one partner's access to the fruits of that collective endeavour more than another's. In other words, both past and current decisions made 'together' – including decisions about collective endeavours seen as in their joint interests – may increase one member's 'financial autonomy' more than another's. For example, a couple's decision that the woman rather than the man should give up employment when they have small children may well be a shared decision. It may reduce the consequent loss of household earnings if she is the lower earner. However, this may nevertheless in practice de-legitimise her access to the household income that he now earns, and thus limit her financial autonomy.

Satisfaction with Household Income

To investigate the determinants of individual financial autonomy, we used answers to the question 'How dissatisfied or satisfied are you with the income of your household?' as our dependent variable. This question was asked in the BHPS through a self-completion questionnaire administered to all adults every year from 1996 to 2005, except in 2001. Answers had to be given on a seven-point scale, from one, 'not satisfied at all' to seven, 'completely satisfied'. We considered that an empirical analysis of the factors influencing our notion of financial autonomy could be carried out better by using data on individuals' satisfaction with household income than by using data on specific household expenditures, as is more usual in economic analyses of intra-household resource distribution.[8]

The assumption behind our analytical method is as follows: one possible cause of differences in how partners report their satisfaction with their common household income is differential access to household resources (see also Alessie et al. 2006; Bonke and Browning 2009). Therefore, if, after controlling for a number of other possible causes of such differences, factors have differential effects on the satisfaction of the man and the woman in a household, this is likely to be because those factors affect relative access to household resources.

Of course, answers to questions about satisfaction depend on a number of other factors, and these must be controlled for. On the one hand, there are relatively stable influences such as personality traits: for example, some people are just inherently more positive (Diener and Lucas 1999). On the other hand, there are processes that are not specifically financial. These include adaptation to existing circumstances and the formation of expectations about the future that can impinge on all satisfaction measures

(Stutzer 2004). Because we had panel data that track individuals through time, we could abstract from any invariant personality traits by using the method of fixed effects regression. This statistical technique takes account of the influences on individuals' responses that vary over time (while eliminating the characteristics that may differ across individuals but are invariant over time for any individual). This method allowed us to strip out the effects of any individually unchanging factors, including personality traits (Ferrer-i-Carbonell and Frijters 2004). There was also a question in the survey about people's overall satisfaction with life. Controlling for responses to this question meant that we were examining the potential causes of variations in satisfaction with household income *over and above* any variation in satisfaction in general. In this way, we hoped to control for the effects of adaptation, and expectation formation, which we assume affected all forms of satisfaction, not just financial, as well as concern for a partner's overall well-being. For more detail of the methods and statistical model used, and the results of a similar analysis, see De Henau and Himmelweit (2009).

Decomposing Individual Answers about Satisfaction

The empirical model is displayed in Figure 4.1. Individual and household financial characteristics (potential and current income, costs, and so on) are seen to be influenced by gender norms and the socio-economic environment. The individual and household characteristics have an influence on an individual's access/entitlement to household resources through (1) the amount of total household resources, current or potential (the size of the pie) and (2) the relative access of each partner to those current and potential resources (the share of the pie). Individual entitlement to household resources cannot be observed directly. However, our assumption is that individuals will report increased (decreased) satisfaction with household income if their own entitlement increases (decreases), provided adequate controls are included for other influences (including own and partner's overall satisfaction, and individual characteristics that do not vary over time).

The BHPS allows us to match the individual answers of partners in a household. We can therefore include not only factors that apply to the household as a whole (such as home ownership or the number and age of children) but also individual-level factors for both partners, such as their employment status or the hours that they spend in housework. The unit of analysis is therefore the household and two fixed effects linear regressions were run: the first regression used the arithmetic average of the man's and the woman's satisfaction with household income as the dependent

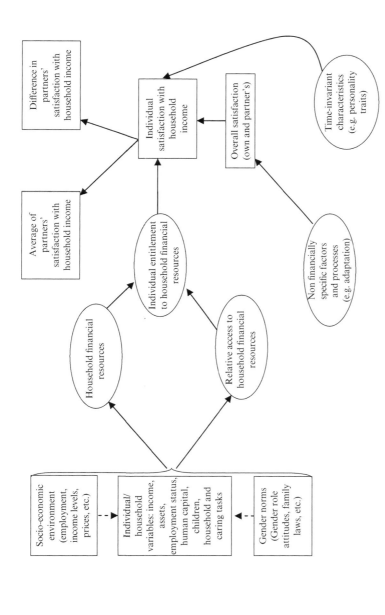

Note: Ovals represent underlying factors (concepts/unobserved) while rectangles represent measurable variables.

Figure 4.1   Conceptual framework of factors influencing partners' satisfaction with household income

variable, and household, man's and woman's individual characteristics as explanatory variables; the second regression used the difference in their satisfaction with household income as the dependent variable and the same explanatory variables.[9]

Therefore we can examine to what extent a change in a factor (such as the man getting a full-time job) has influence in either of two ways: (1) on both partners' answers, through a positive effect on total household resources and hence on both partners' satisfaction with household income, and/or (2) by influencing partners' answers differently, through the man's employment giving him a greater claim on household resources relative to his partner, resulting in his satisfaction with household income increasing more than his partner's. The first of these effects would be captured by a significant coefficient for the average of the man's and the woman's satisfaction with household income, and the second by a significant coefficient for the factor in the difference in the partners' satisfaction scores. The full results are given in the Appendix (Table A4.1, with the significant coefficients summarised in Tables 4.1 and 4.2).

The same factors may, of course, influence both household financial resources and relative access to those resources. The explanatory variables that we investigated[10] were ones that the literature on intra-household allocation models (including Sen's approach mentioned above) suggests could have effects on the current or future economic prosperity of the household on the one hand and/or the relative entitlements of each partner on the other (Bonke and Browning 2009; Pollak 2005; Sen 1990). Variables that have been suggested as affecting relative entitlements generally fall into two categories: those that register the perceived contribution of an individual to household finances, such as individual earnings, and those that register an individual's perceived fall-back position in case intra-household co-operation or the household itself breaks down. These include variables that affect how well an individual could fare on their own (such as eligibility for benefits). Again, of course many variables, notably those to do with employment status and potential wages, fall into both categories.

Effects on Both Partners' Average Satisfaction

The factors that were found to be significantly associated with a couple's average satisfaction with their household income are summarised in Table 4.1. These are the factors that indicate what a couple might value 'together'. Some of these factors apply to the household, while others are individual. For an individual variable its 'symmetric/non-gendered effect' is the average of its effect when it applies to the man and when it applies

Table 4.1   *Factors influencing couple's average satisfaction with household income*

	Impact on couple's average satisfaction with household income	
	Positive	Negative
Household variables	• Household income • Household receives investment income • Home ownership	• Household receives benefits • Children under 5 years old
Individual variables Symmetric/non-gendered effect	• Working full-time • Potential wage • One partner earns more than 75% of household earnings	• Being unemployed • Long-term disabled • Working part-time • Being out of labour market • Reporting poor health • Hours of housework
Additional gendered effect	• Man working full-time • Man's potential wage • Woman earning more than 75% of household income (or receiving more than 75% of its non-labour income)	• Man being unemployed • Man long-term disabled • Man working part-time • Man being out of labour market

Notes: An individual factor is reported as having a non-gendered/symmetric effect if its average effect over the man and the woman on the couple's average satisfaction is significant at the 5 per cent level. A factor is reported as having a gendered effect if its effect on the couple's average satisfaction with household income differs significantly (at the 5 per cent level) according to gender.

Source: Authors' calculations from BHPS 1996–2005.

to the woman, with its gendered effect representing any difference between these two effects.

Table 4.1 shows, for example, that a higher household income, receiving investment income and home ownership were all associated with an increased average level of a couple's satisfaction with their household's income. The presence of young children was associated with a decrease in the average level of the couple's satisfaction with household income. If either partner took a full-time job, average satisfaction with household income increased. If either partner became unemployed or long-term

Table 4.2 *Factors influencing the difference in partners' satisfaction with household income*

	Impact on difference in couple's satisfaction with household income	
	Positive	Negative
Individual variables Non-gendered effects for both men and women	• Potential wage • Working full-time	• Being unemployed • Working part-time • Being out of labour market • Long-term disabled • Reporting poor health • Hours of housework
Gendered effects Household variables	• Favouring the man • Children under 5 years old	• Favouring the woman • Household receives transfer income
Individual variables		• Woman earning more than 75% of household income

Notes: An individual factor is reported as having non-gendered effects if its average effect (over the man and the woman) on the difference in the couple's satisfaction scores is significant at the 5 per cent level. Factors are reported as having gendered effects if their effect on the difference in the couple's satisfaction scores differs significantly (at the 5 per cent level) according to gender.

Source: Authors' calculations from BHPS 1996–2005.

disabled, worked part-time or dropped out of the labour market, average satisfaction with household income decreased. However, these effects are gendered: the positive effect of the man going into full-time employment, and the negative effect of him losing his job, becoming long-term disabled, working part-time or leaving the labour market were all significantly greater than if these changes happened to the woman. Similarly, a higher potential wage for either partner was associated with an increase in average satisfaction with household income. But the effect was stronger for increases in the man's wage. Spending more hours of housework reduced average satisfaction with household income, but there was no significant gender difference in this effect.

There is a great deal that could be unpacked from these results, but the main point is that gender roles matter in what makes couples satisfied with their household income. In particular, the man's current employment status and potential wage have greater effects than the woman's – even after controlling for the level of current household income. Our interpretation of our regression results depends on the implicit assumption that all characteristics that might jointly influence a couple's labour market status and their satisfaction with household income have been included.[11] If this does not hold, our results can be no more than indicative; but they do suggest that when couples make decisions 'together', they are likely to put more weight on the man's employment opportunities than on the woman's.

Effects on Differences in Satisfaction

Table 4.2 shows which factors led to differences in satisfaction, used here as a measure of differences in access to household resources.

Working full time or having a higher potential wage was associated with an increase in *that* partner's satisfaction with household income more than the other's. This was true for both men and women. Given the controls that we have used in our regressions, we can interpret this as indicating greater access to that household income. This is consistent with the findings from other studies (Bonke and Browning 2009; Pollak 2005).

We also found gendered effects. The presence of young children reduced a woman's satisfaction with household income relative to her partner's (even controlling for her employment status). Receipt by the household of transfer income (more likely to be the woman's, since most transfer income is child support) had the opposite effect. In addition, a woman's satisfaction with household income increased relative to her partner's if she earned more than 75 per cent of household income; this did not happen in reverse for a man. In all cases, we interpret such changes in relative satisfaction as reflecting changes in relative entitlements to the couple's joint household income.

Authors' Reflections on Findings

Some of the findings from the quantitative analyses are consistent with the qualitative research findings. In particular, the fact that men's employment status matters more than women's for a couple's satisfaction with household income relates to the differences in how men's and women's earnings are perceived in the qualitative research. The qualitative research found that a woman's earnings were seen as less important but also more likely to be hers to spend (even if that does not necessarily mean that she spends them on herself). The quantitative analysis's finding that couples tend to value the man's employment opportunities over the woman's is consistent with the finding from the qualitative interviews that couples are more likely to see the man's earnings as for the household.

However, employment status also affects relative entitlements. Thus togetherness may well end up not only favouring the man's employment but also thereby improving his relative entitlements within the household. This is consistent with Sen's observation, mentioned earlier, that structural factors internal and external to the household may mean that pursuing a couple's shared view of a household's collective best interests favours one partner or the other in their entitlements to the fruits of that collective endeavour. This outcome is but a modern version of the notion that it is in the whole family's interests that the man eats well even when food is scarce for other family members, because all their fortunes depend on his strength as the family's main breadwinner.

In the quantitative part of the research individuals' experience of financial autonomy was identified with their assessment of the opportunities that their household's financial resources give them, indicated indirectly by their satisfaction with household income. This was influenced by two factors; an assessment of that household income itself, captured by a couple's average satisfaction with household income, and individual access to household resources, captured by differences in that satisfaction. Women's financial autonomy depends therefore in part on their household income, and through that was seen as more affected by their partner's labour market status than their own. However, women's own labour market status is also an important determinant of their access to household resources and through that to their financial autonomy. External constraints, gender norms and the gendered division of labour within households that reduce women's labour market attachment compared with men's also erode women's financial autonomy. This can occur even where such gendered division of labour results from decisions made together on the basis of a shared understanding of what benefits their household financially.[12] Togetherness in pursuit of a higher standard of living by couples may therefore reproduce unequal gender roles and have an impact on the relative financial autonomy of men and women. The economic constraints and/or gender norms giving rise to such shared views thus contribute to a reduction in financial autonomy for women, and the reproduction of gender inequalities both within and beyond households.

Thus togetherness may lead to couples making decisions that reproduce unequal gender roles. These decisions, while not conflictual, may still disadvantage women whether or not their household remains intact. A continuing concern of feminism has been that women make decisions for the short-term benefit of their families that can be to their own long-term disadvantage – for example, if the couple later splits up. This research has shown that there is also another issue: that such decisions made together in what are seen as the couple's joint interests, if they reproduce unequal gender roles, may disadvantage women within their own households by reducing their access to household resources and their financial autonomy overall. This is in addition to any longer-term disadvantage, which this research has not investigated. However, couples' joint decision-making may be one of the key ways in which such longer-term disadvantage accumulates.

This suggests that any effects of household decision-making on gender roles and the opportunities to which these give rise may be more important than the immediate distribution of resources within households. This issue can only be tackled by changing the external conditions, both economic constraints and accepted gender roles, which lead to togetherness resulting in decisions that so often disadvantage women. We return to this issue in the conclusions below.

6.   CONCLUSIONS

As noted in the introduction above, autonomy and togetherness have both been important to feminism. On the one hand, women's financial autonomy has been a long-standing feminist aim: to free women from the financial dependence on men that has often kept them in unsatisfactory relationships and unable to realise their potential. On the other hand, feminism has recognised that individual independence is a myth, whose apparent appeal rests on the non-recognition of the domestic contributions that women make to the so-called 'independence' of male wage earners. Rather than positing such false independence as an ideal, an honest recognition of togetherness, or interdependence, is therefore essential.

This is what we have tried to do in this project, in both the qualitative and quantitative research. We found evidence of togetherness among the couples we studied. However, this was by no means the same as discovering gender equality. Indeed, the loyalty to jointness and mutuality found among these low- to moderate-income couples sometimes seemed closer to a unitary concept of the couple. The common belief in solely family-based care for children, together with a traditional gendered division of labour, and a retreat into coupledom through lack of resources, limited some women's opportunities in particular (for example, for paid work).

The quantitative research findings mirrored these qualitative results. Differences between the joint views of couples and those of the individuals within them have a systematic character. While the shared views endorse more traditional gender roles, the individual views show a relative disadvantage to those who take on the more traditionally female roles within households. Behavioural economics demonstrates that individuals do not always make choices that are in their own longer-term interests. Our results show that couples, especially women, are even less likely to do so. Although these are rarely distinguished, our results imply that there could be a significant difference, in terms of their gendered effects, between policies that give choices to couples to make jointly and those designed to ensure that men and women make their own individual choices (even if individuals take their partners' wishes into account in making such decisions).[13]

The findings from our research suggest that for members of heterosexual couples in the UK today, neither 'togetherness' nor 'autonomy' provides an automatic or unproblematic route to achieving gender equality within the household. As noted above, 'togetherness' can be used to reduce or increase gender inequalities while pursuing a household's collective interests within a gendered society. It can also reproduce or exacerbate gender inequality. On the other hand, attempts to achieve financial autonomy within the household can result in a lower standard of living for women who wish to be financially independent without drawing on their partners' resources (see Stocks et al. 2007).

Moreover, the ways in which both men and women view financial autonomy are integrally related to togetherness. Just as Lewis (2001) found in relation to older men in particular, men in the low- to moderate-income families whom we interviewed tended to make sense of their own behaviour in relation to the family. They also saw financial autonomy (independence) as the family as a whole doing well economically. When women exercised financial agency, this was often done in relation to the family – for example, what they saw as their personal projects often consisted of gifts to family members. To counterpose togetherness and financial autonomy (as we have done here) therefore does not always make sense. The women we interviewed seemed to be more aware of the coexistence of both, and of the tensions between the two.

It can of course be argued – for example, by Lister (2003) – that true interdependence is not possible without some sense of equality and autonomy for both partners. There are examples in the qualitative findings of women in particular who are aware of the tensions between togetherness and autonomy, and who find ways – however limited and constrained – to try to exercise some agency. Some had achieved a degree of independence – not always via paid work, but sometimes through the receipt of benefits in their own name. Women can feel a sense of entitlement as a result of ownership of such income. Also, perhaps because it is more unusual, women can gain more entitlement from having some earnings of their own than men gain through being the couple's main earner, as demonstrated in the quantitative findings.

Rather than seeing this as a zero sum game, it is also clearly possible for both partners to increase their autonomy within a relationship. Previous research, even among low-income families, has found that some have more equal relationships than others (for example, see Goode et al. 1998). Further research could usefully investigate the most important factors influencing both men's and women's ability to achieve this. In addition, our research findings reported here focus on only income. Clearly there is room to extend the discussion to include (gendered) access to resources of all kinds.

NOTES

1. In this chapter, we use 'household' and 'couple'/'family' interchangeably. Technically a household can be made up of more than one 'family' (for example, when a non-dependent adult such as a grown-up child lives in the parental home, this would be one household but two 'families', as an individual is also described as a family unit). In both our qualitative and quantitative samples, some couples did have grown-up children living with them. But in most cases when we use the word 'household' we are referring to the heterosexual couples who are the main focus of our research.
2. This research did not include interviews with members of same-sex couples and the quantitative data set identified too few of them to allow any meaningful analysis.
3. The BHPS followed individuals from a representative clustered sample of British household in 1991, annually interviewing them and all adult members of the households in which they subsequently lived.
4. These households were added for the European Community Household Panel in the late 1990s, and were interviewed each year from 1997 to 2001 inclusive.
5. Couples whose household income differed by more than £1000 from the sum of their individual incomes were excluded (since this could indicate the influence on decision-making of a child with significant individual income) as well as all those living with others beside their own children.
6. Each couple is given a number in this chapter, so that where appropriate men and women in the same couple can be matched.
7. The available data did not allow for exploration of the privacy aspect of 'financial autonomy' in the quantitative analysis.
8. Expenditure data is often used to assess models of household decision-making. However, doing so raises theoretically and empirically difficult questions of how to assign expenditure to individuals, and fails to capture the distinction that we wish to make between the actual use of financial resources and the opportunities which those resources provide.
9. This is essentially the same as running a single linear estimation with satisfaction with household income as the dependent variable using gendered interaction effects. The only difference with such a single estimation is the need for post-estimation tests to identify some of the effects and the choice of one gender as reference (more details on the technique used can be found in De Henau and Himmelweit 2009).
10. These were: log of total annual household income; whether the household receives any state benefit, any other transfer income, any investment income; age and number of children; whether they own their home outright or on a mortgage (ref: home rented); share of household earnings, share of household non-labour income; employment status; potential wage (Essex score, see Gershuny and Kan 2006); hours of housework; subjective health status; providing care inside/outside the household.
11. As mentioned earlier, by using fixed-effects regression our specification controls for

unobserved time-invariant characteristics such as personality traits. Moreover, we assume that any change in unobserved time-varying characteristics that might influence labour market outcomes (such as motivation) is captured by a change in overall satisfaction, which is included as a control.
12. Folbre (1997) makes a similar point about bargaining power.
13. In either case the well-being of other family members may influence decisions.

REFERENCES

Adato, M., B. De la Briere, D. Mindek and A. Quisumbuing (2000), *The Impact of PROGRESA on Women's Status and Intra-household Relations: Final Report*, Washington, DC: International Food Policy Research Institute.

Alessie, R., T. Crossley and V. Hildebrand (2006), 'Estimating a collective household model with survey data on financial satisfaction', IFS Working Paper 06/19, London: Institute for Fiscal Studies.

Ashby, K.J. and C.B. Burgoyne (2008), 'Separate financial entities? Beyond categories of money management', in C.B. Burgoyne (ed.), *Journal of Socio-Economics*, special issue on the household economy, **37** (2), 458–80.

Bennett, F., J. De Henau and S. Sung (2010), 'Within-household inequalities across classes? Management and control of money', in J. Scott, R. Crompton and C. Lyonette (eds), *Gender Inequalities in the 21st Century: New Barriers and Continuing Constraints*, Cheltenham, UK and Northampton, MA, USA: Edward Elgar, pp. 215–41.

Bjornberg, U. and A.-K. Kollind (2005), *Individualism and Families: Equality, Autonomy and Togetherness*, London and New York: Routledge (Taylor and Francis Group).

Bonke, J. and M. Browning (2009), 'The distribution of financial well-being and income within the household', *Review of Economics of the Household*, **7** (1), 31–42.

Browning, M., P.-A. Chiappori and V. Lechene (2006), 'Collective and unitary models: a clarification', *Review of Economics of the Household*, **4**, 5–14.

Cornwall, A. (2007), 'Myths to live by? Female solidarity and female autonomy reconsidered', *Development and Change*, **38** (1), 149–68.

Daly, M. and M. Leonard, with assistance from T. Gorman (2002), *Against All Odds: Family Life on a Low Income*, Dublin: Institute of Public Administration and Combat Poverty Agency.

De Henau, J. and S. Himmelweit (2009), 'Cooperation and conflict within couples: a longitudinal analysis of the gendered distribution of entitlement to household income', Milton Keynes: Open University, mimeo.

Diener, D. and R.E. Lucas (1999), 'Personality and subjective well-being', in D. Kahneman, E. Diener and N. Schwarz (eds), *Foundations of Hedonic Psychology: Scientific Perspectives on Enjoyment and Suffering*, New York: Russell Sage Foundation.

Dwyer, D. and J. Bruce (1988), *A Home Divided: Women and Income in the Third World*, Palo Alto, CA: Stanford University Press.

Ferrer-i-Carbonell, A. and P. Frijters (2004), 'How important is methodology for the estimates of the determinants of happiness?', *The Economic Journal*, **114**, 641–59.

Folbre, N. (1997), 'Gender coalitions: extra-family influences on intra-family inequality', in H. Alderman, L. Haddad and J. Hoddinot (eds), *Intrahousehold Allocation in Developing Countries*, Baltimore, MD: Johns Hopkins University Press, pp. 263–74.

Friedberg, L. and A. Webb (2006), 'Determinants and consequences of bargaining power in households', CRR Research Working Papers 2006-13, Boston: Center for Retirement Research.

Gershuny, J. and M,-Y, Kan (2006), 'Human capital and social position in Britain: creating a measure of wage-earning potential from BHPS data', ISER Working Paper 2006-03, Institute for Social and Economic Research, Colchester: University of Essex.

Goode, J., C. Callender and R. Lister (1998), *Purse or Wallet? Gender Inequalities and Income Distribution Within Families on Benefits*, London: Policy Studies Institute.

Haddad, L. (1999), 'The welfare impacts of the income earned by women', *Agricultural Economics*, **20** (2), 135–42.

Hotchkiss, J. (2005), 'Do husbands and wives pool their resources? Further evidence', *Journal of Human Resources*, **40** (2), 519–31.

Lewis, J. (2001), *The End of Marriage? Individualism and Intimate Relations*, Cheltenham, UK and Northampton, MA, USA: Edward Elgar Publishing.

Lewis, J. and S. Giullari (2005), 'The adult worker model family, gender equality and care: the search for new policy principles and the possibilities and problems of a capabilities approach', *Economy and Society*, **34** (1), 76–104.

Lister, R. (2003), *Citizenship: Feminist Perspectives*, Basingstoke and New York: Palgrave Macmillan.

London Women's Liberation Campaign for Legal and Financial Independence and Rights of Women (1979), 'Disaggregation now! Another battle for women's independence', *Feminist Review*, **2**, 19–31.

Lundberg, S. and R.A. Pollak (1996), 'Bargaining and distribution in marriage', *Journal of Economic Perspectives*, **10** (4), 139–58.

Lundberg, S., R. Pollak and T. Wales (1997), 'Do husbands and wives pool their incomes? Evidence from the United Kingdom child benefit', *Journal of Human Resources*, **32** (3), 463–80.

Peter, F. (2003), 'Gender and the foundations of social choice: the role of situated agency', *Feminist Economics*, **9** (2–3), 13–32.

Pollak, R.A. (2005), 'Bargaining power in marriage: earnings, wage rates and household production', NBER Working Paper Series 11239, Cambridge, MA: US National Bureau of Economic Research.

Rake, K. and G. Jayatilaka (2002), *Home Truths: An Analysis of Financial Decision Making Within the Home*, London: Fawcett Society.

Robeyns, I. (2003), 'Sen's capability approach and gender inequality: selecting relevant capabilities', *Feminist Economics*, **9** (2–3), 61–92.

Sen, A. (1990), 'Gender and cooperative conflicts', in I. Tinker (ed.), *Persistent Inequalities: Women and World Development*, New York and Oxford: Oxford University Press, pp. 123–49.

Sonnenberg, S. (2008), 'Household financial organisation and discursive practice: managing money and identity', in C.B. Burgoyne (ed.), *Journal of Socio-Economics*, **37** (2), 533–51.

Stocks, J., C. Diaz and B. Hallerod (eds) (2007), *Modern Couples Sharing Money, Sharing Life*, Basingstoke: Palgrave Macmillan.

Stutzer, A. (2004), 'The role of income aspirations in individual happiness', *Journal of Economic Behavior and Organization*, **54** (1), 89–109.

Sung, S. and F. Bennett (2007), 'Dealing with money in low- to moderate-income couples: insights from individual interviews', in K. Clarke, T. Maltby and P. Kennett (eds), *Social Policy Review 19*, Bristol: The Policy Press in association with Social Policy Association.

Vogler, C. (1998), 'Money in the household: some underlying issues of power', *The Sociological Review*, **46** (4), 687–713.

Vogler, C., C. Lyonette and R.D. Wiggins (2008), 'Money, power and spending decisions in intimate relationships', *The Sociological Review*, **56** (1), 117–43.

APPENDIX

Table A4.1   Regression results of quantitative analysis

	Average satisfaction		Difference in satisfaction	
	Coeff.	Std err.	Coeff.	Std err.
Household variables				
Log of household income	0.271	0.029***	0.000	0.022
Prop. benefits >0% of hh income	−0.106	0.035***	0.045	0.028
Prop. benefits >50% of hh income	−0.081	0.072	0.069	0.056
Prop. benefits >95% of hh income	0.124	0.091	−0.051	0.072
HH receives investment income	0.090	0.024***	−0.006	0.018
HH receives transfer income	−0.076	0.042*	−0.076	0.033**
Home owned on mortgage	0.113	0.044**	−0.017	0.035
Home owned outright	0.247	0.067***	0.004	0.052
No of children aged 0–4	−0.079	0.023***	0.040	0.018**
No of children aged 5–11	−0.023	0.021	−0.013	0.016
No of children aged 12+	−0.042	0.025*	−0.012	0.019
Constant	1.087	0.141***	−0.160	0.110*
Individual variables				
Symmetric effect [1]				
Share of earnings 75–100%	0.165	0.061***	0.064	0.045
Share of non lab. inc. 75–100%	−0.066	0.040	0.022	0.024
Essex score	0.055	0.012***	0.024	0.010**
Working part-time	−0.347	0.062***	−0.119	0.049**
Inactive (care or other)	−0.444	0.080***	−0.173	0.064***
Unemployed	−1.450	0.090***	−0.250	0.074***
Long-term disabled	−0.632	0.147***	−0.471	0.119***
Reporting poor health	−0.248	0.060***	−0.111	0.048**
Providing care for others within hh	−0.032	0.097	0.040	0.102
Providing care for others outside hh	−0.036	0.046	−0.021	0.046
Weekly hours of housework	−0.015	0.004***	−0.007	0.003**
Weekly hours of housework squared	0.000	0.000***	0.000	0.000**
Overall satisfaction	0.436	0.013***	0.239	0.012***

Table A4.1   (continued)

	Average satisfaction		Difference in satisfaction	
	Coeff.	Std err.	Coeff.	Std err.
Gendered effect [2]				
Share of earnings 75–100%	−0.139	0.057**	−0.094	0.048*
Share of non lab. inc. 75–100%	−0.063	0.031**	0.006	0.032
Essex score	0.026	0.013**	0.005	0.010
Working part-time	−0.103	0.062*	−0.050	0.048
Inactive (care or other)	−0.169	0.082**	0.013	0.063
Unemployed	−0.616	0.095***	−0.102	0.070
Long-term disabled	−0.377	0.151***	−0.093	0.115
Reporting poor health	−0.075	0.061	−0.005	0.047
Providing care for others within hh	−0.131	0.130	0.069	0.076
Providing care for others outside hh	0.068	0.059	0.020	0.036
Weekly hours of housework	−0.006	0.004	−0.002	0.003
Weekly hours of house-work squared	0.000	0.000	0.000	0.000
Overall satisfaction	0.052	0.015***	0.013	0.010
R-sq (within/between)	0.201	0.420	0.059	0.180
Prob>F	0.000		0.000	
Joint stat. sig. fixed-effects (p-value)	0.000		0.000	

Notes:
*** $p < 0.01$; ** $p < 0.05$; * $p < 0.1$. Year dummies are included but not shown.
(1)   Symmetric effects refer to the average effect of male and female characteristics.
(2)   Gendered effects refer to the difference in the effects of male and female characteristics.

5. Global flows and local labour markets: precarious employment and migrant workers in the UK

Linda McDowell, Adina Batnitzky and Sarah Dyer

INTRODUCTION: MIGRATION AND SERVICE SECTOR EMPLOYMENT

In this chapter we explore the world of waged work for both men and women migrants who have come to the UK in search of a better life. Migration for employment was once conceived as a predominantly male affair, and women, if included in analyses at all, were theorised as dependants. However, in recent decades increasing numbers of women worldwide are moving independently, as well as within family groups, to search for waged work. The United Nations Population Fund estimated that in 2005 women comprised half of the world's 191 million transnational migrants, compared with 45 per cent in 1960. This number may look large but it is important to note that migrants constitute less than 3 per cent of the global population.

In Britain in 2008, 250 000 people entered the country as migrants and 87 000 people left, a net inflow of 163 000, not all of whom were economic migrants. Asylum seekers and refugees are also an important part of the new population, but the majority of migrants into the UK are planning to become economically active. This is substantiated by the employment participation rates of the non-British born population, which are substantially higher (9 per cent higher in 2008) than for British-born people. The highest rates of all – at 80 per cent of the working age group – are found among the migrants from the eight East European countries[1] (termed the A8 migrants) that joined the European Union in 2004. Among these both men and women are usually economically active, in part as they are young and often single when they enter the UK. Three-quarters of the people from these A8 countries who entered the UK between 2004 and 2008 were from Poland and about two-thirds of them were aged between 18 and 24.

Some of these Polish migrants are the subject of this chapter. Although men outnumbered women among the A8 entrants, overall men and women are approximately equal in numbers among the migrant population who entered the UK over the past decade, of whom about 50 per cent of both women and men registered for a National Insurance number each year. They joined an existing population of non-British born migrants that has become increasingly diverse in its origins and characteristics as the new millennium progresses (Vertovec 2007). This diversity is reflected in the characteristics of economic migrants. They are differentiated by age, gender, national origin and skin colour as well as by their reasons for migrating, their visa statuses and the types of employment for which they are eligible in the UK.

Some migrants – typically those who are highly educated and often from the 'white' Commonwealth countries and the USA – come to Britain for a limited period to take up specific vacancies in, for example, the financial services sector, the National Health Service (NHS) and other public sector positions, including teaching. Legal recruitment of migrant workers tends to operate in favour of men as schemes that target highly skilled migrants focus on male-dominated occupations, such as information technology (IT) workers and medical doctors. Temporary migrant workers' schemes for semi-skilled and unskilled workers typically focus on male-dominated sectors such as agriculture or construction (Chammartin 2008). Women are typically recruited for nursing or for domestic service and, among exploited and often undocumented workers, for the sex industry. Many migrants, but especially women, are affected by 'brain waste' (Chammartin 2008, p. 5) as, despite relatively high levels of education and skills, many migrants find employment in jobs that they may be overqualified for. Others without skills have no option but to take poorly paid work, which is often precarious or on a temporary or casual contract.

It is this type of low-wage, unskilled employment that is the focus of this chapter: jobs where both men and women provide services to more affluent or needy members of British society in, for example, catering, cleaning, hospitality and care work. This often occurs to replace the labour of British women, who may once have cared for individual members of their households but who now find themselves time-poor but relatively income-rich as they enter or remain in the labour market. What we explore here is the sort of once-private feminised tasks that are now largely commodified and thus available for purchase in the market or as a public service (see McDowell 2009). We show how the rise of the service sector in the UK has created an expanded set of poorly paid 'servicing' jobs at the bottom end of the labour market, many of which are now filled by migrant workers. We explore the ways in which gender and migration intersect so that these 'feminised' servicing jobs are now undertaken by both women and by men. Our empirical focus is on low-paid employment in servicing jobs in hotels and hospitals, where similar types of work – looking after the bodily needs of guests and patients – are provided in the private and public sector respectively, and are often undertaken by migrant workers. These particular local (in the sense of what the poet Adrienne Rich once termed 'the geography closest in') bodily needs are increasingly met by the assembly of a workforce across a wide spatial scale.

THE GROWTH OF SERVICE EMPLOYMENT

Since around 1973, the economic restructuring of the British economy has resulted in the growing dominance of service sector employment, paralleled by a growing diversity among the population working in this sector. Since the early 1970s, women's labour market participation, as we noted above, has grown, as has the employment of students and school children. This diversity is matched by new terms and conditions of employment and a greater variety in hours that are worked. Many workers are now employed on casual and temporary contracts, working part-time on a daily, weekly or annual basis. Their hours are less likely to be the traditional 9 to 5 pattern of previous decades as a 24/7 society demands continuous provision of many services, not only healthcare and transport but also the leisure services that increasingly dominate the so-called 'night economy'. Furthermore, many workers are now born abroad rather than in the UK, as economic growth in the prosperous decades before the 2007–09 financial crisis was based on consumer demand that created growing numbers of these types of precarious, low-paid jobs, often rejected by the British-born population but seen as an opportunity to gain a foothold in the UK labour market by many migrants (Wills et al. 2009). An Organisation for Economic Co-operation and Development (OECD) report in 2009 suggested that 70 per cent of the new jobs created by the Labour governments in the decade after 1997 were filled by migrant workers. The service sector as a whole is characterised by social and income polarisation (Goos and Manning 2007; Green 2005; Toynbee 2004). At the top end of the labour market highly skilled well-paid workers – in 2010 the majority of them still men – are employed in relatively secure positions demanding high educational entry credentials. At the other end of the labour market, poorly paid employees labour in often insecure positions, waiting on, looking after or servicing many of those in more fortunate positions. These jobs at the bottom end employ both growing numbers of male migrants and growing numbers of women, both migrant and UK born.

These types of jobs at the bottom end of the service sector typically can be classified as interactive or body work (Leidner 1993; Wolkowitz 2006). They are jobs in consumer services, almost always where the service provider and the consumer are both present in the exchange and where the service provided is used up in the course of the transaction and so has to be continuously re-provided. Thus, for example, meals and drinks are consumed on the spot, haircuts, massages and sexual services are provided and consumed at the same time, hospital or elder care is used up as it is provided. Thus close contact as well as repetition is a key feature of these services. As a consequence, the social characteristics of workers – their gender, national origins, their social capital – and their embodiment – height, weight, looks, voice, often their sexual attractiveness, sometimes their empathy – all matter, both in acquiring work and in selling the service. Other jobs are less visible and involve little or no contact with customers. Here examples include working in the kitchens in hotels and hospitals, night-portering and room-cleaning in hotels, although these jobs may involve casual contact with service users. Many employers, as we have shown elsewhere in our research (Batnitzky et al. 2008; Dyer et al. 2010; McDowell et al. 2007) draw on sets of stereotypical attributes associated both with the jobs themselves and with the workers in assembling what is regarded as an appropriate workforce. Caring for others and cleaning up dirt, for example, are constructed as low-paid and unskilled work, with the tasks to be completed depending on 'natural' feminine characteristics such as empathy and deference. In a similar way, security and door-keeping are constructed as appropriate jobs for men, drawing on brute male strength, also regarded as natural among working class and men of colour and so also poorly financially remunerated. Workers' bodies and talents are constructed as appropriate for some tasks and not for others: the associations between masculine rationality and female emotions as part of the explanation for gender segregation in the labour market have been explored in detail by feminist scholars (see Wolkowitz 2006). For migrants, as well as gendered embodied attributes, stereotypical associations between ethnicity, skin colour and nationality are acknowledged by employers as part of the reasons for their concentration in particular sectors of the labour market (see Ruhs and Anderson 2010 for a discussion of these associations in different sectors of employment).

Here we explore different aspects of work undertaken by recent and not so recent migrants to the UK in bottom-end service jobs. We address the ways in which migrant workers in the UK are recruited for different types of body work in both the public and private sector. Elsewhere we have shown how patterns of disadvantage and inequality based on gender, class and nationality are re-created and reconstructed. We show the associations that were common in a hotel and hospital in the mid-2000s, not long after European Union (EU) expansion, and explore the ways in which new sets of transnational connections are producing labour forces that increasingly are assembled across a large spatial reach. Our particular focus here is to explore how employment agencies, operating both 'here', that is, in Greater London, and 'there' (in the countries of origin for economic migrants) are part of the process by which a transnational labour force is assembled to provide interactive services.

A significant part of the work of employment agencies is in the provision of what Parker (1994) has termed 'warm bodies' to undertake tasks for an employer who prefers to use this sort of 'lump labour' rather than recruit individuals for permanent jobs. This sort of work has been termed 'generic' work by the urban sociologist Castells (2000), and it is exactly the type of work at issue here: work undertaken by women, and sometimes by men, in the labour market to replace those tasks previously provided in the home by women as part of unwaged domestic labour. Like most 'feminised' jobs, this work is poorly paid and of low status (McDowell 2009), and increasingly provided by men, although gender divisions of labour within this type of work in both hotels and hospitals remain significant.

A NEW TRANSNATIONAL LABOUR FORCE

> It was a quick decision, I had a call from London [from a Polish-owned employment agency], . . . I bought a one way ticket [from Warsaw] . . . it was very cheap, but it was a bus, so 34 hours . . . [I arrived] Saturday morning. I had to go to sign the contract with the agency; that was Monday, the next day I came to work.

This is Stanislaw, one of a growing number of young Polish men and women working as temporary agency employees in the hospitality sector in Greater London. Like many migrants, Stanislaw registered with an employment agency to secure work: in his case through a contact already made before he left Poland.

The rise of employment agencies is perhaps one of the least well-explored, yet significant, phenomena in the assembling of workers, including recent economic migrants, in European labour markets (although see Coe et al. 2006, 2007; Ward 2004). Over the last two decades of the twentieth century, temporary agency work was a significant part of the rapid growth of 'atypical' work. According to Biggs (2005, p. 1) the UK saw 'a phenomenal increase of the (employment agency) industry over the last two decades'. One in five UK businesses used temporary workers in the mid-1980s (Casey 1988), and by the end of the 1990s the figure was one in three (Cully et al. 1999). Many of these temporary workers are either supplied to employers by agencies or directly employed by them, typically with fewer rights than permanent workers. As the labour lawyer Freedland (2003) has argued, the British legal system has been largely unwilling to legislate to control the triangular relationship between workers, employment agencies and end-user employers, leaving workers unsure of their rights, excluded from legal forms of employment protection and often among the most exploited of all groups of workers. The British government dragged its feet in implementing the EU Directive[2] to improve the position of such workers, although since this research was carried out it has changed its stance and implemented the directive.

As employment agencies increase in number and scope, they are having a growing impact on the ways in which labour is recruited and employed in British cities. They have identified and exploited a business opportunity: supplying 'flexible' (and often vulnerable) workers and managing many of the costs and contradictions of employing temporary workers on behalf of the end-employer. Thus, they are 'active institutional agents in the remaking of labour market norms and conventions, brokering as they do between under-employed workers on the one hand and would-be employers of contingent labour on the other, while turning a profit in the process' (Peck and Theodore 2001, p. 474). They also play a key role in assembling the 'servicing' labour market and in reproducing, and perhaps on occasion challenging, conventional divisions of labour in the UK. As we shall show, agencies sometimes provide male workers for what are constructed as quintessentially feminine tasks.

Mirroring the overall polarisation of the service sector outlined above, the market which agencies construct and operate within is also polarised between bottom-end, low-status and 'back street' agencies, supplying 'warm bodies', and high-status and highly skilled specialist workers for professional positions (Peck and Theodore 1998, 2001; Ward 2004). A further division has also been identified between the global and the local reach of the agencies and their clients. At the top end of the labour market, staffing agencies operate across a wide spatial scale, connecting prospective workers and vacancies in skilled occupations in expanding and shortage sectors on a global scale. Recruitment of professionals, for example, for short-term vacancies in high-status work in the National Health Service, in the City of London and in high-status law firms, operates at an international scale (Bach 2007; Kirkpatrick and Hoque 2006). Other studies of globally mobile workers, including research on 'body shopping' in the computer industry for mostly male Indian systems analysts for firms in Australia (Xiang 2006) and studies on 'gap year' workers (Jones 2008), have also begun to document the ways in which global capital, imperial and post-colonial connections, international regulations and national economic and welfare regimes produce particular patterns of uneven geographic connections. However, as Coe et al. (2006, 2007) note, relatively little is currently known about organisational structures, growth strategies or the role these international agencies play in facilitating flexibility in labour markets as part of the growing dominance of neo-liberal policies of labour market deregulation.

At the bottom end of the labour market, research has focused on the role of agencies within urban labour markets, showing how casual workers are assembled for casualised or what Peck et al. (2005) termed 'contingent work'. Based on their research in the 'hiring halls' in Chicago where unskilled temporary labourers are recruited, Peck et al. (2005, p. 23) argued that at this scale, 'most of the transactions are local ones – connecting local job seekers to local employers'. However, as workers were not interviewed, it is not clear where they were born or how mobile they had been in their search for work. Relatively little is known about the role that employment agencies play in the assembling of migrant labour forces across a global spatial scale. Instead, it is usually assumed that the labour market for 'warm bodies' – the contingent workers who fill the vacancies in bottom-end work in the hospitality and healthcare sectors – is a local one, restricted to the spatial reach of a single city or region. We explore this assumption, showing that, even for unskilled and poorly paid positions, agencies working at the bottom end of the labour market operate across a wide spatial reach to recruit workers from an increasingly diverse set of countries. Their actions are part of the production of a new migrant division of labour in Greater London (May et al. 2007), which is characterised by a growing diversity of origins and migrant status.

Through qualitative research, we demonstrate the ways in which migrant agency workers were recruited and assembled as part of the temporary or casualised labour force for a hotel and a hospital, exploring the workers' social characteristics, the length of their employment contract and their conditions of work. The focus is on those workers defined by the British government as 'vulnerable' – that is employees in precarious, low paid work. We argue that even for the most 'local' of service sector jobs, workers are assembled and recruited at a transnational scale. Networks of service sector workers stretching across space are a growing feature of the assemblages of workers who service global cities, keeping hotels open and hospitals clean as well as caring for the bodies of tourists and patients. Thus, although consumer services by definition are geographically 'sticky', that is, tied to specific localities, the labour force involved in the production and exchange of consumer services increasingly is assembled across a wide spatial scale.

The rest of the chapter is structured in four parts. In the next section, the coincidence of agency workers and migrant workers in the UK is briefly outlined before describing the methodological strategy. This is followed by the case study showing how agency workers are recruited and the relationships between the types of work, length of contract, sector of employment and national origins. In the conclusion we explore the significance of our findings and suggest ways in which the emerging divisions of labour documented here may be transformed in the next few years.

AGENCY EMPLOYMENT AND ECONOMIC MIGRATION

Among the significant changes identified by employment theorists, two key trends are too seldom connected. The first is the growing global reach of labour markets as both the internationalisation of firms and the mobility of workers inexorably grow (Dicken 2003). The second is the rise of various forms of temporary, precarious, non-standard or insecure work, of which agency work is an important element (Dex and McCulloch 1997; Goos and Manning 2007; Green 2005; McOrmand 2004; Vosko 2001). It has, however, recently been suggested that the rise of temporary contract and agency employment in the UK in the new millennium was directly related to the former trend. Increases in the supply of transnational migrant workers, prepared to work under less favourable conditions than 'local' workers, were facilitated by and also increased agency work.

An OECD (2006) report on economic migration noted that the growth of the migrant labour force, as well as the rise in participation rates for women and older people, had been a key factor in maintaining overall growth rates in the British economy while containing inflation before the economic crisis of 2007–09 affected both growth rates and migration flows. Proponents of open borders such as the Confederation of British Industry, an employers' organisation, argue that migrants are an essential element in meeting labour shortages in the expanding economy, especially at the bottom end of the labour market, where jobs are low paid, sometimes dangerous and often involve demeaning work or dirty conditions. On the negative side, critics of the (relatively) free movement of labour have argued that economic migration depresses wage levels, although a study by Dustmann et al. (2004) found little support for this contention. However, there is clear evidence that in-migrants are generally paid lower wages than native-born workers, in part because they are concentrated in low-wage/low-status sectors of the economy. As these are the parts of the labour market where agency work is not uncommon, it is not surprising that there is a statistical association between migrant workers and agency workers.

Labour Force Survey data showed that in 2007 about 6 per cent of all British workers were employed on a temporary basis, although it is sometimes difficult to draw a boundary between different forms of temporary and precarious work such as fixed-term contractors, seasonal workers and casual workers. Employees were recorded as agency workers if they held a job acquired through an agency in any given week. They are defined as workers supplied to a third-party organisation through an employment agency. Contract workers are employees who hold fixed-term contracts, directly negotiated with an employing organisation. However, employment agencies operate across the boundaries of these definitions. At the bottom end of the NHS hierarchy, for example, where services are often supplied through a subcontractor, workers may have permanent or temporary contracts, but they may also be agency workers, brought in on a temporary basis to meet urgent needs. In hotels, migrant workers are more likely to be agency workers than fixed-term contract workers. There has also been a shift in the attributes of agency workers. Once dominated by women working mainly in temporary secretarial positions, there is now growing gender balance among these workers, as men, and especially male migrant workers, register with agencies and accept low-paid work in servicing occupations, including in hotels and hospitals.

Agency workers are thus a particular subset of temporary or contract workers. Among them, especially those in bottom-end jobs, are some of the least secure and most exploited workers in the UK, with little direct power to alter the terms and conditions in their workplaces and typically without access through union membership to negotiate rights or achieve formal representation. Drawing on Labour Force Survey estimates, Forde and Slater (2005) suggested that in 2004 agency workers constituted approximately 16 per cent of all temporary workers, or 1 per cent of the total UK labour force: 270 000 individuals in total. However, this figure is likely to be an underestimate. The Department of Trade and Industry's estimate at the turn of the century was closer to 600 000 (Forde 2001) and Biggs (2005) suggested that in 2001 the total may have been as high as 1 million. Almost two-thirds of agency workers are employed in routine, manual jobs or in clerical and secretarial work undertaking a range of menial tasks. Many of them are young – temporary work as a whole is most common among workers under 25 – and they are twice as likely as permanent workers to come from a minority ethnic group (Biggs 2005).

In total, in 2001 foreign-born workers accounted for 5.4 per cent of the total UK workforce, about 1.5 million workers of whom (45.3 per cent) lived in Greater London (Salt and Millar 2006) where they constituted 35 per cent of the workforce. Migrant workers are a particular significant part of the labour supply in Greater London, especially in the service sector and among low-wage workers (May et al. 2007). Labour Force Survey figures for the 2000s show that 2006 was the peak year for the number of foreign workers entering the UK workforce, of whom Poles were the largest single group, reflecting the expansion of the European Union. Since 2008, after the research reported here, numbers have declined reflecting the effects of the recession. In 2006, non-British born workers accounted for 21 per cent of all workers in hospitality, hotels and catering (Salt and Millar 2006), and 40 per cent of all employees in this sector (whether migrants or not) held non-standard contracts. Migrants and contract workers are also employed in significant numbers in the NHS, although here they are as likely to be highly skilled as unskilled workers (Salt and Millar 2006). We now turn to the methodology of our case study.

A HOTEL AND A HOSPITAL IN WEST LONDON

A comparative case study of how organisations assemble their labour force is a useful way to explore emerging migrant divisions of labour in a local labour market. Through interviews with agencies, workers and managers within the service sector, we assessed the ways in which agencies assemble and employ migrant workers with different embodied charac-teristics for different end-users. Our aim was to show why and how the actions of agencies are part of the production of particular migrant divi-sions of labour within different workplaces. To address the intersections of gender and other social divisions in constructing 'appropriate' workers for different types of caring and serving work in the hotel and hospital, we interviewed non-British born workers, employed both directly by the hotel and the hospital and by the employment agencies used by these two organisations. Both the hotel and the hospital provided us with basic quantitative data about their labour force and allowed us to approach their foreign-born workers for an interview. However, we found that not only were the personnel data in the two organisations incomplete, but that details of the characteristics of agency workers were not held by the hospital, as an intermediary organisation acted as their employer. For this reason we approached these workers directly, but in all cases the employer did not know who we approached and to whom we spoke, thus preserving a degree of anonymity for the respondents

We adopted a semi structured interview-based approach, in which the questions progressively became more open, allowing the respondents to tell us about their working lives in their own words. Thus we first collected basic demographic data, followed by work histories and then by questions about the respondents' recruitment to and working lives within the hospital and hotel. Personal interviews are an appropriate way of exploring how migrant workers find their jobs and why they use employment agencies, as well as to address matters such as migration histories and visa statues which often require delicate probing, and as assurances of confidentiality. It became clear, for example, that a number of the people to whom we talked had broken their visa conditions and it was important to reassure them that we would not pass on their details to anyone else, including the agency and their end-employer.

The two workplaces – West Central Hospital (WCH) and Bellman International (BI), the hotel[3] – are in the same geographical vicinity in West London and draw on the same local labour market for migrant workers, as well as recruiting both locally and internationally through agencies. The local labour market was extremely buoyant when we were interviewing in 2005 and 2006. Skill shortages were an issue for both workplaces, which were then experiencing high levels of labour turnover in most categories of employment.

West Central Hospital is a large NHS university hospital that provides specialist care as well as meeting the general medical needs of the locality. It has to conform to national agreements in its direct recruitment of foreign nurses and doctors, although it is also able to draw on a wider pool of migrant labour already resident in London. The hospital uses agencies to recruit both professional and non-professional staff, although the latter group are more likely to remain as agency staff rather than become NHS employees. While professional staff members are likely to belong to trade unions and professional associations, levels of unionisation are minimal among the low-paid agency staff. Bellman International is a non-unionised major branch of an international hotel chain, positioning itself towards the top end of the price range. It relies on agencies to recruit almost all its entry-level staff as well as to fill some professional vacancies, and is unwilling to rely on recruitment from a pool of direct applicants.

In total, the West London BI hotel employed 80 direct employees and 120 agency workers, both groups consisting almost entirely of migrants. Indeed, only three BI employees were UK born. The total employment was more difficult to ascertain at WCH, as services such as catering and cleaning were contracted out to a major international organisation – Greenspan (a pseudonym) – that employed both agency workers and direct temporary contract workers: about 500 in total. The hospital itself employed almost 2000 workers of whom 30 per cent were non-British born and a similar proportion (overlapping but not completely coincident groups) were agency or contract employees. These organisations capture

Table 5.1   Agency workers at BI by gender, nationality and job, 2005–06
(N = 20)

Women		Men	
Room attendants	4 Polish	Porter	1 Polish
	2 Russian	Waiters	3 Polish
	1 Latvian		1 Hungarian
	1 Bulgarian	Underchefs	2 Indian
Room supervisor	1 Ukrainian		1 Hungarian
Waiter	1 South African	Stewards	2 Indian

the range and complexity of temporary contract and agency employment. Here, we focus on low-wage agency workers in each workplace.

Although the two organisations differed in the size of their total labour and in the representation of non-British born workers, 60 interviews in each allowed us to capture the range of occupations. Among the 120 workers whom we interviewed there was significant variation: in employment contracts, in migrant status and in countries of origin (from more than 30 nations), supporting Vertovec's (2007) assertion of a new form of super-diversity among migrants in the new millennium. There were 31 current agency workers, as well as 14 others who were initially employed through an agency but were direct employees at the time of their interview. Twenty-two of these 45 worked at BI and 23 at WCH. After excluding professional workers (doctors and nurses at WCH and managers at BI), there were 20 past and present agency workers at BI and 17 at WCH. These 37 respondents worked in basic entry level jobs in both organisations, requiring no credentials and little training. With the exception of migrants from the A8 countries (of whom 13 were Polish and all but one of them worked at BI) or those who have taken British citizenship (and so have the right to work), they had been employed in the UK for between one and five years, on a range of visas including student, working holiday, two-year working visas, and a five-year skilled workers scheme. We also carried out ten interviews with the owners and/or managers of seven employment agencies in Greater London, all of whom had been involved in recruiting the workers in our survey. Finally, we talked to a representative of Greenspan and to human resources managers at both BI and at WCH. Here we draw on these 'gatekeeper' interviews and interviews with the 37 workers in low-wage jobs. In Tables 5.1 and 5.2 we show the gender, nationality and current job of these 37 at the time of the interviews.

Table 5.1 reveals a conventional division of labour with the majority of women (all but a single woman working as a waiter) in the housekeeping

Table 5.2   Agency workers at WCH by gender, nationality and job, 2006
(N = 17)

Women		Men	
Ward cleaner	2 Jamaican	Ward cleaner	1 Afghani
	1 Barbadian		2 Jamaican
Catering	1 Indian	Catering assistant	2 Indian
assistant		Catering manager	1 Algerian
		Porter	1 Polish
		Security	2 Ghanaian
		Shop assistant	1 Indian
		Domestic supervisor	1 Moroccan
		Coffee shop supervisor	1 Yemini
		IT assistant/clerk	1 Indian

section as room attendants or supervisors and men as various types of underchef, waiters, porters or stewards of function rooms such as the banqueting suite. It is less easy to comment on the gender division of labour at WCH as there were only four women among the hospital's agency staff that we interviewed. As far as we were able to ascertain, this reflected the gender distribution of agency workers as a whole, but Greenspan were reluctant to disclose details of their employees. Both men and women agency employees were employed by WCH as ward cleaners, but Table 5.1 seems to suggest that traditionally masculine jobs that rely on bodily strength, such as security and portering, were held by men only. Men were also supervisors or in white-collar jobs such as IT which perhaps confer higher status, although seldom higher salaries, on their occupants. All the agency workers we interviewed were poorly paid, and also ineligible for holiday and sick pay, as well, of course, as having little job security.

CONSTRUCTING A TRANSNATIONAL LABOUR FORCE: ASSEMBLING WARM BODIES FOR LOW-STATUS 'LOCAL' WORK

Both workplaces used employment agencies to assemble workers for low-status servicing jobs, keeping the rooms of the hotel and the hospital wards clean, making and serving meals and undertaking general maintenance and security. For both BI and WCH, using agencies to recruit casual or temporary workers brought advantages: low labour costs, flexible (or exploitative) employment contracts, and low recruitment and retention costs. They were also able to delegate the decisions about who to employ to the agencies, as well as decisions about replacing one group of workers by another, if they proved unsatisfactory. As Maggie, manager of an agency who supplied hotel workers, also noted, using agency staff enabled rapid responses to changing needs. Thus, she told us 'in the event of a turndown, they (end-employers) will lose our staff. It will be our responsibility to re-employ, not the hotels. If they have permanent staff they have contractual obligations'. She also told us that BI was relatively unspecific when describing potential employees, leaving the choice of employees to the agency. Thus for room attendants Maggie was instructed that 'we don't care about [the ability to speak] English, as long as they are clean and do good work'. Although all the room attendants to whom we spoke were women, gender was also insignificant in the instructions given to the agency and BI accepted both women and men for 'traditionally' female-dominated jobs such as room cleaning. One of the Polish agency workers employed as a waiter told us that he had started as a room attendant at BI, and that he had also done private house-cleaning in London. Despite being a qualified mechanic in Poland, he thought that Polish men, on the whole, were not too proud to take 'women's work' in England as it was a way into the labour market.

What is interesting, however, was the difference between BI and WCH in the mechanisms they used to assemble their temporary labour forces. While both employed agencies to recruit low-paid staff, WCH relied entirely on the local recruitment of foreign workers, using London-based agencies to assemble London-based workers, who then paradoxically became contract workers for an international company, Greenspan. Bellman International, by comparison, used both London-based agencies and offshore agencies that recruited workers in their home countries. Whereas BI recruited workers for particular positions – room attendants, waiters, and so on – who held employment contracts with the agency that recruited them, WCH, in contrast, contracted a service from Greenspan, rather than a particular number of employees, as part of what has become an international industry in service provision for the NHS. However, Greenspan itself used London-based agencies to recruit its temporary workers, and most of them remained agency employees. Thus, although Greenspan is a transnational corporation, it uses London-based employment agencies to assemble its stock of 'warm bodies' to service the hospital.

The different strategies resulted in a migrant labour force in each of the workplaces that in 2005–06 was noticeably different in its national origins, the length of time workers had been in the UK and in their job tenure, as we explore in more detail below. As McGovern (2002) has argued, so-called global labour forces should more accurately be termed international. This is because migrant labour forces vary in composition between and within host nation-states, reflecting earlier patterns of connections established through trade and imperialism, particular systems of regulation, new political alliances and new flows of workers. In the UK, older 'imperial' patterns of migration – from the Caribbean and the Indian subcontinent that influenced the composition of the migrant communities entering the UK in the second half of the twentieth century (Winder 2004) – are being altered by new flows of economic migrants within Europe. The accession to European Union membership of ten new states in May 2004 transformed the pattern of migration into the UK, and into London in particular, creating a new supply of low-wage migrant workers who were white Europeans. Between May 2004 and the middle of 2006, when we finished interviewing workers in WCH and BI, almost 500000 people from the A8 countries were recorded by the Home Office (2006) as employed, under its Worker Registration Scheme (WRS). Of these the majority were Polish (61.5 per cent) and two-thirds of them were men. Over 50000 of these WRS-registered A8 nationals entered the London labour market and 29 per cent of them found jobs in the hospitality sector during the first year after accession (Home Office 2006).

It is perhaps not surprising then that there were several agency workers from A8 states among the interviewees at BI (9 of the 20). However, while they rapidly established themselves in hotel employment, we found workers from the A8 countries were almost completely absent from the agency employees at the hospital (only one of the 17 interviewees). When the national origins of the two sets of agency workers are compared the significance of changes over time in the multiple pathways of migration becomes evident.

A New European Labour Force at BI?

At BI, both London-based and offshore agencies were used to recruit most of the workers for all the positions in the housekeeping section as well as for security and non-career grades in the catering department. All but four of the 20 agency workers interviewed at BI in menial jobs were East Europeans, although they were not all from the accession states. They had entered the UK in a range of different ways – some through the auspices of agencies in their country of origin that seemed to be operating on the edges of legality. A number of interviewees had entered the UK on working holiday visas that had expired by the time of the interviews, others had arrived for a holiday and had never returned. Some of the interviewees from A8 countries, Poles and Hungarians for example, had been in the UK for up to three years before accession in 2004. For this group, accession transformed their legal status and therefore their willingness to consider changing employers. We also interviewed seven Polish hotel workers who had been recruited after May 2004. Some of these workers had entered the UK as individuals without a work offer, registering at an employment agency on their arrival in London, often using personal contacts to identify an appropriate agency. Other European workers, from Ukraine, Belarus and Russia for example, had been recruited by an agency within their own country (some were still agency workers, others held different forms of direct contracts in 2005). For sizeable fees, these agencies had arranged their visas and a potential vacancy. In total, eight of the 20 agency workers at BI had been recruited in their home country, including five East Europeans, two Indian men and a Belgian. The spoken English of many of the East European workers was rather basic, and among the non-A8 workers, their grasp of their legal status and their eligibility to work was not always accurate. Clearly these workers were even more vulnerable to exploitation than the other agency workers.

At the time of our study, two of the agencies used by BI for recruitment for the most menial positions were located in London but were owned by migrants: a Bulgarian and a Pole, who often, though not solely, recruited within their own communities. These agencies used a range of methods to attract putative workers: word of mouth, advertising in foreign language newspapers in London and elsewhere, and direct agreements with sister agencies in other European cities, including in Warsaw and Moscow. They offered a comprehensive service to BI, bearing the initial costs of recruitment, for example, as well as remaining as the end-employer of workers. For an initial fee, these agencies ensured that applicants filled forms in accurately, checked references and previous work experience, undertook job interviews and for potential employees from the new EU accession states ensured that they had applied for permission to work under the Work Registration Scheme (WRS). After vetting, the agencies presented BI with a list of potential workers and although BI had the right to refuse an applicant, all of those who were offered jobs remained employees of the agency. Thus, through a network of contacts stretching across Europe as well as within London, workers were assembled and made ready for work in the hospitality sector by specialist agencies.

It became clear during the research, however, that the BI chain as a whole frequently changed agencies, both because there was rapid turnover among agency staff (overall annual rates of 30–50 per cent are common in hotels) but also to prevent the dominance of the agency labour force by a single nationality. In the housekeeping section at the BI hotel where we interviewed, young Polish women were numerically dominant in 2006. Judith, the Head of Housekeeping, told us that this concentration of employees from a single country sometimes led to problems of maintaining discipline and the requirement to speak in English at all times. Before A8 accession, room attendant vacancies had been filled by Vietnamese men: BI at that time employed a Vietnamese-owned London-based agency in the local area to supply workers for the housekeeping department. Here Judith reflects on the management implications of this change in the national origins of her agency staff.

> The main problem is language barriers and also cultural barriers sometimes, because perhaps what I consider to be rude or abrupt, another person might not see that as being rude or abrupt because that's the way they would generally converse with each other . . . We used to have Vietnamese people before and the Vietnamese people are very soft and compliant, and perhaps they weren't as challenging. So at the moment we're quite challenged because I think the Polish people are quite headstrong, . . . they tend to stick together and suddenly we start to have cliques in housekeeping where we never had cliques before.

Notice here the way in which national stereotypes are used to explain the consequences of shifting to a different staffing agency. Polish workers are regarded as more aggressive than the compliant Vietnamese workers, even though the Vietnamese employees were men and the Polish contingent all women. Thus Judith's claims not only challenge gender stereotypes but also support Waldinger and Lichter's (2003, pp. 176–7) contention that unskilled migrant workers are segmented into particular niches in the low-paying service economy through the operation of employer stereotyping. Here is evidence of the ways in which the intersection of transnational movement and local attitudes construct particular migrant divisions of labour. What is also interesting about this example is its challenge to what we might term 'traditional' gender divisions of labour. Housekeeping and room-cleaning in major hotels is a female-dominated sector of employment (Aguiar and Herod 2006) and, indeed, the employment of Polish women re-established conventional patterns. However, the use of a particular agency that had mainly men on its books led to an all-male room cleaning force for a number of years. Here we see an example of the attributes of ethnic minority men being reinterpreted by employers in feminised terms – these men where according to Judith, the current head of housekeeping, 'adaptable, pliant and keen to please' as well as 'quick, clean and quiet'. Their dismissal was to meet a downturn, as well as a high rate of turnover among these employees, rather than dissatisfaction with their performance.

Further evidence that the rapid labour turnover in hotels affects the composition of the migrant labour force was provided through an interview with Helena, an employee of a branch of a large UK-based international agency that supplied staff for cleaning to a wide range of organisations, including BI. The agency had 700 individuals, all foreign born, on its books in spring 2006, working in 25 London hotels. She confirmed that EU expansion had made a difference to the composition of agency workers in hotels. The majority of new clients then registering with her agency were from the accession states. Although many clients were acquired through personal contacts within migrant communities, the agency also advertised in a range of foreign-language newspapers in London, especially in the expanding Polish press.

Other owners and managers of the agencies employed by BI also told us that labour turnover rates had recently increased. The reason given for the turnover was that as A8 nationals typically had come to the UK to improve their English, they preferred to remain in menial jobs for as short a time as possible, moving into better-paying work as soon as their language skills improved. Helena also reported that her East European clients were significantly better educated than migrants from elsewhere and so more likely to be able to achieve occupational mobility. Most of the A8 workers whom we interviewed were from middle-class backgrounds with higher or further education credentials. They all told us that they were aiming for more professional employment after as short as possible a period of temporary work in the hotel. Raisa, for example, a Russian post-graduate student, Teresa, a Polish young woman with a first degree, and Stanislaw, formerly a soldier, were typical of the young East European agency workers working at BI. Another agency worker, a young Indian man working as a waiter at BI told us of his surprise in discovering that:

> They (East Europeans) are actually very skilled back in their own countries. Some of them are lawyers, some of them are management graduates and well, they don't make that kind of money over there, so they come here to do this, and to learn the language.

As each of these employees planned only a short stay at BI, they were (relatively) content to accept both the low pay and the gender stereotyping that is common in hotel employment. Thus in 2006 Raisa and Teresa were working as room attendants and Stanislaw as a porter.

The interviews we undertook with these three and other East European migrants were within the first two years of EU accession when workers from these states were a relatively unknown entity for employers. However, as other research has shown (Anderson et al. 2006), many British employers, in the hospitality sector as well as in other sectors of the labour market where temporary and casual employees are significant, including construction, quickly expressed favourable attitudes about A8 nationals, regarding them as reliable and hard workers. Whether Raisa, Teresa and Stanislaw managed to acquire better English language skills and move up the occupational hierarchy cannot be established without a longitudinal study but opportunities for mobility for these white European migrants seem more likely than for the post-colonial migrants who preceded them to the UK. Indeed, as we show below through the WCH case study, migrants from Africa, India and the Caribbean were more numerous in the hospital and as they typically had few educational or occupational credentials, they had fewer prospects for occupational mobility.

An Older Post-Colonial Workforce at WCH?

Both WCH and the subcontractor, Greenspan, used agency workers to fill temporary positions in 'servicing' departments in the hospital. As in the hotel, agency employees were used both to meet shortages and as a form of probation for direct employment. If agency workers proved reliable they might then be transferred on to direct contracts, albeit usually on a temporary, time-limited basis. However, unlike the current pool of migrant agency workers at BI, the 17 agency workers at WCH were from more diverse backgrounds. Some had been in the UK for many years, and a number had worked (indirectly) for the hospital for long periods. Others were more recent migrants but all of them, without exception, previously had worked in a wide range of other bottom-end jobs, in both manufacturing and in the service sector. For these workers, employment at WCH was a job among several rather than their first job in the UK, like the majority of contingent workers in the hotel. The national backgrounds of the WCH agency workers were also more varied than among the BI agency workers, with a noticeable absence of East European workers. At WCH, we interviewed agency workers from Afghanistan, India, Sri Lanka, Ghana, Malaysia, Algeria and Turkey, but only one person from the A8 countries. And as we noted earlier, all but four of the interviewees were men. This is different from the gender composition of agency workers as a whole as women dominated among the agency nursing staff and in the health-related professional occupations, such as physiotherapy, although the majority of doctors with agency contracts were men. Here, however, we focus on a group from among the low-wage and unskilled agency workers in WCH.

We explored with agency managers the reasons for the different composition of the WCH unskilled and low-waged workers compared to those at BI. Claire, employed by an agency that recruited for jobs in the catering and cleaning sections of London hospitals, told us that the origins of her client base had changed significantly over the last five years. The hospital and the subcontractor Greenspan used to recruit, she told us, from an older, long-standing migrant population in the locality, predominantly British Asian women most of whom had come to Britain between 1968 and the mid-1970s: 'these ladies are in their late 60s now, so they have been here quite a long time'. More recently her clients included 'Chinese, Afro-Caribbean (*sic*), Portuguese, Polish, Irish – this is where it all starts to change, and now definitely with the East Europeans, that's definitely created a big change'. She noted that on her books now 'there are more East Europeans – Latvians, Lithuanians' but suggested that the new EU workers faced several problems in gaining access to the labour market. Their major disadvantage, she argued, was poor language skills:

> The level of English of East Europeans is quite low and that's one of our biggest issues when it comes to recruitment. A lot of them could barely speak any English [on arrival]. What we try to do is to make sure that there is a basic level [before placing them].

Even so, her success rate in placing Europeans with Greenspan was low.

A second difference between the hotel and hospital was in the rates of turnover among agency staff. The rate for those employed indirectly by Greenspan was much lower than that for BI agency workers. Although agency work in the hospital was badly paid – all of the 17 workers whom we interviewed at WCH employees were paid the minimum wage (£5.20 per hour at the time) or just above – workers were keen to hold on to their jobs. Both at WCH and at BI, agency workers were employed on terms and conditions that were inferior to those of directly hired workers. They did not receive a London allowance, for example, and had lower sick pay and less holiday entitlement than direct employees. Yet most respondents told us that they valued their employment in the hospital and believed that it might eventually offer some degree of security, despite their current position as an agency worker. The majority of the 17 agency workers had managed to construct some degree of employment continuity, working in WCH for relatively long periods (between one and seven years). They achieved this by moving between agencies or accepting a series of time-limited contracts despite being agency and subcontract workers with an average job tenure of eight months. Six of the 17 WCH agency workers were employed on a part-time basis; only one of whom was a woman. Others had a contract of less than 25 hours and several respondents had to take a second job to make ends meet.

Unlike the BI agency workers who were keen to move on, the WCH agency respondents told us they made every effort to hold on to their current job, unless, of course, they were able to transfer to the permanent or direct workforce. Amber, for example, a woman who had entered the UK from the Caribbean in the early 1990s, had been an agency employee in several London hotels. She was then sent by her agency to WCH which she preferred, arguing that even a cleaning job had more social worth when it was in a hospital rather than a hotel, and so conferred dignity on her labour. Despite the insecurity of agency work, Amber told us 'I love my job and I really want to keep my job'. Hafiz, an Afghani man, had also until recently worked as an agency employee for Greenspan. In the month before we talked to him, he had transferred to direct employment with Greenspan, working in both capacities as a ward cleaner. He worked on a part-time basis for Greenspan, as well as doing a second job on an evening shift in a garage where he earned slightly more per hour than at Greenspan. And yet he assured us that 'I love this job; I want to stay' at WCH. He also told us that, although he worked mainly with women, he considered that men were even better ward cleaners as 'we have more strength, we keep it even cleaner'. Unlike Amber, who mentioned the caring aspects that she felt were, or should be, part of her work – 'a kind word makes a difference. I sometimes sit with them (patients), to chat or sing to them' – Hafiz talked only about the technical aspects of his work as a cleaner.

The comparison between the hotel and hospital agency workers reveals the connections between the changes in migration flows, and the relative rates of turnover in different parts of the service sector. At WCH, even the lowest paid agency contracts were seen as relatively desirable jobs by economic migrants. In workplaces where turnover rates are low, the migrant division of labour reflects an earlier pattern of in-migration. But the different origins of agency workers at WCH compared to BI also reflected the human capital of the workers and their future aspirations. As we noted above, EU migrants, especially the new A8 nationals were better educated and intended to move into other than domestic forms of work. The temporary workers in basic positions in the NHS were less well educated (none of them had a degree and most had left school at or before the minimum school-leaving age in their country) and had few occupational credentials. Thus with almost no other options in the London labour market, they were trapped in their current positions. Without skills and training, they were restricted to the least well-paid and most menial job vacancies in the capital (Datta et al. 2007) and unlikely to be able to move.

CONCLUSIONS: LOCAL JOBS, GLOBAL WORKERS

The sorts of jobs undertaken by the agency workers we interviewed in WCH and BI are perhaps the most locally based of all forms of employment. The jobs are local in a threefold way. First, they are local in the sense of providing an immediate embodied service to a set of clients/customers/patients in West London. Secondly, they are local in the sense that the potential workers constitute an immediately available labour force, assembled by staffing agencies at minimum costs to end-user employers. The jobs require no specialist knowledge, skills or training to able to undertaken the work tasks almost instantly on recruitment. Thirdly, they are local jobs in the sense that their low pay means that they attract only those living in the immediate vicinity. And yet the potential and actual labour force in this part of the labour market is a transnational one. New as well as more established economic migrants – some with no skills and few options, and others with an inadequate command of English – are assembled by employment agencies to staff the basic services that keep hospitals running and hotels commercially viable. Agency workers are among the most exploitable and exploited of bottom-end service sector employees, with little security and almost no rights in the labour market.

However, as we have shown here, the migrant labour force employed by agencies to labour in these two different workplaces varies. As other studies of migrants employed both directly and by agencies in low-waged servicing jobs showed (May et al. 2007; Newman 1999; Sherman 2007; Wills et al. 2009) the particular composition of the labour force in different workplaces at different times is constituted through a combination of changing global flows of labour, the differential human capital of migrant workers from different countries of origin and the ways in which low-status work is organised. The interaction of these factors affects the composition of specific local labour forces undertaking service sector employment (see also Lusis and Bauder 2009). And although most of the employees doing this type of 'poor work' are recruited locally, in the sense of not until they arrive in London, typically they are placed in work through the operation of agencies that operate across spatial scales. The agencies that provided workers for BI and for WCH (indirectly through Greenspan) ranged from small, almost informal agencies to large multinational firms that are part of the increasing internationalisation of service provision. Even the smallest, informal London-based agencies utilised a network of trans-European, and often transnational, contacts to mobilise applicants. Thus, internationalisation is not only a feature of the growth of producer services and their global demand for labour, but is also significant in the production of consumer services (those services where the product is 'used up' in the exchange; Bryson and Daniels 2007). This fraction of the global labour force, the workers who are merely warm bodies, is dependent on precarious contracts providing extremely low rewards. Despite their initial transnational mobility, low pay, anti-social working hours and heavy workloads trap them in place within a small part of West London and they are often unable to undertake further travel across national boundaries, or indeed within the UK.

The agency workers at WCH, however, were the most trapped. The relative low costs of travel, especially between London and some of the capital cities of the A8 states, meant that the younger BI workers were more able to maintain contacts with their home nations. They also reported that they planned to return. These migrants might be more accurately classified as transnational workers, able to cross space and return 'home', whether on a permanent or temporary basis. The older migrant workers at WCH, by comparison, had made a permanent move to the UK, many of them had married in Britain and some were raising children in the capital. For these workers, agency work meant that they were trapped at the bottom end of the occupational status hierarchy and relative poverty.

At WCH and BI, as in other parts of the labour market, migration patterns, national origins, gender and skin colour intersect in particular ways to construct workers who are seen as appropriate employees by service sector organisations. As we found in our study, migrant men may have to take 'feminised' work – cleaning and caring for others for example – which in some cases they are able to construct as congruent with stereotypical attributes of masculinity. Some interviewees spoke of their skill in manipulating heavy machinery and of their scientific knowledge of dangerous chemicals, whereas women in these jobs more typically spoke about providing comfort and support. We also found evidence of national stereotyping. Male Indian management trainees, for example, were more highly regarded as they were seen by BI managers as embodying past traditions of colonial hospitality and service (see Batnitzky et al. 2008) and so given greater opportunity for in-house training. Many workers of colour, however, often found themselves excluded from the more visible areas of work in the hotel – from the front desk for example, or actively discriminated against by the new A8 workers. In the hospital, on the other hand, the long association of Caribbean women with nursing seemed to produce an environment in which skin colour was a less significant axis of differentiation between migrant workers. We suggest that in the future in the labour market as a whole, people of colour with longer connections to and within the UK may find themselves in competition for employment in these 'servicing' positions with more recent white-skinned migrants. Since our survey, however, the numbers of A8 migrants who have left Britain, perhaps for a different destination in Western Europe or to return home, has increased and so the competition may have declined.

New patterns of migration in post-millennium Britain are producing distinctive new geographies of inequality. These geographies, at different spatial scales (the continuing North–South divide, within large conurbations and so forth) are being produced and reproduced through the intersection of the global reach of local service sector labour markets and changing economic conditions in sending and receiving countries. Globalisation continually reproduces patterns of social and spatial inequalities rather than vanquishing the significance of geographic differentiation as some of the more optimistic analysts of globalisation have suggested (Friedman 2006). At the local level, the production of particular forms of segmented labour forces, both in towns and cities and within organisations, which are divided by gender, ethnicity, skin colour and class, thus depends on a set of connections between the actions of international agencies that regulate and mediate labour flows, the role of the national and local states, the assumptions and practices of employers, the strategies of employment agencies and the combination of the motivations and decisions of millions of transnational migrants who leave their own country for diverse reasons. This complexity is daunting but, we suggest, needs unpicking through detailed and careful analysis of the specificity of places and sectors in order to protect the interests of the vulnerable and regulate the flow of migrants in ways that produce as socially equitable a division of labour as is possible in capitalist economies.

ACKNOWLEDGEMENTS

We would like to thank the respondents for spending their valuable time talking to us. This is a revised version (with a different introduction and a greater focus on gender divisions) of an article originally published in the *British Journal of Industrial Relations*, **46**, pp. 750–70, 2008, 'Internationalisation and the spaces of temporary labour'. We would like to thank the editor and publisher for permission to reproduce part of that article here.

NOTES

1. Czech Republic, Estonia, Hungary, Latvia, Lithuania, Poland, Slovenia and Slovakia joined in 2004 and Bulgaria and Romania in 2007.
2. EU Part-time workers Directive (Prevention of Less Favourable Treatment) 97/81/EC, 15 December 1997.
3. Both names are pseudonyms to ensure confidentiality. This was a condition of access and means that documents such as the hospital's workforce analysis cannot be fully referenced.

REFERENCES

Aguiar, L and A. Herod (eds) (2006), 'The dirty work of neoliberalism', special issue of *Antipode*, **38**(3), 425–666.

Anderson, B., M. Ruhs and S. Spencer (2006), 'Fair enough? Central and East European migrants in low wage employment in the UK', final report to the Joseph Rowntree Foundation, copies available from the authors on request at COMPAS, University of Oxford.

Bach, S. (2007), 'Going global? The regulation of nurse migration in the UK', *British Journal of Industrial Relations*, **45**, 383–403.

Batnitzky, A., L. McDowell and S. Dyer (2008), 'A middle class global mobility: the working lives of Indian men in a west London hotel', *Global Networks*, **8**, 51–70.

Biggs, D. (2005), 'Satisfaction levels among temporary agency workers', a review of the literature for the Recruitment and Employment Confederation (available from the author at University of Gloucestershire, Cheltenham GL50 4AZ).

Bryson, J. and P. Daniels (2007), *The Handbook of Service Industries*, Cheltenham, UK and Northampton, MA, USA: Edward Elgar.

Casey, B. (1988), 'The extent and nature of temporary employment in Britain', *Cambridge Journal of Economics*, **12**, 487–509.

Castells, M. (2000), 'Materials for an exploratory theory of the network society', *British Journal of Sociology*, **51**, 5–22.

Chammartin, G. (2008), 'Female migrant workers' situation in the labour market', International Migration Programme, ILO, Geneva, available at: www.mutual-learning-employment.net (accessed 6 September 2010).

Coe, N., J. Johns and K. Ward (2006), 'Mapping the globalisation of the temporary staffing industry', *The Globalisation of the Temporary Staffing Industry Working Paper Series*, no. 2, October School of Geography, University of Manchester available at www.sed.manchester.ac.uk/geography/research/tempingindustry/download/wp 2.pdf (accessed 6 September 2010).

Coe, N., J. Johns and K. Ward (2007), 'Managed flexibility: labour regulation, corporate strategies and market dynamics in the Swedish temporary staffing industry', *The Globalisation of the Temporary Staffing Industry Working Paper Series*, no. 3, February, University of Manchester School of Geography www.sed.manchester.ac.uk/geography/research/tempingindustry/download/wp3.pdf (accessed 6 September 2010).

Cully, M., S. Woodland, A. O'Reilly and G. Dix (1999), *Britain at Work*, London: Routledge.

Datta, K., C. McIlwaine, Y. Evans, J. Herbert, J. May and J. Wills (2007), 'From coping strategies to tactics: London's low-pay economy and migrant labour', *British Journal of Industrial Relations*, **45**, 404–32.

Dex, S. and A. McCulloch (1997). *Flexible Employment: The Future of Britain's Jobs*, Basingstoke: Macmillan.

Dicken, P. (2003). *Global Shift*, 3rd edn, London: Sage.

Dustmann, C., F. Fabbri, I. Preston and J. Wadsworth (2004), 'The local labour market effects of immigration in the UK', Home Office online report 06/03, London: Home Office.

Dyer, S., L. McDowell and A. Batnitzky (2010), 'The impact of migration on the gendering of service work: the case of a West London hotel', *Gender Work and Organisation*, **17** (6), 635–57.

Forde, C. (2001), 'Temporary arrangements: the activities of employment agencies in the UK', *Work, Employment and Society*, **15**, 631–44.

Forde, C. and G. Slater (2005), 'Agency working in Britain: character, consequences and regulation', *British Journal of Industrial Relations*, **43**, 249–72.

Freedland, M. (2003), *The Personal Employment Contract*, Oxford: Oxford University Press.

Friedman, T.L. (2006), *The World is Flat*, New York: Farrar, Srauss, Giroux.

Goos, M. and A. Manning (2007), 'Lousy and lovely jobs: the rising polarisation of work in Britain', *Oxford Review of Economic Policy*, **7**, 49–62.

Green, F. (2005), *Demanding Work: The Paradox of Job Quality in the Affluent Economy*, Princeton, NJ: Princeton University Press.

Home Office (2006), 'Accession monitoring report, May 2004–September 2006', a joint online report by the Home Office, the Department of Work and Pensions, HM Revenue and Customs and the Department of Communities and Local Government, London, 21 November, available at: www.ind.homeoffice.gov.uk/6353/aboutus/accessionmonitoringreprt9/pdf (accessed 6 September 2010).

Jones, A. (2008), 'The rise of global work', *Transactions of the Institute of British Geographers*, **33**, 12–26.

Kirkpatrick, I. and K. Hoque (2006), 'A retreat from permanent employment? Accounting for the rise of professional agency work in UK public services', *Work, Employment and Society*, **20**, 649–66.

Leidner, R. (1993), *Fast Food, Fast Talk: Interactive Service Work and The Routinization of Every-Day Life*, Berkeley, CA: University of California Press.

Lusis, T. and H. Bauder (2009), 'Immigrants in the labour market: transnationalism and segmentation', *Geography Compass*, **4** (1), 28–44.

May, J., J. Wills, K. Datta, Y. Evans, J. Herbert and C. McIlwaine (2007), 'Keeping London working: global cities, the British state and London's new migrant division of labour', *Transactions, Institute of British Geographers*, **32**, 151–67.

McDowell, L. (2009), *Working Bodies: Interactive Service Employment and Workplace Identities*, Oxford: Wiley-Blackwell.

McDowell, L., A. Batnitzky and S. Dyer (2007), 'Division, segmentation and interpellation: the embodied labours of migrant workers in a Greater London hotel', *Economic Geography*, **82** (1), 1–26

McGovern, P. (2002), 'Globalization or internationalization? Foreign footballers in the English league, 1946–95', *Sociology*, **36**, 23–42.

McOrmand, T. (2004), 'Changes in working trends over the past decade', *Labour Market Trends*, January, 25–35.

Newman, K.S. (1999), *No Shame in My Game: The Working Poor in the Inner City*, New York: Alfred Knopf.

Organisation for Economic Co-operation and Development (OECD) (2006), *Economic Outlook*, no. 80, November, Paris: OECD, available at: www.oecd.org/document/18/0 (accessed 6 September 2010).

Parker, R. (1994), *Flesh Peddlers and Warm Bodies: The Temporary Help Industry and Its Workers*, New Brunswick, NJ: Rutgers University Press.

Peck, J. and N. Theodore (1998), 'The business of contingent work: growth and restructuring in Chicago's temporary employment industry', *Work, Employment and Society*, **12**, 655–74.

Peck, J. and N. Theodore (2001), 'Contingent Chicago: restructuring the spaces of temporary labour', *International Journal of Urban and Regional Research*, **25**, 471–96.

Peck, J., N. Theodore and K. Ward (2005), 'Constructing markets for temporary employment: employment liberalisation and the internationalization of the staffing industry', *Global Networks*, **5**, 3–26.

Ruhs, M. and B. Anderson (eds) (2010), *Who Needs Migrant Workers? Labour Shortages, Immigration and Public Policy*, Oxford: Oxford University Press.

Salt, J. and Millar, J. (2006), 'Foreign labour in the United Kingdom: current patterns and trends', *Labour Market Trends*, **114** (10), 335–53.

Sherman, R. (2007), *Class Acts: Service and Inequality in Luxury Hotels*, Los Angeles, CA, and London: University of California Press.

Toynbee, P. (2004), *Hard Work: Life in Low-Pay Britain*, London: Bloomsbury.

Vertovec, S. (2007), 'Super-diversity and its implications', *Ethnic and Racial Studies*, **30** (6), 1024–54.

Vosko, L. (2001), *Precarious Work*, Toronto: Toronto University Press.

Waldinger, R. and M.I. Lichter (2003), *How the Other Half Works: Immigrants and the Social Organisation of Labour*, Berkeley, CA: University of California Press.

Ward, K. (2004), 'Going global? Internationalisation and diversification in the temporary staffing industry', *Journal of Economic Geography*, **4**, 251–73.

Wills, J., K. Datta, Y. Evans, J. Herbert, J. May and K. McIlwaine (2009), *Global Cities at Work: New Migrant Divisions of Labour*, London: Pluto Press.

Winder, R. (2004), *Bloody Foreigners: The Story of Immigration to Britain*, New York: Little Brown.

Wolkowitz, C. (2006), *Bodies at Work*, London: Sage.

Xiang, B. (2006), *Global Body Shopping: An Indian Labour System in the Information Technology Industry*, Princeton, NJ: Princeton University Press.

PART III

Gender Inequalites in a Changing World

6. Equality law and the limits of the 'business case' for addressing gender inequalities

Colm McLaughlin and Simon Deakin

1. INTRODUCTION

How best to align the interests of society with corporate behaviour has been a contentious issue in the context of gender inequality throughout the 1990s and 2000s. In the UK context, the traditional, rights-based rationale for anti-discrimination law has had to compete with an officially sanctioned 'business case' for equality. The business case rests on the premise that addressing gender inequality is good for an organisation's competitiveness and performance. Gender equality policies and practices, it is argued, can help organisations attract and retain valued employees, understand diverse customer needs, reduce costs associated with staff turnover and low morale, and minimise the reputational and litigation risks of discriminatory behaviour. Organisations can present their progressive policies of this kind as part of a wider agenda to promote corporate social responsibility (CSR).

As part of the CSR agenda, a number of corporate governance mechanisms have been suggested as means for advancing progressive employer practices. Pension funds and other institutional owners of shares in UK-listed companies have been encouraged to take a long-term view of their holdings and to engage more actively with investee companies (Myners 2001). Part of this process is a growing emphasis on socially responsible investment (SRI) practices, according to which institutional investors not only may but, in some circumstances, must take into account the social and environmental performance of their investee companies, alongside benchmarks based on more narrowly focused financial returns (Watchman 2010). Changes to the law made by the Companies Act 2006 required boards of large companies to pay explicit regard to the interests of employees alongside those of other corporate constituencies when discharging their wider duty to promote the success of the company. This 'enlightened shareholder value' position gives boards leeway to adopt human resource management (HRM) strategies which address issues of workplace equity, including gender inequalities, where they legitimately consider that to do so is in the long-term interests of the company's investors (Armour et al. 2003; Company Law Review Committee 2001).

Interest in the business case for gender equality has also intersected with changing attitudes towards legal regulation as a means of delivering policy goals. A discourse of 'better regulation' has developed which associates 'hard law' with overly prescriptive and inflexible controls. 'Light touch' regulation and self-regulation, with organisations encouraged to go 'beyond compliance' in order to improve competitiveness, have been put forward as appropriate techniques for the implementation of a range of government policies, including those in the area of employment equality (DCLG 2007).

In the 2000s these tendencies converged to produce a lively debate on the most effective means of tackling gender inequalities in the workplace. The Equal Pay Taskforce (2001) recommended that employers should be legally required to carry out equal pay audits, clarifying the extent of the gender pay gap in their organisations, and to act on the results. The Kingsmill Report of the same year, on the other hand, recommended a more voluntarist approach, pointing to the business case for equal pay and to the potential impact of corporate governance and CSR mechanisms, including shareholder activism, on employer behaviour (Kingsmill 2001). By the end of the decade, the principle of legal compulsion had apparently prevailed with the introduction of a legal requirement for employers to report on the gender pay gap in the Equality Act 2010, but this part of the Act was not immediately brought into force and remains controversial.

In this chapter we examine the growing use of a business logic to address gender inequalities. We assess the effectiveness of the business case in practice by drawing on interviews with institutional investors involved in the practice of SRI and with managers in a range of organisations in both the private and public sector. We also make use of material from interviews with trade unions, policy-makers and other relevant actors.

Section 2 below briefly reviews relevant legal and policy initiatives of the last ten years, culminating in the 2010 Equality Act. Section 3 presents some of the main critiques of the business case for addressing gender inequalities. Section 4 sets out the methods used in our empirical research. In sections 5 and 6 we present our empirical evidence on the impact of different regulatory approaches, looking in turn at the responses of investors and managers in the interviews we conducted. Section 7 concludes.

2. LEGAL AND POLICY INITIATIVES ADDRESSING THE GENDER PAY GAP IN THE 2000S

Thirty-five years after the Equal Pay Act came into effect in the UK, there remains a significant gender pay gap. For full-time employees across the whole economy (that is, including both the public and private sectors), the difference between the median hourly pay of men and women was 10.2 per cent in 2010, while the gap for all employees (both full-time and part-time) was 19.8 per cent. In the private sector, the hourly gap was wider at 19.8 per cent for full-time employees and 27.5 per cent for all employees (ONS 2010). In certain sectors, the pay gap is even more pronounced. A recent study of the finance sector commissioned by the Equalities and Human Rights Commission (Metcalf and Rolfe 2009) revealed an hourly pay gap of 40 per cent for full-time employees.

While there are a number of wider societal explanations for the pay gap, including occupational segregation and the unequal division of family responsibilities, it is generally accepted in policy circles that discriminatory practices by employers continue to play a role. Although pay discrimination may sometimes be intentional, it is more likely in practice to be systemic, and as such only identifiable through the evaluation of payment systems. Following the approach first adopted in Ontario under its 1987 Pay Equity Act (McColgan 1997), the argument for mandatory equal pay audits has been increasingly made in the UK over the past decade. The argument was first put forward by the Equal Pay Taskforce (2001), which claimed that as most managers did not believe their pay systems were discriminatory employers would only conduct an equal pay audit if it were made compulsory.

Compulsion, however, was rejected by the government, and two months after the Equal Pay Taskforce released its report it commissioned Denise Kingsmill to undertake a further review into women's pay and employment. Kingsmill's terms of reference were limited to an examination of non-legislative proposals for addressing the pay gap (Kingsmill 2001). Given this, it is not surprising that her report should recommend a voluntarist approach in relation to equal pay audits. She based her arguments for voluntarism on an HRM perspective which stressed the link between good managerial practice and the attainment of organisations' strategic objectives. From this point of view, the persistent pay gap reflected human capital mismanagement by UK organisations. Even where equal pay audits did not uncover systemic discrimination, Kingsmill argued that they could be expected to reveal the clustering of women into lower roles within an organisation. Moreover, a deeper analysis of the data was likely to reveal a disparity between the abilities and talents of women employees and the positions they occupied within the firm. Pay audits, in addition, offered the opportunity for organisations to examine various barriers to the full utilisation of the talents and skills of their employees, such as promotional structures that disadvantaged those who took career breaks or rewarded those who worked long hours.

Kingsmill drew on the language of CSR in pointing to the Turnbull Report of 1999 and its requirement that company boards should report to shareholders on their assessment of, and response to, significant business risks. Kingsmill argued that the failure to manage human capital effectively exposed an organisation to the same level of risk as a failure to manage financial resources. Good human capital management would reduce the risks associated with equal pay and sex discrimination litigation, and the costs of staff turnover. It should also lead to an organisational composition that reflected the company's consumer base. In this vein, Kingsmill pointed to the increased interest of institutional and individual investors in how effective companies were at managing their non-financial resources. She implied that 'reputational effects' and shareholder activism would help drive human capital management reform.

The issue of compulsory pay audits was revisited by both the Women and Work Commission (2006) and the Discrimination Law Review (DCLG 2007). The Women and Work Commission was unable to arrive at a consensus on the issue and thus simply set out the arguments for and against making pay audits mandatory. It also recommended various policy supports to raise awareness, promote best practice and build employer capacity to address equality issues. The Discrimination Law Review rejected mandatory pay audits on the grounds that the potential costs would outweigh any benefits. These would 'contravene better regulation principles' (DCLG 2007, p. 54). Instead, it recommended the promotion of best practice and the introduction of mechanisms that would increase the 'reputational benefits' for organisations that voluntarily carried them out (DCLG 2007, p. 112).

Following on from these various commissions and reviews, a number of public policy supports were implemented during the 2000s to encourage employers to conduct equal pay audits and address gender diversity more widely. The Equal Opportunities Commission (EOC) published various toolkits and codes of practice on conducting equal pay audits and complying with equal pay legislation. Government departments began working with a number of networks of 'fair pay champions', such as Opportunity Now, to promote best practice and reward exemplar employers. In 2003 legislation extended the right of individual workers bringing equal pay claims to obtain information on pay practices from their employer, using an equal pay questionnaire. Taken together, these various supports had significantly raised the profile of equal pay audits in the private sector by the mid-2000s (Neathey et al. 2005).

In the public sector, meanwhile, pay audits became de facto mandatory through the Civil Service Reward Principles, the National Joint Council pay agreement for local authorities, and the Agenda for Change programme in the National Health Service (NHS). Legislation which came into force in 2006 introduced the public sector gender equality duty. This placed a duty on public bodies proactively to promote gender equality as part of a wider legal obligation to eliminate unlawful discrimination. During the same period, equal pay litigation in the public sector saw a significant increase. A number of high-profile cases highlighted the potential liabilities for employers and unions who were found to have contravened the requirement of equal pay through discriminatory collective bargaining (Deakin and Morris 2009, pp. 629–30).

However, despite this range of public policy supports, and the various governance and business case-based arguments put forward for a voluntary approach, empirical evidence suggests that its influence on private sector organisations had been limited. The EOC commissioned a number of surveys between 2002 and 2005 examining the extent of equal pay audits among organisations. Eighty-two per cent of organisations in the 2005 survey reported that they had not conducted an equal pay review, did not have one in progress and did not intend to conduct one (Adams et al. 2006). This evidence helped shift opinion in favour of legal compulsion once again, with the inclusion of a mandatory reporting requirement in the Equality Act 2010. Section 78 of the Act provided that with effect from 2013, organisations with more than 250 employees would be required to report on their gender pay gap on a regular basis (GEO 2009). The 2010 Act was passed in the final days of the Labour government, and it was left to the new administration to decide when and how far to bring it into force. In late 2010 the coalition government announced that it would not be implementing section 78, although it stopped short of proposing its outright repeal, leaving open the possibility of its adoption at a later date (GEO 2010). Meanwhile, the Equalities and Human Rights Commission (EHRC) published new research indicating a continued low use of pay audits, with only a marginal improvement on take-up levels of the mid-2000s. It also found very low levels of internal or external disclosure of findings by those organisations conducting equal pay reviews (Adams et al. 2010).

3. THE BUSINESS CASE FOR ADDRESSING GENDER INEQUALITY

There is empirical evidence to suggest that addressing gender inequality can have positive effects on a firm's financial performance (see Herring 2009). The reason for this, as Kirton and Greene (2000, p. 180) succinctly put it, is that 'inequality is inefficient'. The following more specific organisational benefits have been identified (cf. Hutchings and Thomas 2005; Kirton and Greene 2010; Monks 2007):

1. Increased competitive advantage through recruitment and retention for organisations which become 'employers of choice'.
2. Improved morale and productivity through flexible work practices and perceptions of fairness.
3. Improved human capital management and full utilisation of employee skills and experience.
4. Reductions in hiring and training costs associated with high turnover.
5. New insights into customer requirements and attracting new customers in organisations with a more diverse employee base.
6. Increased creativity and innovation in organisations which prioritise workplace equity.
7. Reduced litigation risk.
8. Reputational effects arising from reduced reputational risks associated with discrimination claims and organisations' raised CSR profiles.

Critics of the business case do not deny these potential benefits exist. Rather, they argue that the business case is ineffective in bringing about organisational change on a widespread scale. One of the most articulate critiques has come from Dickens (1994, 1999) who argues that the business case is 'inevitably contingent, variable, selective and partial' (Dickens 1999, p. 9). She argues that the advantages of the business case are contingent on the competitive strategy of the firm. While some organisations may see attracting and retaining talented employees as an important part of the HR and wider managerial strategies, addressing gender inequalities is likely to be less important for firms operating a cost-minimisation strategy. Indeed, it may be more cost-effective for some organisations not to address gender inequalities where they benefit from discriminatory behaviour or the utilisation of women in roles that are undervalued by the market. Thus, while the business case can support progressive practices in some organisations, it can be seen as justifying regressive and discriminatory practices in others. It is also contingent on the economic climate, with recruitment and retention less of an issue for firms in times of recession.

The business case is also selective and partial in its impact *within* organisations: it can be invoked to bring more women into senior management while not addressing the needs of those lower down the organisational hierarchy. Thus many gender initiatives 'show a greater concern for the glass ceiling than the "sticky floor"' (Dickens 1999, p. 10), with insufficient emphasis being placed on the interests of low-paid women, the issue of the over-representation of women in lower levels of the organisation, and power differentials (Colling and Dickens 1998).

The business case approach also assumes that organisations can readily be convinced of the potential benefits. As Noon (2007) argues, it is based on the premise that managers just have to be educated, when in fact some may have already considered the arguments and decided that the business case benefits do not outweigh the costs involved. It also ignores the role of continuing, deeply held prejudices on the part of some managers and employers. Thus 'it assumes irrationality where rationality might prevail, and assumes rationality where irrationality might prevail' (Noon 2007, p. 779).

A further critique of the business case for gender equality is that it serves to dilute and depoliticise the rights-based goals of equality law. One of the principal functions of equality law has been to identify and remedy structures which systemically disadvantage certain social groups. The business case, by comparison, emphasises the role individuals can play in overcoming discrimination with a view to contributing to enhanced organisational performance (Hutchings and Thomas 2005). Kirton and Greene examined this shift in focus by studying the effects of the displacement of equality officers by diversity management specialists with a generalist HRM background during the 2000s. They found that the greater legitimacy enjoyed by diversity managers meant that senior managers were more ready to give them public backing than they had been with equality officers, and that line managers were more prepared to take equality issues seriously. However, they also reported a 'considerable risk that if diversity practitioners over-identify with management and management interests, the changes they drive are more likely to serve organisational objectives than improve working lives' (Kirton and Greene 2009, p. 173).

Support for the business case, on the other hand, can be derived from a consideration of the limits of strategies based on legal enforcement. A major criticism of UK equality law has been that it is reactive rather than proactive. Litigation largely takes the form of individual claims. Following the judicial restriction, in the late 1970s, and then abolition, in the mid-1980s, of the powers of the Central Arbitration Committee to revise discriminatory payment structures, there have been few legal means available for tackling inequality at an organisational or sectoral level (Dickens 1999). This was the context in which mandatory pay audits were advanced as a possible legal solution in the early 2000s (see section 2, above). The introduction of the gender equality duty in the mid-2000s, building on an earlier, similar duty in the context of race discrimination, marked a limited step forward, but its impact was confined to the public sector (Deakin and Morris 2009, pp. 604–5).

With some exceptions (see Epstein 2002), the critique of UK equality law has been concerned mostly with particular shortcomings of the legal framework, rather than taking the form of criticism of the principle of legal intervention as such. Critics have argued that, rather than leaving it up to individuals to make a claim through a tribunal, the law should require employers to take positive steps to overcome discrimination inherent in organisational systems. Doing so would, it is suggested, change attitudes and behaviours and lessen the role of costly and confrontational litigation (Hepple et al. 2000; O'Cinneide 2003). This legal critique is consistent with aspects of the business case in arguing that employer practice can be a vehicle for change, but it departs from it by stressing the need for external regulation to alter the incentive structure facing employers, and in particular to increase the litigation and reputational costs of not addressing persistent gender inequalities.

4.   RESEARCH METHODS

We now turn to examine empirical evidence on the reaction of employers to the pressure to address gender inequality through organisational change during the 2000s. These pressures included corporate governance mechanisms, including investor pressure; government support for the 'business case' for change; legal pressures deriving from individual litigation and the gender equality duty; pressure from trade unions and employees; and the procurement process. Our results are based on 40 interviews conducted between late 2007 and early 2010.

At the organisational level, we carried out interviews with eight public sector organisations (six local authorities and two civil service departments), eight private sector organisations (five listed companies and three professional partnerships), two universities, and two not-for-profit organisations (a housing association and a charity). Here our interviewees consisted of a mix of HR managers and diversity champions, most of whom occupied senior positions in the relevant organisations. Our sample consisted mostly of organisations which had made a public commitment to greater gender equality, as it proved difficult to persuade other organisations to participate in the research. Forty-five private sector organisations were approached to take part in the study across a range of sectors. Initially, a large proportion of these were chosen because they were *not* part of an employer gender network organisation such as Opportunity Now. However, all of these declined to participate. We therefore approached firms that were on public record as being committed to improving gender equality.

As Kirton and Greene (2010) also found, access to private sector organisations on gender equality issues is problematic because of concerns that public statements of commitment to gender equality might be seen to amount to window dressing, given that policies might not always be reflected in practice. Given increasing levels of equal pay litigation and the high profile of a number of controversial equal pay cases in recent years (see Deakin and Morris 2009, pp. 623–30), it is not surprising that employers appear to be hesitant to talk about gender inequalities and equal pay.

We also carried out interviews with five investment funds undertaking a range of approaches to SRI, and two trade unions engaging in SRI issues either through their own pension funds (that is, those providing pensions for their own employees) or on behalf of their members. In addition we interviewed a range of union officials at the local, regional and national level and a number of national-level stakeholders in order to gauge views on the policy-making process.

5. GENDER INEQUALITY, CSR AND SRI: ATTITUDES OF INVESTORS

As we have seen (see section 2 above), the Kingsmill report (2001) placed considerable emphasis on the role of institutional mechanisms of corporate governance and corporate social responsibility in putting pressure on employers to address the question of gender inequality. Our interviews were aimed at elucidating, first, the importance of SRI-based strategies as a whole in the practice of asset managers and pension fund trustees, and, secondly, the extent to which investors were paying specific regard to gender equality and related issues of workplace equity.

There is evidence that CSR has become an important issue for large companies and in particular for those with a stock exchange listing. A KPMG (2008) survey showed that 80 per cent of Global Fortune 250 companies and over 90 per cent of the UK's largest 100 corporations reported CSR-related information. Increasingly, responsibility for CSR lies with a board member. Additionally, firms are employing CSR managers, joining CSR membership associations, such as Business in the Community, and participating in CSR performance indices such as FTSE4Good (Grosser and Moon 2008).

On the investor side, shareholder engagement has grown significantly. The United Nations Principles for Responsible Investment was launched in 2006. By 2008 it had over 360 institutional signatories representing US$14 trillion in assets, up from US$4 trillion in 2006 (UNPRI 2008). In the UK, the SRI fund market is estimated to be worth around €331 billion (Waring and Edwards 2008). These developments have been supported by various national reporting requirements, which would have raised awareness of the importance of social, ethical and environmental issues on the part of pension fund trustees. In particular, pension disclosure regulations which came into force in the UK in 2000 required pension funds (on a 'comply or explain' basis) to disclose the content of their investment mandates and to report annually on how they were implementing them.

These developments, however, have largely taken place at the level of policy initiatives, or of formal corporate reporting. Our interviews were aimed at finding out how far they were shaping practice. The evidence we gathered suggests that the impact of SRI on investment practice remains limited, both in general and with specific regard to the issue of gender equality.

A first reason for this is that despite significant growth in recent years, SRI remains very much a niche market. Even among some of the larger UK investment firms which employ SRI-based approaches, SRI-specific funds range between only 2 and 8 per cent of their total equity assets under management. These figures may understate the size of the SRI market, as other, non-SRI funds may have a CSR engagement overlay, or engage on specific CSR-related issues that are perceived to have some financial risk. Even allowing for this margin of error, the SRI market occupies a peripheral role within investment practice as a whole.

Secondly, the extent of investor activism, or active engagement with investee companies, is restricted. Most interviewees were able to cite to us examples of investor activism which had led a fund manager to engage with a company on an issue, or to file or support a shareholder resolution. However, the general view was that the asset managers who held shares on behalf of pension funds were not being challenged to any great extent by those funds' trustees. There was some evidence that the trustees of unions' pension funds were beginning to raise employment-related issues with investee companies. However, UK unions were perceived to be a long way behind their US counterparts in realising the potential to influence organisational change through this route. United Kingdom unions are now offering their members training in relation to being a pension fund trustee, and over time this may lead to more institutional activism. However, a union official told us that it is difficult to persuade senior union officials in the UK to accept the potential role of pension funds in addressing workplace issues, and then to dedicate appropriate resources to pension fund activism.

Two investment firms took the view that there was a disconnect between the way pension fund trustees saw their role, and the missions of the organisations they represented. Even public-interest organisations such as charities, campaign groups, and public sector organisations in the education and health sectors rarely used SRI-based approaches when setting out their investment mandates. As a result, campaign groups and charities might well be 'investing in an activity which they are campaigning against . . . you would have thought of any sector . . . they would have got it before anybody else' (fund manager). While non-governmental organisations (NGOs) were thought to be effective in influencing the engagement of SRI funds, they did this most often by lobbying SRI funds directly, rather than in their capacity as investors through their own funds.

Pension fund trustees were seen as being more conservative on SRI issues than the members and beneficiaries of their funds. This conservatism was highlighted by a union official who had recently attended a meeting of a large pension fund. An actuary stated publicly at the meeting that 'the downfall of the fund was when you let women in'. As the union official put it to us, in relation to using pension funds as a vehicle for bringing about social and ethical change, 'there are some severe barriers to overcome'. Uncertainty over the future defined benefit pension schemes, many of which have recently been closed to new members and/or to new contributions from existing members, was also seen as making trustees more risk averse on the issue of SRI.

Engagement with companies was in some cases driven not by the mandates set by institutional investors, but by SRI investment funds themselves as part of their own strategic aims. One investment firm talked about their aim being to educate fund managers and 'transform the capital markets and get them to [have] sustainability issues . . . reflected in investment decisions'. Socially responsible investment firms draw up their own engagement plans around key social, ethical and environmental issues and then build sector and issue expertise so they can engage not only with companies, but also with fund managers and brokers.

However, even in the SRI sector, a problem is that fund managers are rewarded for short-term gains, and that the gains from CSR-based activism are not always visible. As one interviewee noted, the stock market price of a firm may drop in response to some negative CSR-related news, but it often returns to its previous level after a short period. This suggests that the initial decrease was 'a market reaction to unexpected news as opposed to the market really factoring in what the impact is of a company not managing [CSR] issues'.

A factor limiting the impact of SRI-based approaches on gender diversity is the existence of a hierarchy of concerns within CSR. Employee issues are generally viewed as one of the four clusters of significant CSR issues along with governance, environmental and wider social issues. But within the employee cluster, issues including use of child labour, supply chain employment conditions and health and safety are seen as carrying the greatest reputational risk and are the easiest to engage on. Issues such as gender equality and union recognition are regarded as more problematic because of the lower public profile they enjoy.

We had some reports of engagement with companies in relation to issues of workplace diversity and equality. However, there were no reports of significant engagement over equal pay issues. A fund manager told us that while the fund had raised concerns about the low numbers of women on boards of directors, asking questions about whether a firm had conducted a pay audit would constitute unacceptable micro-management: 'there are limits to what we think we can achieve as corporate owners'. He acknowledged that some niche SRI firms might try to engage at this level because it fitted in with the requirement of certain ethical retail investment products. However, this approach did not work well, he thought, within a mainstream investment context. Thus, the multiplicity of issues that investors took into account had led to the relative marginalisation of diversity issues even within the SRI segment of the market.

It is also not clear to what extent the danger of litigation over equal pay is seen to give rise to a significant financial risk for investors or the companies they hold shares in. A union official with responsibility for pension funds to whom we spoke had approached a number of SRI fund managers from different investment firms in relation to equal pay. These specific listed companies, he claimed, had inherited discriminatory pay systems from the public sector without conducting a non-discriminatory job evaluation scheme. He provided fund managers with a number of questions on equal pay practice to put to firms, taken from the EHRC website. One fund manager told him that the estimated risk liability from breaches of equal pay legislation was simply too small: it 'would have no material impact on the share price; no one would be interested'. Only one fund manager raised the questions concerned with the specified companies, but according to the union official we spoke to the issues were not acted upon by the organisation.

We also spoke with an SRI investment firm that had raised questions about pay audits on behalf of a trade union. The companies they had spoken to responded to the effect that equal pay issues or conducting a pay audit were not part of the contract negotiations with the public sector. They did not feel that the public sector bodies awarding the contracts for service provision gave the issue much weight. One SRI investment firm had produced a document about using SRI to close the gender pay gap, but had regarded this as very much exploratory work, and it had not been possible to present the information in a quantitative form that fund managers could process as part of investment decisions.

The lack of quantitative information that third parties could use to make meaningful investment decisions was seen by most interviewees as the biggest barrier to significant levels of institutional activism in relation to CSR issue. As one interviewee noted, currently 'companies choose what they are going to report on . . . when it comes to environmental and social issues'. The lack of standardised performance indicators means the CSR performance of companies could not be assessed, ranked and challenged by civil society and by investors: 'transparency is a fundamental tenet of responsibility; without transparency you can't have accountability [and] third parties have no way of judging what you have been doing'.

The lack of meaningful reporting on the issue of CSR is a consistent theme. A PricewaterhouseCoopers survey of annual reports in the UK found that while 83 per cent of companies included a CSR section in their annual reports, only 17 per cent connected CSR issues to their strategic objectives (PWC 2007). Sixty per cent of companies claimed that their employees were an essential asset for achieving their strategic objectives, but only around 20 per cent included relevant performance indicators in their annual reports.

At the same time, most of the investor firms we spoke with were not opposed to greater levels of regulation. As one interviewee noted, 'companies operate within a society which itself has laws and rules . . . and to suppose that the control of companies can be left entirely to the shareholders as owners seems to me wrong and rather dangerous'. Thus they saw regulation as potentially important, both in facilitating institutional activism and in helping firms understand society's expectations of employer behaviour.

6. GENDER INEQUALITY, THE 'BUSINESS CASE' AND LEGAL COMPLIANCE: ATTITUDES OF MANAGERS

Given the bias in our sample towards organisations with a stated commitment to diversity, it is significant that none of the listed companies we spoke to reported significant engagement with investors on SRI issues.

Only one interviewee was aware of any questions from shareholders relating to gender equalities issues, which resulted in their head office requesting each subsidiary organisation to produce a diversity policy. However, it appeared to be a one-off directive to ensure that managers were not 'embarrassed in front of the shareholders again', and there had been no follow-up or monitoring of the policy in the intervening years.

A more significant driver of change was the highlighting of the business case for equality by government and by business groups such as Opportunity Now. In practice, the business case was by far the most dominant driver of gender equality pointed to by the diversity managers and champions we interviewed, in both the public and private sector. Recruitment and retention of talent, reflecting the customer base of the organisation, delivering a better product or service, reputation and, to a lesser extent, litigation risk, were all seen as well-embedded justifications. These motivations were frequently combined with a strong sense that reducing inequalities was the right approach for ethical reasons. One interviewee commented that the business case ultimately came back to an underlying belief system. The organisation's maternity policies had been justified on the grounds of protecting the investment in staff, in getting female employees to return to work and to be the 'leaders of the future'. But as the company had no problem recruiting talented employees, there was also a strong belief that 'we want more women in our senior management teams' simply because it was 'the right thing to do'. For some respondents, the ethical rationale was explicitly stated in the terminology of 'right and wrong', but mostly it came through in a passion for changing the organisation culture that was very personal and went well beyond the business case. It was also evident in the frustration and disappointment some respondents expressed in response to the lack of progress they felt they were making, or in their experience of the attitudes of some male colleagues.

However, while the diversity and HR managers we interviewed were motivated by both the business case and a sense of justice, the same could not be said for all of their chief executive officers (CEOs) and senior management teams. In one company, which had won awards in relation to its gender equality policy, the 'buy-in' from the CEO had come about only when he had been convinced by diversity champions about the impact upon the 'bottom line'. Every initiative they implemented had to be 'cost neutral', so that 'if I want to introduce anything new, something else has to go or I have to find a way of funding it a different way'. This respondent talked about working out 'what kept the CEO awake at night' and tapping into that in order to bring about change. Following a significant employment tribunal award against the company, she had told the CEO that 'one way we could protect ourselves at tribunals was to say we did diversity training . . . and that was my hook in'. The same CEO viewed 'work-life balance as part-time work and less commitment from staff', so making the business case was essential to changing his perception.

In another organisation, changing a 'laddish culture' meant convincing managers that diversity was 'a business critical issue'. This also involved changing perceptions. A common response to diversity initiatives from male colleagues was, 'it's not that we've been held back because we didn't have more women, so what are women going to contribute that is going to make us even more successful?' Yet another spoke of the difficulty in justifying maternity leave policies in excess of legal minimum requirements to the organisation's accountants. Arguments based on protecting the organisation's investment in human resources were difficult in a context where the company did not find it hard to recruit well-qualified staff. So while for this respondent good maternity leave was simply the right thing to do in that it would lead to more women in the senior management team, the justifications he gave senior management were framed in terms of the firm's business needs.

The business case was often seen to be an effective tool for bringing gender equality into mainstream managerial thinking. However, we also found evidence that the rhetoric of organisational success was framing the discussion of gender inequalities in a limiting and depoliticising way. First, while many organisations reported they were working on changing behaviours and attitudes, most noted this was a slow process, requiring a 'major organisational transformation'. In the interim, significant energy and resources had to be invested in supporting women employees to 'survive in a political environment [and] to play the game'. This implied a need for building women's support networks and training and personal development programmes in order for them to developing relevant skills and confidence. One interviewee told us, 'women just have this tendency to think that their hard work will get them noticed and get them promoted whereas men think differently . . . most of our men don't even realise that women want promotion'. Mechanisms that might bring about cultural change, such as target-setting around promotions, were reported as being resisted by many line managers, particularly in professional services companies. In contrast, two engineering-based companies reported having achieved significant cultural change in part through the setting of targets. The public sector was also noticeably different in this regard. Managers in the civil service departments we interviewed reported target-setting and robust monitoring from the Cabinet Office, and saw this as an effective driver of change.

Evidence of a depoliticisation of the equalities agenda was also present in the prioritising of business values over right-based approaches to diversity. In the public sector, there was a strong sense of diversity initiatives helping employees to balance work and their private lives. In many of the private sector firms, on the other hand, work–life balance policies were about helping employees fit the demands of their job around their private lives. This involved an acceptance that the way work was organised was a given, which could not be questioned. For one interviewee, the issue was: 'so if the pace is relentless, what can we do to help you fit that around your life?' This respondent went on to say, 'if you say to someone do you have work–life balance they'll say no because they're working long hours. If you actually ask the questions – are you able to go home if you need to, can you work from home some days, does your boss ask where you are . . . then I think they do have work–life balance'. In the professional services sector firms we interviewed, long hours and working away from home were just the nature of the business:

> our industry . . . is not the most conducive to having children . . . It means working a lot of hours and also a lot of hours away from home . . . We do try to allow people to have a preference . . . but at the end of the day we are a business and . . . so we do try and be as flexible as we can but there is a limit I think and you really have to balance the business need.

Others spoke of the 'resentment' that was caused when women returning from maternity leave were reluctant to travel or work long hours as this increased the pressure on their colleagues: according to one respondent, this gave 'working women a bad press'. Some also reported that because of the demands of professional work, women returning from maternity leave often gravitated to parts of the business with greater predictability of hours and less travel. However, these were often the less profitable parts of the business and thus provided lower remuneration and fewer opportunities for promotion. So there was no deeper questioning of the prevailing work culture or the organisation of work and whether it was these that needed to change. This was all the more surprising in that the main gender issue these firms reported was the lack of women in senior positions, while long hours of work were one of the primary explanations given for their inability to retain female employees.

A third aspect of depoliticisation was the priority given to addressing gender inequality at the top of organisations, to the detriment of employees outside the higher managerial ranks. This lack of women in senior roles was the most common 'pressing' issue, often mentioned by respondents at the very start of the interview indicating it was uppermost in their minds. Concern for women in junior or administrative roles was not as pressing. A common response to questions about administrative and junior positions was that these workers had the same access to the female networks and flexible working policies as their more senior colleagues, and then the discussion quickly returned to the issue of getting women promoted into senior roles. A number of respondents argued that the solution to the gender pay gap was not pay audits but dealing with the issue of women's progression within the organisation 'so that they can earn higher salaries'. Occupational segregation was seen as a wider societal responsibility, beyond the scope of what the organisation could address, while low pay was viewed as simply a reflection of the market. Little has changed, it would seem, since Colling and Dickens (1998) argued that business case initiatives would tend to focus on promoting women into senior management roles at the expense of addressing the position of low-paid women in the organisation, the undervaluation of women's work, or power differentials; now as then, the 'exclusive reliance upon management action risks promoting conceptions of equality that are partial and insecure' (Colling and Dickens 1998, p. 403).

We then asked respondents how far they saw the law as driving organisational change. Most of the private sector respondents bridled at the suggestion that the law played any role at all in shaping organisational practice. A typical response was, 'we would very rarely refer to the law as the reason for doing something . . . our aspiration is best in class approach . . . We would want to do better than that'. Another commented, 'we would want to be ahead of the law', while another said that if they were to be driven by the law 'then I think we would be failing'.

However, upon probing it became clear that these respondents had interpreted the question as being 'caught out' by the law, and that they could, in other circumstances, see legislative developments as a way of educating their organisations and 'as a platform for a change of behaviour'. Several private sector interviewees pointed to the requirement under public procurement rules of disclosing diversity information as a driver of change. Additionally, the statutory right to request flexible working was mentioned spontaneously by a number of interviewees as a legal development that had enabled the HR department to enter into dialogue with operational managers. The need to be compliant with the law had provided them with the opportunity to educate their managers about the issues that employees with caring responsibilities face.

Despite many of the private sector respondents reporting that they were always ahead of the law, of the eight private sector organisations interviewed, only one had published any pay-gap data. This was also the only private sector organisation in which an interviewee was in favour of pay audits being made mandatory. At the time of our interviews, it was known that future legislation on pay disclosure rules was likely, and the decision of the UK coalition government to put the law on hold could not have been anticipated. In this context, the lack of anticipation of legal change among most of our interviewees is striking.

The partial application of the business case that Dickens (1999) referred to was also confirmed in our interviews. The private sector firms we spoke to were all strongly committed to addressing gender inequality and reducing the pay gap, but yet they were not convinced of the business case justifications for publishing their pay gap data, either internally with staff or externally in their annual reports. In some cases, the business case pointed to *not* publishing the data because of the possibility of litigation risk and the reputational risk associated with negative public perceptions of persistent inequalities which had previously been concealed from view. As one HR manager said to us: 'we would only do it voluntarily if it showed us in a good light . . . without the law we would never do it'. Some of our respondents accepted that legal change would be helpful for addressing the pay gap. As one respondent put it: 'publicly I don't like transparency, privately I think it can only help' indicating that in this instance, the business imperative and practices for addressing the pay gap do not coincide.

7. CONCLUSION

Our findings provide mixed evidence on the use of the business case to address gender inequalities. Shareholder engagement has so far proved to have very little impact in this area. The practice of SRI remains limited to a niche market, and even within the SRI sector, employment issues in general and gender inequalities in particular do not receive a high priority from asset managers and pension fund trustees. Within organisations, on the other hand, a growing stress has been placed on the business-related rationale for addressing gender equality. As part of the practice of diversity management, organisations have responded to the argument that persistent gender inequalities represent a form of mismanagement of human resources, with negative implications for the delivery of services, in the public sector, and for the efficiency of the firm, in the private sector. At the same time, the increased legitimacy of diversity management has come at a cost in terms of the deradicalisation of gender policies. This trend is particularly pronounced in organisations where diversity management practices are being applied in a way which takes as a given the organisational structures which are principally responsible for creating gender inequalities.

The legal critique of equality law mounted by Hepple et al. (2000)

focused on the relative effectiveness of particular regulatory mechanisms in inducing organisational change. From this point of view, the problem with the existing framework of equality law is the failure to integrate legal strategies with the potential for internal reform within organisations. Our interview material suggests that diversity managers increasingly acknowledge the role that legal compulsion and the threat of litigation can play in shifting managerial attitudes. On the specific issue of pay audits, there is some evidence that managers would be willing to move in the direction of more systematic investigation and disclosure of pay gaps in their organisations if there was a legal trigger for doing so. Similarly, some SRI investors see legal rules mandating disclosure by companies on gender inequality issues as a crucial step for raising awareness of social and ethical issues within asset management and pension fund practice. Thus, targeted legal reforms could in future operate *in conjunction with* the business case to stimulate changes in organisational and investment practice. Making anti-discrimination legislation more proactive could also help to counter the depoliticisation of equality law which has been associated with the rise of the business case. A first step in this direction would be for the UK coalition government to revisit the issue of mandatory pay disclosure and bring section 78 of the Equality Act into force.

REFERENCES

Adams, L., K. Carter and S. Schäfer (2006), *Equal Pay Reviews Survey 2005*, Manchester: Equal Opportunities Commission.

Adams, L., K. Gore and J. Shury (2010), *Gender Pay Gap Reporting Survey 2009*, Manchester: Equality and Human Rights Commission.

Armour, J., S. Deakin and S. Konzelmann (2003), 'Shareholder primacy and the trajectory of UK corporate governance', *British Journal of Industrial Relations*, **41**, 531–55.

Colling, T. and L. Dickens (1998), 'Selling the case for gender equality: deregulation and equality bargaining', *British Journal of Industrial Relations*, **36**, 389–411.

Company Law Review Committee (2001), *Modern Company Law for a Competitive Economy: Developing the Framework*, London: The Stationery Office.

Deakin, S. and G. Morris (2009), *Labour Law*, 5th edn, Oxford: Hart.

Department for Communities and Local Government (DCLG) (2007), *Discrimination Law Review. A Framework for Fairness: Proposals for a Single Equality Bill for Great Britain*, London: Department for Communities and Local Government.

Dickens, L. (1994), 'The business case for women's equality: is the carrot better than the stick?', *Employee Relations*, **16** (8), 5–18.

Dickens, L. (1999), 'Beyond the business case: a three-pronged approach to equality action', *Human Resource Management Journal*, **9** (1), 9–19.

Epstein, R. (2002), *Equal Opportunity or No Opportunity? The Good Thing about Discrimination*, London: Institute for the Study of Civil Society.

Equal Pay Task Force (2001), *Just Pay*, Manchester: Equal Opportunities Commission.

Government Equalities Office (GEO) (2009), *A Fairer Future: The Equality Bill and Other Action to Make Equality a Reality*, London: Government Equalities Office.

Government Equalities Office (GEO) (2010), 'Equality Act 2010', available at: http://www.equalities.gov.uk/equality_act_2010.aspx (accessed 6 August 2010).

Grosser, K. and J. Moon (2008), 'Developments in company reporting on workplace gender equality? A corporate social responsibility perspective', *Accounting Forum*, **32**, 179–98.

Hepple, B., M. Coussey and T. Chowdhury (2000), *Equality: A New Framework. Report of the Independent Review of the Enforcement of UK Anti-Discrimination Legislation*, Oxford: Hart.

Herring, C. (2009), 'Does diversity pay? Race, gender and the business case for diversity', *American Sociological Review*, **74** (2), 208–24.

Hutchings, E. and H. Thomas (2005), 'The business case for equality and diversity: a UK case study of private consultancy and race equality', *Planning, Practice & Research*, **20** (3), 263–78.

Kingsmill, D. (2001), *Review of Women's Employment and Pay*, London: DTI.

Kirton, G. and A. Greene (2000), *The Dynamics of Managing Diversity: A Critical Approach*, Oxford: Butterworth-Heinemann.

Kirton, G. and A. Greene (2009), 'The costs and opportunities of doing diversity work in mainstream organisations', *Human Resource Management Journal*, **19**, 159–75.

Kirton, G. and A. Greene (2010), *The Dynamics of Managing Diversity: A Critical Approach*, 3rd edn, Oxford: Elsevier.

KPMG (2008), *KPMG International Survey of Corporate Responsibility Reporting 2008*, Amstelveen: KPMG.

McColgan, A. (1997), *Just Wages for Women*, Oxford: Clarendon Press.

Metcalf, H. and H. Rolfe (2009), *Employment and Earnings in the Finance Sector: A Gender Analysis*, Manchester: Equalities and Human Rights Commission.

Monks, K. (2007), *The Business Impact of Equality and Diversity: The International Evidence*, Dublin: The Equality Authority and NCPP.

Myners, P. (2001), *Institutional Investment in the UK: A Review*, London: HM Treasury.

Neathey, F., R. Willison, K. Akroyd, J. Regan and D. Hill (2005), *Equal Pay Reviews in Practice*, Manchester: Equal Opportunities Commission.

Noon, M. (2007), 'The fatal flaws of diversity and the business case for ethnic minorities', *Work, Employment & Society*, **21** (4), 773–84.

O'Cinneide, C. (2003), *Taking Equal Opportunities Seriously: The Extension of Positive Duties to Promote Equality*, London: Equality and Diversity Forum.

Office for National Statistics (ONS) (2010), 'Full-time gender pay gap narrows', available at: http://www.statistics.gov.uk/cci/nugget.asp?id=167 (accessed 2 March 2011).

PriceWaterhouseCoopers (PWC) (2007), *Business Review: Has it Made a Difference*, London: PricewaterhouseCoopers.

United Nations Principles for Responsible Investment (UNPRI) (2008), *PRI*

Report on Progress 2008, New York: United Nations Principles for Responsible Investment.

Waring, P. and T. Edwards (2008), 'Socially responsible investment: explaining its uneven development and human resource management consequences', *Corporate Governance*, **16** (3), 135–45.

Watchman, P. (2010), 'Social responsibility and fiduciary duties of trustees', in P. Thornton (ed.), *Good Governance for Pension Schemes*, Cambridge: Cambridge University Press, pp. 48–66.

Women and Work Commission (2006), *Shaping a Fairer Future*, London: Women and Equality Unit.

7. Work–family conflict and well-being in Northern Europe

Jacqueline Scott and Anke C. Plagnol

INTRODUCTION

Work–family conflict is a crucial issue for quality of life. Moreover, public interest in work–family balance policies has expanded significantly in recent years. From the policy-maker's perspective the issue concerns the extent to which the state can and should intervene to help men and women reconcile work and family responsibilities. This issue has become urgent because, as Esping-Andersen asserts, there is an incomplete revolution in gender roles that threatens societal stability (Esping-Andersen 2009). What is meant by such a claim? The idea is that in modern societies women are facing severe problems of reconciling their dual preference for children and careers. For a growing proportion of women and men, women's employment and less gender specialisation is desirable, both ideologically and pragmatically. Thus the dual-earner based partnership is becoming normative – it is the 'thing to do'.

Yet, we know only too well from time-budget studies that changes in the domestic sphere lag well behind the changing realities of women's employment. Women, faced with only 24 hours in a day, find they have to reduce the time they spend on unpaid work such as housework and family care, when they increase their hours of paid work. While women's paid work activity has been on the rise, time-budget studies reveal that, on average, men are not compensating by an equivalent take-up of unpaid work (Gershuny and Kan, Chapter 3 in this volume). So what is the solution? While housework can be outsourced to some extent, caring implies an ongoing presence and emotional relationship that makes paid care different to family care.

The fact that current debates about work–family conflict in the UK and elsewhere in Europe have tended to focus on the relationship between paid work, parenting and caring is understandable. As Taylor (2001) points out, the decades since the 1970s have seen a feminisation of the UK labour market. The greatest rise in employment in the 1990s was among mothers with children aged 4 or under. At the start of the new millennium, almost half of the country's lone mothers are in some form of part-time work, although only one in five of them are in full-time employment, a much lower proportion than in the USA or even France. This change in the gender make-up of the workforce raises inevitable concerns about how women and men can raise families successfully, while contributing as fully as possible to the labour force.

Family life depends greatly on the quality of relationships between and across generations – within partnerships and between parents and children. Traditionally it was the woman who took responsibility for the home, while the man provided the income on which home-life depends. As dual-earner partnerships become increasingly common, the cost for both men and women in terms of work–family conflict and well-being comes under scrutiny. Do women opt out of the labour force during early motherhood because work–family conflicts have become unbearable? Is life less stressful for them than for mothers who are employed? Is part-time work the panacea that some hope, enabling a better balance of work and family and thereby increasing well-being?

An interesting irony is that although gender relations are one of the most important aspects of work–family conflict, much of the existing policy rhetoric about the need to balance work and family life remains deliberately gender neutral. Indeed, as Lewis (2009) asserts, governments have diverse goals for promoting work-balance policies but, outside of Scandinavia, gender inequality is rarely a priority. Lewis further suggests that in the UK gender equality has hardly been discussed; rather, policy documents have striven for gender neutrality. One problem is that, in the domain of work–family balance policies, the thorny problem of 'equality-as-sameness' or 'equality-as-difference' is core. If the aim is sameness then this translates into an equal division of paid and unpaid work between men and women: a citizen worker/carer model. This position has been championed by Fraser (1994) on the basis of philosophical arguments, and by Gornick and Meyers (2009) on the basis of empirical work. But if, as Orloff suggests (2009), equality consists of differences and diversity, then policy may seek to mitigate any detrimental consequences of caring, albeit at the risk of perpetuating caring work as women's responsibility. Lewis (2009), Orloff (2009) and others, following Sen (1999), advocate that policy should not be equality of outcome but instead focus on *realisable opportunities* that allow people to put their preferences into action.

Disentangling preference from constraint is hugely difficult and beyond the scope of this chapter. We cannot delve into the extent to which men and women are fulfilling their choices in work–family balance (our data do not permit this). Instead we are constrained to look at how the particular contexts in which individuals' lives are situated influence their experience of work–family conflict (WFC) and well-being. Our goal is to examine how WFC and well-being differ by gender and across the family life course. We use data from the 2004 European Social Survey (ESS) to explore these issues in seven countries: Sweden, Norway, Denmark, the Netherlands, Germany, France and the UK. These countries are selected, in part, because they have very different traditions and policies regarding work and family reconciliation.

One of our aims is to examine whether WFC and well-being varies between countries that differ in their support for maternal employment and a more equitable divide of family work between men and women. We also explore how a couple's division of paid and unpaid work across the family life course influences WFC, separately by country and for all seven countries combined. We are particularly interested in examining how both the experience of WFC and well-being is gendered in ways that reflect, in part, the gendered division of paid and unpaid labour that is manifest throughout Northern Europe.

In the next section we review briefly some of the relevant background literature and present our specific hypotheses. We then describe our measures and the approach to the analyses before we present our results. In the summary and concluding section we bring together our main findings and revisit the challenging problem of what policy can and should do to mitigate gender differences in WFC and how this might impinge on policy efforts that seek to enhance citizens' well-being.

BACKGROUND LITERATURE

There has been a veritable explosion of research on 'work–life balance' or 'work–family conflict' in the past couple of decades, and much of the literature deals with how policy differences across Europe affect people's work–life balance and associated well-being. These literatures can be divided into two main camps of substantive focus, although the two interlink. The first focus is on employment and working conditions. Many studies have been concerned with the way employment has been changing as a result of new processes of intensification and flexibilisation (Beck 2000; Burchell et al. 2002; Cappelli et al. 1997; Green and McIntosh 2001). It seems plausible that these developments have severe implications both for personal well-being and for the risks of WFC. There is now increasing evidence that this is indeed the case (Gallie and Russell 2009; Hildebrandt 2006). The second focus is on the changing nature of the family and the position of women, in particular. There are concerns about issues of gender equality; specifically in the way men and women divide paid and unpaid work (Harkness 2008; Kan and Gershuny 2010; Lewis 2008). Much of the focus has been on women's difficulties in combining full-time paid employment with motherhood (Crompton and Lyonette 2008; Fagan et al. 2008; McRae 2008). However, concerns that women's employment conflicts with care for frail elderly parents are also important for ageing societies.

In the 1990s the UK Economic and Social Research Council sponsored a research programme, the 'Future of Work'. A working paper by Taylor (2001) brought together insights into the future of work–life balance. This emphasised that a focus on the difficulties of balancing paid work and parental responsibilities is too narrow an approach for understanding the importance of the work–life debate. It urged that a broader discussion was needed looking more rigorously at the changing character of paid employment under the pressure it is facing from intensive business competition and technological innovation. Job intensification and increasing job insecurity were thought likely to have negative implications for well-being. Moreover, there was concern that this might be particularly marked in the UK, because, until recently, the UK lacked the kind of legally enforceable individual and collective rights at work enjoyed by our mainland European neighbours. Taylor cites the example of Nordic countries, where policies have tilted the so-called 'balance' between work and life towards the protection of the perceived interests of employees, while at the same time benefiting corporate performance.

Gallie and Russell (2009) took up the challenge of examining WFC and working conditions in Western Europe. They found that working conditions make a huge difference to WFC among married cohabiting employees across the same seven European countries that are examined in this chapter. They suggest that there is a clear Nordic effect for men. Perceived WFC is lowest in the Nordic countries where co-ordinated production regimes and social policies are more supportive of combining paid work and care demands. Paradoxically they found that for women 'raw' levels of WFC are particularly high in France, Denmark and Sweden, where supports for reconciling work and family life are good. In the case of France, they suggest that the high conflict is due to higher levels of family pressures associated with household composition. However, in Denmark and Sweden the high WFC among women appears to be associated with long work hours. Gallie and Russell (2009) found that when looking at seven Northern European countries combined, working conditions explained almost 30 per cent of the variance in WFC for both men and women, while 'family variables' explained less than 5 per cent of the variance. The fact that length of working hours, the prevalence of asocial working hours, the intensity of work and job insecurity all had strong negative effects for work–family conflict is not surprising. But what is surprising is their finding that working conditions accounted for much of the inter-country variation in WFC. This raises the question of whether their measures are overly work-centric and fail to capture the realities of gender-related conflicts between paid and unpaid work.

One important concern is how working mothers and fathers can rear their children while at the same time performing paid work effectively. Lewis (2008) argues that in the UK the balance between family and employment responsibilities was historically considered to be a private responsibility. This is not the case in some countries of Europe where gender equality enters the frame as a policy goal (see also Lewis, Chapter 8 in this volume). In Nordic countries in particular, policies have been based on the assumption that men and women will be fully engaged in the labour market. The Nordic model treats women as workers, but then makes allowance for difference by grafting on transfers and services in respect of care work for partnered and unpartnered mothers alike. Hobson (2004) has described the Swedish variant as a 'gender participation model' focusing as it does on promoting gender equality in employment and providing cash support for parental leave and services of childcare and the care of older adults. As a result of this 'supported adult worker model', high proportions of women work (long) part-time hours exercising their right to work a six-hour day when they have pre-school children. In many European countries including the UK, Germany and the Netherlands, part-time work remains the main way for women to reconcile work and family demands.

In recent decades, both in the UK and in other European countries, policies have explicitly been designed to raise employment participation among women. Thus for example, in Lisbon in March 2000 the heads of government of the European Union subscribed to the goal of raising the employment rate of women to 60 per cent by 2010 (Lewis et al. 2008). In the UK, the Netherlands and the Nordic countries the goal was already met by 2000 (Boeri et al. 2005), with France and Germany also close to the target in 2000. There have also been concerns that reduced fertility is problematic when the population is ageing. For example, Esping-Andersen (2009) noted that the quality of people's retirement years will depend on the productivity of increasingly small cohorts of workers. He goes on to suggest that, without any need of resort to feminist arguments, a rational utility model would point to a normative shift towards dual-career couples. He argues that in contemporary societies welfare systems should support a more gender equitable divide in paid and unpaid work. This would allow men and women to reconcile the competing demands they face as partners, parents and workers.

Boye (2009) studied how paid and unpaid work affects patterns of well-being in Europe. She found that while men's well-being appears to be unaffected by hours of paid work and housework, women's well-being increases with increased paid working hours and decreases with increased hours of housework. Gender differences in time spent on paid work and housework accounted for one-third of the European gender difference in well-being and helped to explain why women have lower well-being than men. In a more recent paper, Boye (2011) investigated whether associations between well-being and paid work and housework differed between European countries with different family policy models, and how this related to WFC.

Boye followed Korpi's (2000) typology of welfare state classification and differentiated three family models: dual-earner, traditional and market orientated. *Dual-earner models* are characterised by Scandinavian policies; these have strong support for female labour force participation as well as male participation in unpaid reproduction work in the family, but weaker support for women as homemakers. The *traditional family models* (found in France, Germany and Netherlands) have high levels of traditional family support and low levels of dual-earner support. The *market-orientated family model* is typical of the UK where reproduction work is allocated to the family or the market and 'choices' of how to combine family and employment are seen mainly as a private concern. Boye finds, counter-intuitively, that countries with the traditional family policies show the most positive association between women's well-being and paid work hours, although this association is concealed by WFC.

HYPOTHESES

From the literature, we derive ten hypotheses concerning the relationship between gender, paid and unpaid work, and well-being in Northern Europe. These are as follows:

H1. Full-time employed women will have higher WFC than employed men. This is because in the UK and other developed countries women still undertake the bulk of the housework. This 'second shift' phenomenon was first named by Hochschild (1989). While there is some evidence that the years since 1989 have seen some erosion of the gender gap in household labour, the overwhelming bulk of housework is still done by women (Kan and Gershuny 2010).

H2. Part-time employed women will have less WFC than full-time employed women as part-time work is often used to reconcile work and family demands.

H3. Gender patterns of well-being will be less pronounced than for WFC because the well-being measure does not tap directly gender inequalities in paid and unpaid work.

H4. WFC and well-being will be negatively correlated because high levels of conflict reduce well-being.

H5. Country differences in both WFC and well-being will remain strong even when individual characteristics and couple work strategies and family conditions are accounted for because the different welfare systems/family policies vary in their support for combining work and family life.

H6. Work conditions will be more important predictors than family conditions for the WFC of both men and women. Thus we expect to confirm Gallie and Russell's (2009) findings, even when couples' paid and unpaid work strategies across the life course are included in the models.

H7. Work and family factors will explain more of the variance in WFC than in well-being, because well-being is more individualistic. For example, health is an important predictor of well-being (Boye 2011).

H8. There will be gender differences in the way family life stage affects WFC and well-being. Mothers' are expected to display heightened WFC and lower levels of well-being relative to fathers' during the child-rearing phase, because women tend to remain the primary carer, regardless of their employment status.

H9. There will be gender differences in the way a couple's paid work strategies affect WFC and well-being. Boye's findings suggest that men's well-being will be unaffected by work hours, whereas work hours increase women's well-being (Boye 2011). This sounds plausible because work gives women an independence, which men may take for granted.

H10. We expect men's WFC and well-being to be more negatively affected than women's by a less traditional divide of unpaid housework. Theories of 'doing gender' (West and Zimmerman 1987) suggest that for women but not men to engage in housework is acting out what is seen as the 'essential nature' of male and female roles. Thus engaging in housework will have an adverse effect on the WFC and well-being of men, but not women.

DATA AND MEASURES

Our data are from the 'Family, work and well-being' module in the European Social Survey (ESS) (Jowell 2005), which was created for the second round of this cross-sectional survey conducted in 2004–05. Our main variables of interest – the questions relating to WFC – were only asked of people who were employed at the time of the survey, and we limit our sample to those of prime working age, aged 18 to 65. We restrict our sample to those in partnerships as we are particularly interested in the way heterosexual couples arrange paid and unpaid work within a household. We exclude same-sex partnerships as there was only a very small number of same-sex couples. We further restrict our sample to include only seven of the original 25 ESS countries, namely, Germany, France, the Netherlands, the UK, Denmark, Norway and Sweden. The survey's response rates in these countries were 65 per cent in Sweden; 66 per cent in Norway; 64 per cent in Denmark; 64 per cent in the Netherlands; 51 per cent in Germany; 51 per cent in the UK, and 44 per cent in France. In our analysis we use both design weights and population weights (for more details see European Social Survey 2004). The sample characteristics of variables in our analyses are shown in the Appendix, Table A7.1.

KEY VARIABLES

Work–Family Conflict

The ESS contains five indicators which measure various aspects of WFC (see Table A7.2, in the Appendix). These items are supposed to measure work-to-family conflict as well as family-to-work conflict. However, the wording of the items emphasise mostly paid work. Not surprisingly previous research has found that work–life conflict (or work–life balance) is most closely associated with paid work hours (for an overview see Pichler 2009). These five indicators are often lumped together into a composite measure of WFC. However, we chose to include only the first four items in our composite measure of WFC because the last item – which asks the respondent about their difficulty to concentrate on work because of family responsibilities – is rarely mentioned as being a problem. The responses to each item range from 'never' (coded as 1) to 'always' (coded as 5). Our composite measure of work–family conflict consists of the mean score of these first four items with values ranging from 1 to 5 (5 is the highest amount of work family conflict).

Table 7.1   Paid work strategies

Paid work hours strategy:	His weekly hours	Her weekly hours
Dual earner	30 or more	30 or more
Male breadwinner	Only male works	0
Modified male breadwinner	More than female	Less than 30 hours
Female breadwinner	Less hours than female	More hours than male

Well-being (WHO-5)

We also consider a further measure of psychological well-being which is less work-centric than WFC. This variable is a composite measure representing the mean of five items, which are often referred to as the WHO-5 well-being index (Bech 1998). The WHO-5 well-being index is constructed to measure positive well-being such as positive mood, vitality and general interests (Psychiatric Research Unit 2008). The five items comprising the measure are reverse coded from the original, ranging from 1 (at no time) to 6 (all of the time). Our composite measure of well-being consists of the mean score of these five items with values ranging from 1 to 6 such that a high score reflects high well-being (Appendix, Table A7.3).

Paid Work Strategies

We are particularly interested in whether couples' division of work significantly affects their perceived WFC. We define four distinct paid work strategies which are derived from the male and female partners' usual weekly hours of work. A couple in which both partners work 30 hours or more per week is classified as a 'dual earner' couple. 'Modified male breadwinner' couples consist of a female partner who works part time at less than 30 hours per week, and a male who works more hours than the female partner. If the female partner does not do any paid work, the couple is denoted as a 'male breadwinner' couple. Couples in which the female partner works more weekly hours than the male partner are 'female breadwinner' couples. Table 7.1 summarises our paid work strategies.

Unpaid Work Division

Individual male and female respondents (not living together) were asked how many hours a week are usually spent on activities such as cooking, washing, cleaning, shopping and maintenance of property (but not including childcare) by members of the household. This question is followed by the respondent's assessment of what proportion of this time is spent on housework by the respondent him/herself and his/her partner. The six response categories range from 'None or almost none' to 'All or nearly all of the time'. We derive from these questions whether the division of unpaid labour in a household is 'balanced', 'mostly male', 'mostly female' or whether housework is done primarily by 'others'. However, this measure is not very precise and respondents tend to overestimate their own contribution to unpaid work within a household. While most male respondents state that the housework is done mostly by their female partner, male are still more likely than female partners to state that the division of housework is balanced or largely done by the male partner. (Our data do not allow us to compare or reconcile potential differences in male or female partners' views about their respective shares of unpaid work since we only have data on one partner's views.)

Family Life Course

Our family life course variable has four categories – younger couples (where the woman is aged under 45) with no dependent children; couples with children under 5; couples with children 5 to 18; older couples (with women aged 45 or over) with no dependent children.

In addition to these key variables our multivariate analysis, which we report in the final part of our results section, includes measures of household income (quintiles). We include several measures about the respondents only, including their years of full-time education, log work hours, unsocial hours and task discretion. The unsocial hours index combines three questions that tap the frequency of weekend work, evening work and overtime, which are combined to form a scale of 1 to 5 where 1 represents those who never engage in these three activities and 5 represents participation in all three on a weekly basis. Task discretion is measured by a question which asks people how much 'the management at your work allows you: (1) to decide how your daily work is organised, (2) to influence policy decisions about the activities of the organisation and (3) to choose or change your pace of work'. The resulting index is a scale of zero to 10 with zero no influence and 10 complete control.

Our analytical strategy is to first examine the bivariate associations between WFC, gender and work status in the seven countries. We then examine, for descriptive purposes, country differences in the way family life stage and dual-earner work status are related. We also examine the relationship between WFC and well-being across countries and by gender. This initial section on work status, family life course and gender allows us to address the first four hypotheses. The remaining six hypotheses require multivariate regression analyses of WFC and well-being. For each, we introduce three models: model 1 examines country differences only; model 2 includes both country and family variables, along with gender, age, education and household income; and model 3 adds in characteristics of employment along with gender interactions for family life course, couples' paid work strategies and unpaid work division.

WORK STATUS, FAMILY LIFE COURSE AND GENDER

In Figure 7.1 we can see the mean scores of WFC by gender and work status across each country among this sample of employed men and women, aged 18–65 living in heterosexual partnerships. Contrary to our expectations in Hypothesis 1, which derived from the 'double shift' ideas of Hochschild (1989), the difference in WFC between women who work full-time and men is very small. (We do not differentiate in this bivari-ate analysis between full-time and part-time work for men, because the vast majority of employed men have full-time jobs). In accordance with Hypothesis 2, we find that women who work part-time have significantly

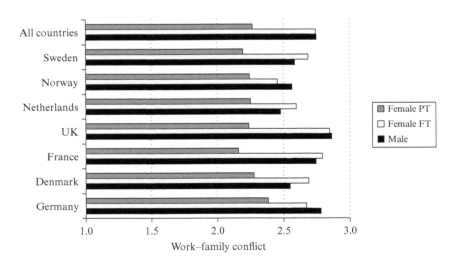

Figure 7.1   Work–family conflict by country, work status and gender

Table 7.2   Percentage reporting division of unpaid work by paid work strategy for all seven countries

Paid work strategy	Unpaid work strategy				
	Balanced	Mostly female	Mostly male	Other	Total per cent
Dual earners	19.62	68.37	8.62	3.39	100
Male breadwinner	4.97	88.10	4.14	2.79	100
Modified male breadwinner	9.21	84.82	3.56	2.42	100
Female breadwinner	15.12	57.45	22.44	4.99	100
Total	14.30	74.67	7.84	3.19	100

lower WFC than women who are in full-time employment (all countries $p < 0.000$, except Norway $p < 0.026$).

So what of this 'double shift' theory? In our data, as Table 7.2 shows for the seven countries combined, women do the bulk of the unpaid work, regardless of the couple's paid-work strategy. It is not surprising that housework is done by 'mostly female' in three-quarters of our couple households. Perhaps more surprising is that outsourcing most of domestic labour is so rare – approximately 3 per cent in total. Our definition of unpaid work includes cooking and shopping which are probably less frequently outsourced than cleaning, which is also included. It may also be the case that domestic labour is viewed as too expensive or too intrusive by most. The reports of a 'balanced' division of housework are quite high – including one in five of our dual-earner couple households.

Table 7.3 shows the percentage of dual-earner couples by family life-course stage for each of the seven countries and for all countries combined. In all countries combined across all stages of the family life course 50 per cent are dual-earner couples. This percentage rises to over 72 per cent for younger couples without children. The dual-earner model is most common in Sweden (73 per cent) and Denmark (75 per cent of all couples) and least common in the Netherlands (30 per cent). It is clear from Table 7.3 that most women work full-time before having children and many women cut back on their paid work hours or drop out of the labour force altogether when they have children. However, family paid-work strategies vary considerably across countries. In Denmark and Sweden over three-quarters of couples with young children are dual-earner couples, compared with approximately 20 per cent in Germany and the Netherlands. France has relatively high maternal employment with dual earners making

Table 7.3   Percentage of dual earners couples by family life stage for the seven countries

Countries	Before children	Children <5	Children 5–18	Older couples	All
Germany	57.38	21.15	43.64	44.06	42.65
Denmark	73.85	75.45	82.80	65.70	74.67
France	83.08	65.38	63.89	51.88	63.49
UK	79.44	27.58	36.56	41.19	43.77
Netherlands	68.66	18.89	20.06	23.71	29.92
Norway	65.96	58.94	61.45	54.66	59.28
Sweden	73.74	74.03	77.65	66.37	72.95
All countries	72.03	42.23	49.36	45.57	50.35

up 65 per cent of couples with young children. In the UK the equivalent is 28 per cent.

The high proportion of dual earners among couples in the child-rearing years in Sweden and Denmark is as we would expect. The Nordic countries' public provision of childcare is very high for under-3-year-olds, due to the assumption that childcare is a legal right of every child (De Henau et al. 2008). Interestingly, France shows a much higher proportion of dual-earner couples with children than would be expected of a country classified as following the traditional family model (Boye 2011). This classification needs updating as there is relatively good state provision for childcare in France (Gallie and Russell 2009). In the Netherlands, the UK and Germany, dual-earner families are rare when children are young. In Germany mothers are expected to care for infants (De Henau et al. 2008), whereas in the UK childcare provision remains mostly private and relatively expensive (Schober and Scott, forthcoming).

Figure 7.2 shows, confirming Hypothesis 3, that the gender differentiation of well-being is much less marked than for WFC across all countries. The striking finding from this figure is the relatively low well-being of UK men and women, compared with the other six countries. This is something we return to in our multivariate analysis.

ASSOCIATION OF WFC AND WELL-BEING

Hypothesis 4 suggested that WFC and well-being would be negatively correlated and this is indeed the case as we can see in Table 7.4. The correlation is strongest in Denmark and weakest in France, with the UK

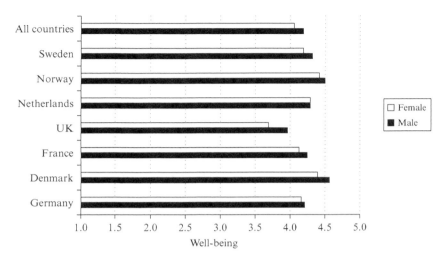

Figure 7.2   Well-being by country and gender

Table 7.4   Correlations between work–family conflict and well-being measures

	Correlation		
	All	Male	Female
Germany	−0.284***	−0.330***	−0.249***
Denmark	−0.424***	−0.459***	−0.373***
France	−0.217***	−0.265***	−0.177**
UK	−0.251***	−0.329***	−0.231***
Netherlands	−0.288***	−0.336***	−0.223**
Norway	−0.270***	−0.251***	−0.319***
Sweden	−0.318***	−0.341***	−0.289***
All	−0.265***	−0.324***	−0.221***

Note: * p < 0.05, ** p < 0.01, *** p < 0.001.

neither strong nor weak. Possibly a relative absence of 'Protestant work ethic' in France may contribute to this pattern, but the country differences are not large. In all countries the correlation is stronger for men than for women, except in Norway (where the gender pattern is reversed). The gender difference is more pronounced in the UK, France, Germany and the Netherlands, and somewhat less marked in Sweden and Denmark.

This is not surprising given the strong support in Scandinavian countries for the citizen worker model.

MULTIVARIATE REGRESSION ANALYSIS OF WFC AND WELL-BEING

Tables 7.5a–c show three different regression models for WFC and well-being for both genders combined (Table 7.5a) and men and women separately (Tables 7.5b and 7.5c). The country differences are shown in model 1; family variables along with gender, age, education and household income are added to country dummy variables in model 2; characteristics of employment are added in, along with gender interaction effects with couples' paid work strategy, unpaid work division, and family life-course stages in model 3. The reference categories are the UK for country differences; dual-earner couples for paid work strategies (see Table 7.1 for definition); balanced housework for the division of unpaid work; and women under 45 without children for family life course.

WORK FAMILY CONFLICT AND WELL-BEING

Our fifth hypothesis predicted that country differences in both WFC and well-being will remain strong even after controlling for other differences; controls include individual characteristics, couple work strategies, and family and employment conditions, because the different welfare systems/family policies vary in their support for combining work and family life. It can be seen in model 1 in Table 7.5a that the Netherlands, Norway, Sweden and Denmark have significantly lower WFC than the UK (the omitted category). In Table 7.5b, which shows men only, we can see that men in all other countries have lower WFC than UK men. Table 7.5c shows this country pattern is not the same for women, as only Dutch women have less WFC than UK women. However, this difference between the Netherlands and the UK disappears in model 3, once employment conditions are accounted for. In addition, once employment conditions are controlled, WFC is not significantly different between France and the UK, for either men or women. Despite the overall country patterns differing across models, the Netherlands and Scandinavian countries have consistently lower WFC than the UK for both women and men.

A similar picture emerges as we examine psychological well-being. The highest well-being levels are found in Denmark, Norway, Sweden and the Netherlands. The UK is by far the lowest – significantly lower than any

Table 7.5a   OLS regressions, both genders

	Work–family conflict			Well-being		
	Model 1 Countries only	Model 2 Family variables	Model 3 Full model	Model 1 Countries only	Model 2 Family variables	Model 3 Full model
Denmark	-0.146*	-0.269***	-0.258***	0.652***	0.656***	0.649***
	(-2.11)	(-3.93)	(-4.16)	(8.62)	(8.59)	(8.50)
France	-0.032	-0.063*	-0.009	0.358***	0.375***	0.370***
	(-0.99)	(-1.97)	(-0.31)	(10.26)	(10.52)	(10.30)
Germany	-0.049	-0.118***	-0.127***	0.356***	0.380***	0.389***
	(-1.60)	(-3.80)	(-4.48)	(10.59)	(10.92)	(11.17)
Netherlands	-0.297***	-0.288***	-0.218***	0.457***	0.481***	0.480***
	(-6.37)	(-6.24)	(-5.20)	(8.95)	(9.33)	(9.29)
Norway	-0.252***	-0.331***	-0.350***	0.625***	0.651***	0.639***
	(-3.65)	(-4.87)	(-5.67)	(8.28)	(8.56)	(8.40)
Sweden	-0.152**	-0.207***	-0.213***	0.427***	0.413***	0.401***
	(-2.82)	(-3.89)	(-4.40)	(7.26)	(6.93)	(6.73)
Age		0.003	0.004*		-0.001	-0.002
		(1.35)	(2.24)		(-0.69)	(-0.92)
Female		-0.171***	0.091		-0.120***	-0.123
		(-6.61)	(1.31)		(-4.14)	(-1.43)
Income quintiles		0.022*	0.002		0.052***	0.046***
		(2.11)	(0.23)		(4.38)	(3.82)
Years of full-time education		0.043***	0.035***		-0.008	-0.010*
		(11.33)	(10.00)		(-1.89)	(-2.40)
Male breadwinner		-0.117**	-0.067		-0.013	0.002
		(-3.20)	(-1.89)		(-0.33)	(0.05)

189

Table 7.5a (continued)

	Work–family conflict			Well-being		
	Model 1 Countries only	Model 2 Family variables	Model 3 Full model	Model 1 Countries only	Model 2 Family variables	Model 3 Full model
Modified male breadwinner		−0.249*** (−8.51)	−0.037 (−1.01)		−0.054 (−1.64)	−0.051 (−1.13)
Female breadwinner		−0.015 (−0.34)	0.009 (0.09)		−0.109* (−2.19)	0.168 (1.31)
Mostly female		0.128*** (3.84)	0.160*** (4.03)		−0.097** (−2.60)	−0.150** (−3.06)
Mostly male		0.047 (0.95)	0.044 (0.75)		−0.078 (−1.39)	−0.061 (−0.85)
Outside help		0.002 (0.03)	0.056 (0.60)		−0.216** (−2.78)	−0.345** (−3.01)
Couples with children under 5		0.050 (1.26)	0.012 (0.25)		−0.039 (−0.88)	−0.029 (−0.48)
Couples with children 5–18		0.019 (0.47)	−0.038 (−0.82)		0.020 (0.46)	0.028 (0.49)
Older couples (women over 44) with no dep children		−0.036 (−0.68)	−0.054 (−0.96)		0.080 (1.36)	0.162* (2.33)
Mod male breadwinner × female			0.030 (0.50)			0.065 (0.90)
Female breadwinner × female			0.096 (0.87)			−0.254 (−1.86)

	(1)	(2)	(3)	(4)	(5)
Mostly female × female			-0.161**		0.116
			(-2.66)		(1.55)
Mostly male × female			-0.011		-0.052
			(-0.12)		(-0.45)
Mostly outside help × female			-0.020		0.273
			(-0.15)		(1.75)
Couples with child under 5 × female			0.169*		-0.015
			(2.37)		(-0.17)
Couples with child 5–18 × female			0.163*		-0.016
			(2.57)		(-0.21)
Older couples × female			0.158*		-0.162*
			(2.47)		(-2.06)
Log work hours			0.537***		0.094
			(12.74)		(1.82)
Unsocial hours index			0.204***		0.000
			(21.59)		(0.04)
Task discretion index			0.014***		0.018***
			(3.35)		(3.54)
Constant	2.748***	2.083***	-0.580***	3.958***	3.550***
	(122.43)	(23.24)	(-3.37)	(39.49)	(16.71)
r^2	0.0108	0.0690	0.2380	0.0563	0.0628
Weighted N	5151	5151	5151	5151	5151

Notes:
Ref.: UK, Dual earner, balanced, no children.
* $p < 0.05$, ** $p < 0.01$, *** $p < 0.001$.

Table 7.5b   OLS regressions, only men

	Work–family conflict			Well-being		
	Model 1 Countries only	Model 2 Family variables	Model 3 Full model	Model 1 Countries only	Model 2 Family variables	Model 3 Full model
Denmark	−0.318***	−0.371***	−0.301***	0.612***	0.629***	0.629***
	(−3.43)	(−4.06)	(−3.56)	(6.13)	(6.24)	(6.22)
France	−0.123**	−0.118**	−0.013	0.299***	0.307***	0.313***
	(−2.85)	(−2.75)	(−0.32)	(6.45)	(6.50)	(6.56)
Germany	−0.082*	−0.152***	−0.139***	0.254***	0.300***	0.299***
	(−2.03)	(−3.71)	(−3.66)	(5.85)	(6.60)	(6.58)
Netherlands	−0.388***	−0.425***	−0.310***	0.336***	0.369***	0.372***
	(−6.34)	(−7.02)	(−5.49)	(5.10)	(5.52)	(5.52)
Norway	−0.304***	−0.335***	−0.314***	0.539***	0.576***	0.571***
	(−3.39)	(−3.80)	(−3.84)	(5.57)	(5.92)	(5.84)
Sweden	−0.278***	−0.251***	−0.220***	0.361***	0.336***	0.333***
	(−3.94)	(−3.59)	(−3.39)	(4.75)	(4.34)	(4.29)
Age		0.004	0.005*		−0.003	−0.003
		(1.55)	(2.48)		(−1.03)	(−1.09)
Income quintiles		0.039**	0.009		0.047**	0.041**
		(2.86)	(0.66)		(3.11)	(2.67)
Years of full-time education		0.035***	0.033***		−0.014**	−0.015**
		(7.30)	(7.28)		(−2.71)	(−2.81)
Male breadwinner		−0.077*	−0.051		−0.010	−0.004
		(−1.98)	(−1.43)		(−0.24)	(−0.09)
Modified male breadwinner		−0.024	−0.023		−0.044	−0.043
		(−0.61)	(−0.63)		(−0.99)	(−0.97)

192

	(1)	(2)	(3)	(4)
Female breadwinner	-0.690***	0.070	0.034	0.167
	(-6.56)	(0.62)	(0.29)	(1.24)
Mostly female	0.253***	0.162***	-0.134**	-0.145**
	(5.90)	(4.05)	(-2.83)	(-3.05)
Mostly male	0.113	0.050	-0.059	-0.064
	(1.80)	(0.87)	(-0.86)	(-0.92)
Outside help	0.076	0.055	-0.341**	-0.339**
	(0.76)	(0.60)	(-3.09)	(-3.07)
Couples with children under 5	0.009	0.010	-0.028	-0.025
	(0.17)	(0.20)	(-0.48)	(-0.43)
Couples with children 5–18	-0.011	-0.063	0.046	0.039
	(-0.21)	(-1.31)	(0.79)	(0.67)
Older couples (women over 44) with no dep children	-0.126	-0.103	0.187*	0.188*
	(-1.87)	(-1.65)	(2.51)	(2.53)
Log work hours		0.626***		
		(9.28)		
Unsocial hours index		0.168***		
		(12.77)		
Task discretion index		0.019**		
		(3.24)		
Constant	2.871***	-0.883***	4.149***	3.651***
	(96.17)	(-3.40)	(33.63)	(11.75)
r^2	0.0207	0.2197	0.0489	0.0511
N	2809	2809	2809	2809

Notes:
Ref.: UK, Dual earner, balanced, no children.
$p < 0.05$, ** $p < 0.01$, *** $p < 0.001$.

Table 7.5c OLS regressions, only women

	Work–family conflict			Well-being		
	Model 1 Countries only	Model 2 Family variables	Model 3 Full model	Model 1 Countries only	Model 2 Family variables	Model 3 Full model
Denmark	0.051	−0.187	−0.216*	0.702***	0.688***	0.669***
	(0.50)	(−1.87)	(−2.36)	(6.14)	(5.91)	(5.75)
France	0.079	−0.043	−0.010	0.435***	0.444***	0.431***
	(1.67)	(−0.91)	(−0.24)	(8.29)	(8.16)	(7.92)
Germany	−0.029	−0.118*	−0.120**	0.471***	0.487***	0.502***
	(−0.63)	(−2.54)	(−2.84)	(8.99)	(9.02)	(9.30)
Netherlands	−0.195**	−0.157*	−0.115	0.598***	0.615***	0.614***
	(−2.74)	(−2.29)	(−1.83)	(7.52)	(7.68)	(7.67)
Norway	−0.204	−0.341***	−0.402***	0.721***	0.737***	0.716***
	(−1.91)	(−3.31)	(−4.26)	(6.06)	(6.13)	(5.96)
Sweden	−0.004	−0.146	−0.208**	0.498***	0.496***	0.479***
	(−0.05)	(−1.85)	(−2.86)	(5.47)	(5.36)	(5.18)
Age		0.000	0.001		0.001	−0.000
		(0.14)	(0.35)		(0.39)	(−0.03)
Income quintiles		0.009	−0.008		0.054**	0.048**
		(0.54)	(−0.51)		(2.91)	(2.58)
Years of full-time education		0.048***	0.038***		0.002	−0.000
		(8.00)	(6.84)		(0.33)	(−0.07)
Modified male breadwinner		−0.467***	−0.031		−0.051	0.004
		(−11.12)	(−0.57)		(−1.03)	(0.05)
Female breadwinner		0.013	0.097*		−0.104	−0.088
		(0.26)	(2.04)		(−1.73)	(−1.45)

	(1)	(2)	(3)	(4)	(5)	(6)
Mostly female		−0.025 (−0.48)		0.011 (0.23)	−0.035 (−0.59)	−0.026 (−0.44)
Mostly male		0.029 (0.37)		0.042 (0.58)	−0.116 (−1.25)	−0.108 (−1.16)
Outside help		−0.088 (−0.93)		0.057 (0.65)	−0.078 (−0.70)	−0.054 (−0.48)
Couples with children under 5		0.130* (2.21)		0.198*** (3.70)	−0.052 (−0.76)	−0.051 (−0.74)
Couples with children 5–18		0.104 (1.70)		0.174** (3.11)	−0.011 (−0.16)	−0.000 (−0.01)
Older couples (women over 44) with no dep children		0.116 (1.41)		0.184** (2.44)	−0.055 (−0.57)	−0.026 (−0.27)
Log work hours				0.498*** (9.15)		0.072 (1.04)
Unsocial hours index				0.238*** (17.04)		−0.007 (−0.40)
Task discretion index				0.010 (1.71)		0.029*** (3.67)
Constant	2.606*** (77.60)	2.037*** (14.83)	3.694*** (98.62)	−0.362 (−1.58)	3.513*** (21.91)	3.187*** (10.90)
r^2	0.0087	0.1047	0.0566	0.2528	0.0660	0.0721
N	2342	2342	2342	2342	2342	2342

195

Notes:
Ref.: UK, Dual earner, balanced, no children.
* $p < 0.05$, ** $p < 0.01$, *** $p < 0.001$.

of the other six nations, including France and Germany. This holds true for both men and women, across all three models. In all countries, except Sweden and Denmark, the country differences become even more pronounced in models 2 and 3 when family circumstances and employment are accounted for.

Hypothesis 6 suggested that work conditions would be more important predictors than family conditions for the WFC of both men and women. This is indeed the case. If we look at the explained variance (r^2) we can see that for our total sample combined (Table 7.5a), once employment conditions are introduced in model 3, we explain 23 per cent of the variance in WFC, as compared to only 6 per cent explained by family conditions (model 2) and less than 2 per cent by country differences alone (model 1). The pattern is similar for both men (Table 7.5b) and women (Table 7.5c). Thus we can confirm Gallie and Russell's (2009) findings about the relative importance of employment conditions, even after couples' paid and unpaid work strategies and family life-course stage are included in the models.

Hypothesis 7 suggested that work and family factors would explain more of the variance in WFC than in well-being, because well-being is more individualistic. This is also confirmed. Again looking at the explained variance (r^2), we can see that for the combined sample (Table 7.5a) all three models for psychological well-being explain less than 4 per cent of the variance. The models do marginally better when broken down by gender (explaining up to 5 per cent of the variance for men and 7 per cent for women). However, compared with WFC, the explanatory power of these family and employment variables is slight. This is not surprising, as psychological well-being is likely to be far more closely linked to individual factors such as subjective health (Boye 2011).

Hypothesis 8 suggested that there would be gender differences in the way family life stage affects WFC and well-being. Mothers' WFC is expected to be heightened and well-being reduced relative to that of fathers during the child-rearing phase, because women tend to remain the primary carer, regardless of their employment status. If we look at the gender interaction effects of family life stage, we see that women's but not men's WFC increases after they have children. The same is not true however for psychological well-being. The well-being of men, but not that of women, is enhanced for older couples without dependent children, where children have likely left the home. Perhaps mothers, because they are primary carers, suffer 'the empty nest syndrome' in ways that fathers do not.

Hypothesis 9 suggested that there would be gender differences in the way a couple's paid work strategies affect WFC and well-being. Compared with dual-earner couples, WFC is lower for men in male breadwinner households and for women in modified male breadwinner households. However, both of these effects disappear when accounting for employment conditions that include work hours (model 3). Long work hours increase the WFC for both men and for women. The same is not true for psychological well-being. Here work hours have no discernable effect for either men or women. In terms of other employment conditions there are some interesting findings. Unsocial hours, as might be expected, increase the WFC of both men and women. However, counter-intuitively, task discretion also increases WFC, but only for men. This might be because the WFC measure includes a question about 'how often your partner/ family gets fed up with the pressure of your job'. Family disapproval of men spending long hours at work may intensify when their task discretion is high. For both men and women, task discretion significantly increases psychological well-being (p <0.001). This is not surprising because task-discretion is likely to boost a person's self-esteem and sense of control which in turn heightens well-being.

According to Hypothesis 10, we would expect men's WFC and well-being to be more negatively affected than women's by a less traditional divide of unpaid housework. Engaging in housework may be more demeaning for men than for women. The findings indicate that our expectation is completely wrong. Men's but not women's WFC is increased when couples adopt a 'mostly female' division of unpaid labour compared to a 'balanced' division of household labour. This average increase in men's WFC ranges from 0.128 (Table 7.5a, model 2) to 0.16 points (Table 7.5a, model 3) on our WFC scale (which ranges from 1 to 5). The same gender pattern is found for psychological well-being. The well-being of men is significantly reduced when the housework is done mainly by women, but this is not the case for women. For well-being, the gender interaction term is not significant, but for WFC it is significant (p <0.01).

This unexpected finding may reflect partners' dissatisfaction with the pressures of men's jobs. Men who leave the chores to women may be subject to more complaints than are men who do their share of home chores. We consider other possible explanations in the concluding section which discusses our findings in more detail and draws out possible policy implications. First however, we briefly review the other findings from our multivariate analyses that are not related to our hypotheses.

In Table 7.5a, model 2, we see that being female reduces both WFC and well-being, but this gender effect disappears once work indicators are introduced in model 3. Older people experience more WFC (p <.05) once work hours and employment conditions are included (Table 7.5a, model 3), although this only applies to men, not to women (Tables 7.5b and 7.5c). Age has no effect on psychological well-being for this sample of working couples. Years of education are positively related to WFC for men and women combined (Table 7.5a) and for men and women separately (Tables 7.5b and 7.5c). This may reflect the higher ambitions that are associated with higher education and the gap between aspirations and reality may lead to greater conflicts for more educated men and women. Oddly, income increases WFC in model 2, but this disappears when employment is controlled in model 3. However, higher levels of income markedly increase the psychological well-being, for men and women.

SUMMARY, DISCUSSION AND CONCLUSIONS

In this chapter, one particular focus has been on how the experiences of WFC and well-being are gendered in ways that reflect, in part, the gendered division of paid and unpaid work in Northern Europe. We also wanted to explore whether WFC and well-being vary between seven countries with very different family policies, particularly in terms of their support for maternal employment and for a more equitable share of family work between men and women.

Our study is set against a background of family change. We note that family life has changed markedly from the traditional male breadwinner family of the past and that the rise of dual-earner couples implies both an ideological and pragmatic move towards less gender-role specialisation. However, we also note that there has been a structural and cultural lag in terms of gender role change, with women still doing the bulk of the housework and unpaid family care. We concur with Esping-Andersen (2009) that there has been an 'incomplete revolution in gender roles' and we tested ten hypotheses concerning the way the divisions of paid and unpaid work among couples relate to each partner's experience of WFC and well-being.

Six of our hypotheses were confirmed by our data, one hypothesis was partially confirmed and partially refuted, and three were not supported. Hypotheses that were confirmed included that women who work part-time have markedly lower WFC than women who are in full-time employment (H2). We also found that well-being is less gender differentiated than WFC (H3) and that WFC and well-being are negatively correlated (H4). In addition, we confirmed the Gallie and Russell (2009) finding that work conditions are more important predictors than family conditions for both men and women (H6). Also, work and family factors explain more of the variance in WFC than in well-being (H7).

We confirmed that country differences in both WFC and well-being remain even when individual characteristics, couple work strategies, family life stage and employment conditions are accounted for (H5). However, this finding went well beyond our expectations. It is not at all surprising that the UK comes out significantly higher than Scandinavian countries for WFC, given how much support Scandinavian countries provide in terms of high-quality childcare and generous parental leave, argued to reduce WFC. However, what is surprising is that the UK is significantly worse than other countries for the more general well-being measure (WHO-5). Moreover, our analysis shows that this relatively dismal UK well-being result remains after controlling for differences in gendered patterns of paid and unpaid work. Undoubtedly, this measure is likely to be strongly influenced by individual factors not investigated here, such as physical and subjective health. However, the fact that UK citizens (both men and women) in our sample have significantly less positive psychological well-being than equivalent couples in the other six Northern European countries is something that merits further investigation.

The hypothesis which was only partially confirmed suggested there would be gender differences in the way family life-course stage affects WFC and well-being (H8). Women's WFC was indeed increased after they had children, compared with when they were younger and without children. Moreover, the effect of family life-course variables only enhanced the WFC of women not men. However, family life course had the reverse gender effect in terms of influencing psychological well-being, enhancing men's but not women's well-being.

The three hypotheses that were not supported are in many ways the most interesting findings. Contrary to our expectations derived from the theories of the 'double shift' we expected women who worked full-time to have more conflict than men (H1). While we found clear evidence that regardless of paid work strategy, women remain primarily responsible for unpaid work, we also found that women in full-time employment had very similar levels of WFC to that of men. Our expectation, following the research by Boye (2011), that men's well-being is unaffected by work hours, whereas work hours benefit women's well-being (H9) was not supported by our data. We found that long work hours affected the WFC of men and women in similar ways. Also, work hours did not affect the psychological well-being of either men or women in our sample. In addition, couple's paid work strategies did not affect the WFC or well-being of men or women, once employment conditions were accounted for.

This lack of a gendered effect of paid work strategies on WFC and well-being makes it even more surprising that the division of unpaid work does affect men's, but not women's, WFC and well-being. Our expectation that men's well-being would be more negatively affected than women's by a less traditional divide of unpaid work (H10) was overturned. It may be that women accept their 'double shift' as a fact of life and therefore do not show the same reduction in WFC or increased well-being as men when the gender division of housework is less traditional (that is, not mainly female).

What is particularly interesting, however, is the way that Northern European men's WFC increases when the female partner is doing most of the unpaid chores. The perceived conflict may result from the dissonance of practice being at odds with normative gender equality beliefs. Or it may be that men's heightened WFC reflects their partners' dissatisfactions. Gershuny et al. (2005) suggest that women could adapt to changing employment patterns in one of three different ways: exit, voice and suffering. The three strategies concern stark choices: exiting from their marriage or quitting their job; expressing dissatisfaction to their husband or partner and pressing for a more equitable division of domestic labour; or suffering their 'second shift' of doing both their paid job and the bulk of the unpaid household chores. Few women would see the extreme option of quitting their marriage or their job as feasible or desirable. Our data provide some evidence that women combine the second and third strategies. The bulk of the household chores are done mainly by women, even in dual-earner couples. However, perhaps one reason that men feel increased WFC when the housework is done mainly by women is that their partner complains. It is also plausible that some men want a more equitable role in the home and their well-being is reduced when the pressure of their job gets in the way. It certainly bodes well for more equitable gender role change in Northern Europe when men's WFC is increased and their well-being is reduced when the housework is left mainly to women.

No country in our sample has reached a position of gender equality. However, our findings are reinforcing other research that suggests that we need to pay closer attention to the gender division of unpaid work in order to examine how changes in family life and employment impinge on well-being. In a recent study based on analysis of the British cohort studies, Sigle-Rushton (2010) found that in the UK a more equitable divide of housework offsets the enhanced risk of divorce associated with female employment. Our study points to wider benefits for men who do their fair share of the housework. Change is slow and, on average, men still play a somewhat minimal role in unpaid domestic labour. However, men today play a far greater role in home and childcare than did their fathers or grandfathers. It might help change move faster if the benefits of a more equitable divide became more widely known.

Can policies help nudge men and women towards greater gender equality in paid and unpaid work? This is a thorny issue and one that has been discussed elsewhere (for example, Dex 2010; Scott and Dex 2009). These authors conclude that the political will is often lacking for the radical steps that would reduce gender inequalities in the division of labour. However, in our view, token and symbolic gestures do matter and state encouragement towards greater male participation in unpaid work could help advance gender convergence. The UK Equality and Human Rights Commission (2009) has also urged reform of policies that perpetuate the traditional gender role division of labour and leave women doing the bulk of family care and prevent men from doing a more equitable share of parenting. The report argued the social and economic benefits of integrating work and care. It called for more financial support for paternity and parental leave and more affordable childcare. In the UK, political rhetoric is supportive, but actions to eradicate the economic inequalities that underpin the traditional gender divide of paid and unpaid labour are less forthcoming. Yet the logic of addressing the inequalities that arise from what Esping-Andersen (2009) calls the 'incomplete revolution' gets stronger as couples aspire to share work and parenting across the life course. By demonstrating that gender equality in paid and unpaid work is associated with enhanced well-being, our study hopes to strengthen the cumulative evidence about potential costs of not tackling the pronounced gender inequalities in employment and family care.

ACKNOWLEDGEMENTS

This work was supported by a grant by the Economic and Social Research Council (RES-225-25-1001). Anke Plagnol is grateful for financial support from the Leverhulme Trust through an Early Career Fellowship and the Isaac Newton Trust, Cambridge.

REFERENCES

Bech, P. (1998), *Quality of Life in the Psychiatric Patient*, London: Mosby-Wolfe.
Beck, U. (2000), *The Brave New World of Work*, Cambridge: Polity Press.
Boeri, T., D. Del Boca and C. Pissarides (eds) (2005), *Women at Work: An Economic Perspective*, Oxford: Oxford University Press.
Boye, K. (2009), 'Relatively different? How do gender differences in well-being depend on paid and unpaid work in Europe?', *Social Indicators Research*, **93**, 509–25.
Boye, K. (2011), 'Work and well-being in a comparative perspective – the role of family policy', *European Sociological Review*, **27** (1), 16–30.
Burchell, B., D. Lapido and F. Wilkinson (2002), *Job Insecurity and Work Intensification*, London: London.

Cappelli, P., L. Bassi, H. Katz, D. Knoke, P. Osterman and M. Unseem (1997), *Change at Work*, Oxford: Oxford University Press.

Crompton, R. and C. Lyonette (2008), 'Mothers' employment, work-life conflict, careers and class', in J. Scott, S. Dex and H. Joshi (eds), *Women and Employment: Changing Lives and New Challenges*, Cheltenham, UK and Northampton, MA, USA: Edward Elgar.

De Henau, J., D. Meulders and S. O'Dorchai (eds) (2008), *Making Time for Working Parents. Comparing Public Childcare Provision across EU-15*, Cambridge: Cambridge University Press.

Dex, S. (2010), 'Can state policies produce equality in housework?', in J. Treas and S. Drobnic (eds), *Dividing the Domestic: Men, Women, and Housework in Cross-National Perspective*, Stanford, CA: Stanford University Press, pp. 79–104.

Equality and Human Rights Commission (2009), 'Working better: meeting the changing needs of families, workers and employers in the 21st century', available at: http://www.equalityhumanrights.com/uploaded_files/working_better_final_pdf_250309.pdf (accessed 6 July 2011).

Esping-Andersen, G. (2009), *The Incomplete Revolution: Adapting Welfare States to Women's New Roles*, Cambridge: Polity Press.

European Social Survey (2004), 'Weighting European Social Survey data', available at: http://ess.nsd.uib.no/streamer/?module=main&year=2005&country= null & download = % 5CSurvey + documentation % 5C2005 % 5C06 %23ESS2+-+Weighting+ESS+Data%5CLanguages%5CEnglish%5CWeightingESS.pdf (accessed April 2011).

Fagan, C., L. McDowell, D. Perrons, K. Ray and K. Ward (2008), 'Class differences in mothers' work schedules and assessments of their work-life balance in dual-earner couples in Britain', in J. Scott, S. Dex and H. Joshi (eds), *Women and Employment: Changing Lives and New Challenges*, Cheltenham, UK and Northampton, MA, USA: Edward Elgar.

Fraser, N. (1994), 'After the family wage: gender equity and the welfare state', *Political Theory*, **22** (4), 591–618.

Gallie, D. and H. Russell (2009), 'Work-family conflict and working conditions in Western Europe', *Social Indicators Research*, **93** (3), 445–67.

Gershuny, J., M. Bittman and J. Brice (2005), 'Exit, voice, and suffering: do couples adapt to changing employment patterns?', *Journal of Marriage and Family*, **67** (3), 656–65.

Gornick, J.C. and M.K. Meyers (2009), *Gender Equality: Transforming Family Divisions of Labor. Volume 6, Real Utopias Project*. New York: Verso Press.

Green, F. and S. McIntosh (2001), 'The intensification of work in Europe', *Labour Economics*, **8**, 291–308.

Harkness, S. (2008), 'The household division of labour: changes in families' allocation of paid and unpaid work', in J. Scott, S. Dex and H. Joshi (eds), *Women and Employment: Changing Lives and New Challenges*, Cheltenham, UK and Northampton, MA, USA: Edward Elgar.

Hildebrandt, E. (2006), 'Balance between work and life – new corporate impositions through flexible working time or opportunity for time sovereignty', *European Societies*, **8** (2), 251–72.

Hobson, B. (2004), 'The individualised workers, the gender partipatory and the gender equity models in Sweden', *Social Policies and Society*, **3** (1), 75–84.

Hochschild, A.R. (1989), *The Second Shift: Working Parents and the Revolution at Home*, New York: Viking.

Jowell, R. and the Central Coordinating Team (2005), *European Social Survey 2004–2005: Technical Report*, London: Centre for Comparative Social Surveys, City University.

Kan, M.Y. and J. Gershuny (2010), 'Gender segregation and bargaining in domestic labour: evidence from longitudinal time use data', in J. Scott, R. Crompton and C. Lyonette (eds), *Gender Inequalities in the 21st Century*, Cheltenham, UK and Northampton, MA, USA: Edward Elgar.

Korpi, W. (2000), 'Faces of inequality: gender, class and patterns of inequalities in different types of welfare states', *Social Politics: International Studies in Gender, State Society*, **7**, 127–91.

Lewis, J. (2008), 'Work–family balance policies: issues and development in the UK 1997–2005 in comparative perspective', in J. Scott, S. Dex and H. Joshi (eds), *Women and Employment: Changing Lives and New Challenges*, Cheltenham, UK and Northampton, MA,USA: Edward Elgar.

Lewis, J. (2009), *Work–Family Balance, Gender and Policy*, Cheltenham, UK and Northampton, MA, USA: Edward Elgar.

Lewis, J., M. Campbell and C. Huerta (2008), 'Patterns of paid and unpaid work in Western Europe: gender, commodification, preferences and the implications for policy', *Journal of European Social Policy*, **18** (1), 21–37.

McRae, S. (2008), 'Working full-time after motherhood', in J. Scott, S. Dex and H. Joshi (eds), *Women and Employment: Changing Lives and New Challenges*, Cheltenham, UK and Northampton, MA, USA: Edward Elgar.

Orloff, A.S. (2009), 'Should feminists aim for gender symmetry? Why a dual-earner/dual-caregiver society is not every feminist's utopia', in J.C. Gornick and M.K. Meyers (eds), *Gender Equality: Transforming Family Divisions of Labor. Volume 6, Real Utopias Project*. New York: Verso Press.

Pichler, F. (2009), 'Determinants of work-life balance: shortcomings in the contemporary measurement of WLB in large-scale surveys', *Social Indicators Research*, **92** (3), 449–69.

Psychiatric Research Unit (2008), 'WHO-Five Well-being Index', available at: http://www.who-5.org/ (accessed April 2011).

Schober, P. and J. Scott (forthcoming), 'Maternal employment and gender role attitudes: dissonance among British men and women in the transition to parenthood', *Work, Employment and Society*.

Scott, J. and S. Dex (2009), 'Paid and unpaid work: can policy improve gender inequalities?', in J. Miles and R. Probert (eds), *Sharing Lives, Dividing Assets*, Oxford: Hart.

Sen, A. (1999), *Development as Freedom*, New York: Knopf.

Sigle-Rushton, W. (2010), 'Men's unpaid work and divorce: reassessing specialization and trade in British families', *Feminist Economics*, **16** (2), 1–26.

Taylor, R. (2001), *The Future of Work-Life Balance*, Swindon: ESRC.

West, C. and D.H. Zimmerman (1987), 'Doing gender', *Gender and Society*, **1** (2), 125–51.

APPENDIX

Table A7.1   Sample characteristics (N = 4065; weighted N = 5151)

Variable	Mean	Std. dev.	Min.	Max.
WFC	2.68	0.82	1	5
Well-being	4.13	0.91	1	6
Age	43.10	10.17	19	65
Female	0.45	0.50	0	1
Income quintile	3.38	1.17	1	5
Years of full-time education completed	13.35	3.27	1	30
Paid work strategy				
Dual earner	0.50	0.50	0	1
Male breadwinner	0.17	0.37	0	1
Modified male breadwinner	0.24	0.43	0	1
Female breadwinner	0.09	0.28	0	1
Unpaid work division				
Balanced	0.14	0.35	0	1
Mostly female	0.75	0.43	0	1
Mostly male	0.08	0.27	0	1
Other/outside help	0.03	0.18	0	1
Family life stage				
Before children, woman <45	0.15	0.36	0	1
Couples with children under 5	0.18	0.39	0	1
Couples with children 5–18	0.35	0.48	0	1
Older couples (women >44) with no dependent children	0.32	0.47	0	1
Log work hours	3.64	0.38	0	4.39
Unsocial hours index	2.60	1.20	1	5
Task discretion index	6.44	2.51	0	10

Table A7.2   Indicators of work–family conflict (WFC) in the ESS Round 2

ESS 2004/05

1. How often do you keep worrying about work problems when you are not working?
2. How often do you feel too tired after work to enjoy the things you would like to do at home?
3. How often do you find that your job prevents you from giving the time you want to your partner or family?
4. How often do you find that your partner or family gets fed up with the pressure of your job?

Not included in composite measure:
5. How often do you find it difficult to concentrate on work because of your family responsibilities?

Answer categories: Never, hardly ever, sometimes, often, always

Table A7.3   Indicators of well-being (WHO-5) in the ESS Round 2

ESS 2004/05

I would like you to say how often you have felt like this over the last two weeks.
1. I have felt cheerful and in good spirits
2. I have felt calm and relaxed
3. I have felt active and vigorous
4. I have woken up feeling fresh and rested
5. My daily life has been filled with things that interest me

Answer categories: All of the time, most of the time, more than half of the time, less than half of the time, some of the time, at no time
Reverse coded from the original.

8. Gender equality and work–family balance in a cross-national perspective[1]

Jane Lewis

The development of modern social policies can be seen as attempts to address certain kinds of risk collectively: typically those of unemployment, ill health and old age. These arrangements were elaborated in the first half of the twentieth century, but by the end of the century the nature of social risks was looking rather different. Labour markets had changed, becoming more 'flexible', with much less expectation of a 'job for life'. Families had changed, both in form, becoming much more 'fluid', and at the household level in terms of the kinds of contributions made by men and, more especially, women. Families have become increasingly dependent on two earners, with women increasing their employment rate and hours of work dramatically, while men have continued to work full-time and often long hours (particularly fathers), and have failed substantially to increase the time they devote to childcare and housework. Welfare systems were built on the assumption of stable families in which men would take primary responsibility for earning and women for the unpaid work of care, and on a commitment to full employment, but are now faced with a new landscape of social risks (Brush 2002).

Family and labour market changes have been accompanied by wider changes in social provision. Since the 1990s, welfare state change in Western Europe has been driven largely by the aim of promoting employment as a means of ensuring competitiveness and growth (CEC 2000). In the face of common economic and demographic challenges, European welfare states have sought to increase the proportion of adults, especially women, active in the labour market and to expand the length of working life for men and women. In this context, policies to balance the responsibility for work and family are seen as serving a wide – probably impossibly wide (Dex 2003) – range of policy goals: addressing the challenges of an ageing society (by enabling women to work and thereby improve the dependency ratio), and falling fertility rates (thought to be exacerbated by lack of supports for women as workers). In some places work–family balance policies have been seen additionally as the best way of tackling child poverty (in the UK, by encouraging and enabling mothers – especially lone mothers – to work), and of raising children's educational achievement (in the UK and Germany, by promoting high-quality early learning in nursery settings). In all this, the issues pertaining to care work in and for itself – in terms of how to compensate it, how to organise it, how to ensure greater equality between men and women, and greater benefits for young children – figure less prominently on the agendas of most governments.

But one of the most striking new social risks *is* the matter of care for dependants, young and old. As women have entered the post-war labour market in increasing numbers, there has been a surge in commentaries on the problems of 'juggling' family and work and of 'time pressure' (Jacobs and Gerson 2004; Gershuny and Kan, Chapter 3 in this volume; Scott and Plagnol, Chapter 7 in this volume), probably more accurately described as 'care pressure' (Ellingsaeter 2006). In some continental European countries, notably France, Belgium and the Scandinavian countries, the matter of work/family 'reconciliation' or work/family 'balance' has long been considered a suitable field for state intervention. However, in the English-speaking countries in particular it has traditionally been seen as a matter for private responsibility and decision-making. In the UK, substantial state effort in this policy field only began ten years ago.

In regard to children, governments have intervened in two basic ways: to provide leave and to encourage flexible working in order to give working parents 'time to care' on the one hand, and to provide and/or finance formal childcare to give parents 'time to work' on the other. This fundamental policy choice reflects the much larger debates on the proper nature of care for pre-schoolers in particular. Family policies often entail competition between different values, probably to a greater extent than in other policy fields (Strohmeier 2002). Thus, men, women, different social classes, ethnicities and regions, as well as academic researchers, politicians and policy-makers, may all have different views on how childcare should be provided and by whom. The main debate is about the extent to which pre-school children of different ages should be cared for at home (usually by their mothers) or in formal childcare institutions. The argument may be fundamentally about the welfare of the child in terms of cognitive, social and emotional development and well-being, and/or about the proper role of mothers. For while it has become the norm for mothers to enter the labour market, the number of hours they work varies enormously between countries.

The substantive part of this chapter charts the way in which time to care and time to work have been balanced over the past decade, focusing on the role played by part-time work and different forms of care leave (maternity, paternity and parental) in respect of the first, and the role of childcare services and care by kin in respect of the second. The chapter draws attention to the different patterns of provision that exist in Western European countries, and to those that characterise the UK in particular. The final section probes in more detail the tension between the interests of the parties involved – mothers, fathers and children – and their implications for gender equality. For while mothers have increased their participation in paid work, fathers have not made a similar change in their contributions to unpaid work. Furthermore, it is commonly acknowledged that children need one-to-one care for their first year.

PATTERNS OF WORK AND CARE IN EU15

Given the traditional gender division of unpaid and paid work, policies designed to balance work and family responsibilities have tended to target women, whether by seeking to provide time to care via shorter working hours and childcare leaves, or time to work via the provision and/ or finance of (in most countries) childcare services, which often permit mothers to work only part-time hours.

Only in the USA and in some of the Nordic countries (Denmark, Finland and to a considerable extent Sweden) has it been assumed by policy-makers (and people) that men and women will be fully engaged in the labour market, but these models work in very different ways. In the US case, the obligation to enter the labour market is embedded in a residual welfare system that often borders on the punitive, whereas in the Nordic countries it is supported by an extensive range of cash benefits for children and care leave entitlements. Other Western European countries have moved substantially towards assuming the existence of an adult worker model family, but in practice still operate a mixed model of 'partial individualisation' with mothers working fewer hours than fathers, and with varying amounts of state support for care leaves and childcare services. In these different 'policy logics' it is possible to discern ideas about what has been and is considered appropriate by and for mothers above all to do in respect of balancing work and care. However, in recent years, policy-makers have demonstrated their desire to develop policy that promotes paid work for mothers as well as fathers, an approach that might have outrun changes in the views of both mothers and fathers.

Time to Care

Historically, the main way in which paid work and family responsibilities have been balanced has been by the expansion of *part-time work* for women. In some countries, such as the UK and Germany, this form of employment emerged spontaneously, but in a country such as the Netherlands it received considerable support from the state in a deliberate effort to create a one-and-a-half breadwinner model family, rather than a full dual-earner model (Visser 2002). All three countries have sought further to embed part-time work by introducing legislation in the 2000s to give some form of entitlement to flexible working patterns, particularly reduced working hours. The Scandinavian countries have also had a long tradition of part-time working, often by women exercising their right to reduce their hours until their children reach school age. By contrast, in the Southern European countries, women still tend to work full-time or not at all; there is little demand for part-time workers. The employment rate of mothers of dependent children varies hugely between countries: in the early 2000s it was 80 per cent in Denmark and 50 per cent in Italy (Eurostat 2005), where the lack of availability of part-time work is a major explanatory factor. In many Western European countries the mothers of young children in particular are likely to work part-time, but in the UK, the Netherlands and Germany particularly, large proportions of *all* adult women work part-time, from which it may be concluded that part-time working is normative for women in these countries.

Table 8.1 shows the differences between countries and makes clear that a high aggregate female employment rate – for example, in the Netherlands – must be considered in relation to the full-time equivalent (FTE) employment rate. For behind the statistics on employment rates lie major differences in the weekly hours of work. Scandinavian women tend to work 'long part-time' (over 25 hours), whereas as many as 33 per cent of Dutch women and 21 per cent of British women work fewer than 20 hours. Fathers in Germany and the UK (but not in the Netherlands) tend to work long hours; more than a third reported working over 46 hours a week to the 2004–05 European Social Survey (Lewis et al. 2008), which affects their capacity to do care work. The gender employment gap in FTE employment (Table 8.1) is bigger when women's employment rates are lower (or men's rates higher) and/or women's part-time employment is higher.

The impact of part-time work as a primary means of providing time to care depends first on its characteristics. Ashiagbor (2006) has argued that there has been insufficient attention paid both to guaranteeing the conditions of such work, which has often remained 'precarious' despite the European 1997 Part-Time Work Directive 97/81 designed to improve its

Table 8.1 Employment rates for men, women and mothers (percentage of men/women aged 15–64 years), and part-time employment rates that are involuntary and due to family care (percentage of men/women aged 25–49 years)

	Employment						Involuntary PT[5]		Family care reasons for PT[6]	
	Men All (a) 2007	Women All (b) 2007	Women Part-time[1] (c) 2007	Women FTE[2] (d) 2008	Gender Gap[3] FTE (e) 2008	Mothers[4] Part-time (f) 2007	Men (g) 2007	Women (h) 2007	Men (i) 2007	Women (i) 2007
Austria	78.4	64.4	31.5	52.1	22.7	53.8	20.7	9.7	6.9u	52.9
Belgium	68.8	54.9	32.9	46.9	21.5	35.2	27.0	13.0	9.4	28.9
Denmark	81.3	73.3	23.9	63.8	13.3	:	16.1	17.5	:	15.8
Finland	72.4	68.5	15.5	65.4	7.5	9.4	35.5	33.0	7.0u	28.2
France	69.1‡	59.8‡	23.1‡	53.7	14.1	24.3	47.2u	30.9	11.4u	49.8
Germany	74.8‡	62.9‡	39.2‡	49.5	22.7	60.9	44.3u	17.9	4.2u	31.0
Greece	74.9	48.1	13.6	47.0	28.7	15.7	58.5	48.9	:	22.5
Ireland	77.4	60.3	35.6	51.1	23.8	:	:	1.6u	:	6.3
Italy	70.7	46.6	29.9	41.8	27.6	38.2	61.9	34.8	1.9u	40.1
Luxembourg	72.4	53.5	28.8	47.7	26.1	43.5	:	4.4u	:	22.8
Netherlands	80.0	68.1	60.0	45.4	29.1	77.5	10.8u	4.0	28.8u	64.8
Portugal	73.9	61.9	14.3	59.0	15.1	7.6	46.6	50.4	:	9.4
Spain	77.4‡	55.5‡	20.9‡	49.9	24.1	25.6	41.7	32.5	2.5	26.6
Sweden	78.0‡	73.2‡	19.7‡	62.5	11.3	:	33.4	25.7	13.2	39.6
UK	78.4‡	66.3‡	38.6‡	52.2	21.2	55.3	34.1	6.8	18.6	68.6
EU-15	74.0	59.1	7.6	50.1	21.6	:	40.1u	19.7	9.0u	43.5
USA	77.8‡	65.9‡	7.2‡							

Notes:

1. Part-time (PT) employment refers to persons who usually work less than 30 hours per week in their main job. Figures show the percentage of women who work PT as percentage of all employed and self-employed women in the OECD sample who declare their usual hours of work.

2. FTE = full-time equivalent: that is, total hours worked divided by the average annual number of hours worked in full-time jobs in each country, calculated as a proportion of total female population in the 15–64 age group.

3. The FTE employment gap is the difference in employment rates measured in full-time equivalent between men and women in percentage points.

4. Mothers include only mothers in couple families, that is, families with two married or cohabiting adults of the opposite sex with a child/children. Data on single parent families are not disaggregated by sex of the parent. Numbers reported indicate the percentage of mothers in couple families working PT over all working mothers in couple families.

5. Involuntary part-time: those who declare that they work part-time because they are unable to find full-time work: 'Could not find a full-time job'.

6. Family care: those who declare that they work part-time because they need to care for family members: 'Looking after children or incapacitated adults'.

† Data are OECD Secretariat estimates obtained by applying percentage point changes between 2006 and 2007 estimates from the European Labour Force Survey to national estimates for 2006.

‡ Refers to persons aged 16 to 64.

u Indicates unreliable data.

: Indicates unavailable data.

Sources:

Columns (a)–(c): OECD (2008) *Employment Outlook: Statistical Annex*, Paris: OECD (Tables B and E).

Columns (d)–(i): European Commission (2009) *Indicators for Monitoring the Employment Guidelines Including Indicators for Additional Employment Analysis. Compendium*, Brussels: DG Employment, Social Affairs and Equal Opportunities (Tables 17.A1, 18.A2).

Column (f): OECD (2007) 'Family database' (www.oecd.org/els/social/family/database, Table LMF8.2) (accessed 21 January 2010).

Columns (g)–(j): Eurostat (2007), *European Labour Force Survey Series Annual Results*.

quality. The Directive permits considerable latitude in interpretation and implementation (Kilaptrick and Freedland 2004). In the UK, Manning and Petrongolo (2008) have shown the extent to which high levels of sexual segregation and poor wages are associated with part-time work.

Second, it matters in some measure as to how far part-time work is 'voluntary'. According to the 2007 report *Employment in Europe*, 'part-time work is largely voluntary' (CEC 2007, p. 133). Not surprisingly, Table 8.1 shows that involuntary part-time work is much more often reported among women aged 25–49 in some countries than in others. Countries with a long history of full-time work for women (France and Finland) and where it is usual for women to work full-time (or not at all) – as in the Southern European countries – report high percentages of involuntary part-time work. These figures need to be linked to the proportions saying that they work part-time in order to carry out care work, which Table 8.1 shows are particularly high (for men as well as women) in the Netherlands and the UK (where care services have been relatively slow to develop), and low (for women) in Denmark and Portugal.[2] Thus in countries where women *expect* to work part-time and to care, the proportions reporting 'voluntary' part-time work are also high. Given the importance of cultural and institutional contexts, it may therefore not be possible to treat such figures as the simple expression of preferences (Hakim 2000).

Childcare leave in the form of maternity leave has been a long-standing commitment in most Western European countries. Paternity leave tends to be short in most countries, from two to 14 days. At the EU level, maternity leave is treated as a health and safety issue. All Western European countries have had some kind of provision for maternity leave since the late nineteenth or early twentieth centuries, but even today this form of leave varies in terms of length and is subject to different eligibility criteria and amounts of payment. In most countries outside Scandinavia, better-paid maternity leave is conditional on a substantial record of paid work. Contract workers (particularly numerous in Spain) and self-employed workers (particularly numerous in Greece) often have only limited rights to maternity leave. Maternity leave was not legislated in the USA, where it was felt to run counter to strict feminist interpretations as to what constitutes 'same treatment'. The 1993 US Family and Medical Leave Act offers only the possibility of 12 weeks unpaid leave to mothers and fathers alike. In the UK, maternity leave was dramatically extended to 12 months in 2003, and payments have been made much more generous, but there is only a very short, unpaid period of parental leave. In contrast, in Sweden, maternity leave consists of 12 weeks prior to the birth, while post-natal leave is formally defined as a gender neutral 'parental' entitlement, which, including the leave taken prior to the birth, can run as long as 18 months and is generously remunerated.

When the European Commission issued its 1996 Directive on Parental Leave, it laid down a minimum individual right to three months parental leave for men and women, but member states were left to determine the conditions of access, whether the leave should be compensated and whether it should be full- or part-time. The fact that no minimum remuneration requirements were specified (a victory for employers) made it likely that men would not take it (as proved to be the case: Bruning and Plantenga 1999), and that it would tend in practice to be 'reconciliation for women'. In law, parental leave is a 'family right' to be divided between parents as they see fit in Austria, Denmark, Finland and Luxembourg, and an individual entitlement in Belgium, France, Germany, Greece, Italy, Ireland, Portugal, Spain, the Netherlands and the UK. In Iceland, Norway and Sweden it is a mixed entitlement, part family and part individual – these countries are distinguished by having a specific 'daddy leave', which is an entitlement for the father and which is lost if he fails to take it. The take-up of parental leave by men is low in all countries. In 2006, 20.6 per cent of leave days were taken by men in Sweden (the highest proportion) followed by 19 per cent by Dutch men. Elsewhere in Europe, including Denmark, fewer than 5 per cent are taken by fathers.[3] Interestingly in Iceland, where one-third of the nine-month parental leave is allocated to the father alone, the figure rose to 80 per cent after the introduction of the three-month quota. While job protection tends to be strong for those taking parental leave, it is much weaker for those taking long home-care leaves (almost always mothers), which can run on after parental leave and which are also poorly compensated.

The trend in parental leave policies has tended to be consistent across countries and signals an important shift in the balance between policies to promote time to care and time to work. Germany is a good example. Germany introduced means-tested parental leave in 1986. By the late 1990s it was possible to take three years parental leave (the third year was unpaid). But in 2007 Germany moved to a parental leave system that strongly resembles that of Sweden. The leave is now earnings-related, paying 67 per cent of income, but the duration has been reduced to 12 months, with an additional two months reserved for the father. The higher rate of compensation has pushed up fathers' take-up of parental leave to 10.5 per cent (Henninger et al. 2008). At the same time, recent policy effort in Germany has focused much more on the provision of childcare services. Thus parental leave policy (and family policy generally) has come into line with the broader trend in social policies of promoting labour market activation: labour market participation is rewarded with an earnings-related policy instrument and prolonged absences from the labour market on the part of mothers are not encouraged. However, it must be noted that this kind of earnings related leave is aimed at and benefits better qualified mothers.

Most Western European countries now tend towards supporting a shorter period at home with the child, followed by the greater provision of childcare services; the nature of provision for children aged 1–3 causes the greatest debate. Only Finland provides the possibility of making a choice between taking a long, three-year leave or using publicly funded childcare. A greater proportion of mothers opt for the leave, particularly less well-educated mothers. However, the tradition of full-time work for women in Finland is strong, and as Table 8.1 shows, the full-time equivalent employment rate for Finnish women is high because of the numbers that return to full-time employment after the leave. National contexts and norms regarding the behaviour of parents, particularly mothers, are important and make radical policy change – such as that in Germany – difficult to implement.

The UK is exceptional in its treatment of childcare leave policies. These were developed incrementally alongside childcare services from 1999 and were aimed mainly at mothers; very little has been done in respect of fathers. Policy change was presented in such a way as to take account of the gap between policy goals regarding mothers' employment on the one hand, and behaviour on the other. Parental leave was implemented only in minimal compliance with the EU Directive in 1999. Instead, the UK focused on providing longer and much better paid maternity leave, which has been increased in stages from 14 weeks to 12 months in 2003. It is the longest in the EU, but it needs to be noted that other European countries have replaced maternity leave by parental leave, which, as described above, sometimes exceeds 12 months. UK maternity pay has been doubled. The 2006 Work and Family Act made it possible for the mother to transfer the last six months of what was by 2010 a 12-month maternity leave to the father if she returns to work. This additional paternity leave was implemented in 2011. In any case, the rate of compensation envisaged for fathers is low and take-up may therefore also be expected to be low.

Successive UK Labour governments wanted to promote mothers' employment. However, in face of labour market behaviour that is not dissimilar to that of German women, albeit attitudes in the UK tend to be less traditional, it has actually been more cautious in terms of its choice of policy instruments and the presentation of policy goals. Thus it has improved leaves for mothers and promoted flexible working – effectively also for mothers, who usually choose to reduce their working hours post-childbirth.

Time to Work

Formal childcare provision has been increased in all Western European countries as policies designed to provide time to work have become more central to the trajectory of social policy. In 2000, the Lisbon Council set a target of 60 per cent for female labour market participation in member states by 2010, albeit without any specification as to the number of hours to be worked. Following this, the 2002 Barcelona Council set targets for the provision of childcare places to reach 90 per cent of children between 3 and school age, and 33 per cent of under 3s.

Table 8.2 presents Organisation for Economic Co-operation and Development (OECD) and Eurostat data on pre-school day care and early education enrolments and public expenditure on these. The Nordic countries and France have the highest rates of public expenditure, which have had a positive impact on not only the levels of provision, but also their quality.[4]

By age 5 (when school begins in the UK[5]), the vast majority of children attend some kind of formal provision in all countries, although the USA is something of a laggard at this point in the child's life (the Finnish data, which are surprisingly low, are suspect, see note to Table 8.2). Parents in Finland, France, Germany, the Netherlands and working parents in the UK since April 2008 have a legal entitlement to a part-time childcare place. In the UK this is for children aged 3 and 4. Unsurprisingly the variation between countries in regard to 3- and 4-year-olds is greater. Again, Finland is very unlike its Scandinavian neighbours. Some countries – France, Belgium, Italy and Spain – have virtually all 3- to 5-year-olds in institutional provision. The English-speaking countries have provision for only 50 per cent or fewer of 3-year-olds, with Austria, Finland, Ireland, the Netherlands and Luxembourg falling below that.

The proportion of under 3s in formal care is particularly high in Denmark (61.7 per cent), with the only other countries recording percentages higher than 30 per cent being Sweden and Belgium. In the OECD data-set, only these countries meet the EU's Barcelona Council target of provision for one-third of under 3s. However, there are important differences in usage within countries that have high levels of enrolment: for example, in Denmark, minority ethnic families tend not to use formal childcare (Kremer 2007). Figures for the proportion of under 3s in formal care are particularly low for Italy and Greece (but not Spain), and for Austria and Germany. In all these countries the tradition of family (maternal) care for young children has been particularly strong. In the UK, childminders have been important in covering at least some of mothers' part-time working hours.

Table 8.2   Enrolment rates in childcare, pre-school and school for children under 6, 2006 (percentage over the population of each age group)

	Enrolment in formal childcare, pre-school and school*				Average weekly hours in childcare Under 3 yrs	Public expenditure as % of GDP**
	Under 3 yrs	3 yrs	4 yrs	5 yrs		
Austria	10.5	48.5	83.2	93.0	23	0.30
Belgium	41.7	99.8	100.0	99.7	30	0.79
Denmark	70.5	93.7	93.4	85.1	34	1.35
Finland***	25.0	39.5	48.5	56.6	35	0.94
France	42.9	99.3	100.0	100.0	30	1.00
Germany	21.2	81.9	93.1	93.0	22	0.38
Greece	18.2	0.0	56.1	85.8	31	0.13
Ireland	25.2	1.9	46.9	99.5	25	0.26
Italy	28.6	96.6	100.0	100.0	30	0.61
Luxembourg	43.4	65.6	94.0	96.0	31	0.39
Netherlands	53.9	0.1	74.2	98.4	17	0.47
Portugal	43.6	63.1	80.6	93.0	40	0.40
Spain	33.9	96.2	97.1	99.8	28	0.44
Sweden	44.0	81.9	86.5	88.3	29	0.98
UK	39.7	79.5	91.3	100.0	18	0.58
USA[†]	31.4	38.5	58.2	78.4	31	0.35

Notes:
Figures in this table are not directly comparable because different sources use different methods of data collection. Data on the participation of children under three in European countries are collected through household surveys, whereas data of children aged 3–5 are based upon headcounts and are therefore more reliable.

    *   OECD's definition of childcare includes, for under 3 years old: centre-based care, childminders and care by non-family members in the child's own home; for 3- to 5-year-olds: all daycare facilities and schools except for EU countries where data relate to pre-primary and primary education only. Note that compulsory school starts at different ages.

  **   Public expenditure figures: public expenditure on childcare and early educational services is all public financial support (in cash, in-kind or through the tax system) for families with children participating in formal day-care services and pre-school institutions. Local public expenditure may or may not be fully included.

 ***   These figures appear to understate the proportions of children over 3 in childcare in Finland. Finnish data for 2004 reported 73 per cent of children aged 5 in childcare, 69 per cent aged 4 and 62 per cent aged 3.

   †   Figure for children under 3 concerns 2005.

Sources: 'OECD family database' (www.oecd.org/els/social/family/database, Tables PF10.1, PF11.1 and PF11.2) (accessed 21 January 2010), except for enrolment for 3- to 5-year-olds in EU countries: 'Eurostat, UOE' (http://eacea.ec.europa.eu/about/eurydice/documents/098EN.pdf, Figure 2.9).

In addition, the nature of entitlements to different forms of care varies between countries. In the UK, subventions for day care are largely confined to working parents by virtue of the way in which such care is funded: parents who claim the childcare element of working tax credit must be working more than 16 hours per week (raised to 24 hours by the coalition government in 2010). Whereas in a country such as Sweden the right to a place attaches to the child. The percentage of childcare costs covered by the childcare tax credit was reduced from 80 to 70 per cent by the UK's coalition government in 2010.

In fact, informal childcare by parents and by grandparents remains enormously important in the vast majority of countries. The 2004–05 European Social Survey shows that care by the mother or partner is particularly important in Britain, where a high proportion of fathers working atypical hours provide a significant amount of informal care, notwithstanding the lack of access to paid parental leave (Lewis et al. 2008). Grandparents (most often grandmothers) are a highly significant source of childcare everywhere except in Sweden, Denmark and France. In Sweden and Denmark, a high proportion of older women aged 55–64 (67 and 54 per cent respectively) are in the workforce and are therefore not available to provide care. Informal childcare, whether supported by parental leave provision or not, remains dominant outside France and the Nordic countries.

In the UK, an enormous amount of money has been pumped into childcare via both the demand-side (via working tax credit) and supply-side subsidies, even though expenditure on childcare and early years education remains slightly lower than the OECD average of 0.7 per cent of gross domestic product (GDP) (Table 8.2). By 2004, free part-time nursery education was being offered to all over 3s, but an obligation on local authorities to ensure provision of early years education and care did not come into operation until 2008, and then only to parents in work or training. Provision for under 3s is mainly in the hands of parents, grandparents and childminders. However, it is not possible to use the childcare element of working tax credit to pay grandparents. This tax credit goes only to parents who are in work or training, which has major implications for the 15.3 per cent of children who live in workless households.

The decision to provide more public finance for formal childcare but to channel this through the existing mixed economy of private, voluntary and public providers has had major implications for parents and children. First, the cost of childcare to parents is very high in the UK compared to other Western European states (Ireland excepted) (OECD 2007), and high childcare costs have been shown to have an impact on the hours mothers work (Cleveland and Krashinsky 2003). Second the quality of care, shown to be crucial to the achievement of longer-lasting benefits for children (Sylva et al. 2004), is still an issue. Compared to the Scandinavian countries in particular, the UK childcare workforce has long been low paid and poorly qualified. Third, while parents are likely to value continuity in care, sustainability of privately provided childcare has been a problem, with high closure rates for private sector providers of day care. Childcare provision has expanded, but remains fragmented, expensive and intended more to enable mothers to work at least part-time than for the child *qua* child's benefit.

DISCUSSION AND CONCLUSION

Many countries laid down time-to-work and time-to-care policies 30 or more years ago (particularly the Scandinavian countries, France and Belgium), during a period in which welfare states were expanding. Thus in Denmark the policy priority in developing childcare services was explicitly the welfare of the child, and to this day Danish children are regarded as disadvantaged if they do not attend (what is high-quality) formal childcare. In Sweden, work–family balance policies were introduced with an explicit regard to achieving greater gender equality. But in the last decade, the main priority of governments in promoting a work/family policy agenda has been clear: to increase labour market participation, particularly of women. In Western European countries this has been justified in terms of economic arguments regarding the need to increase competitiveness and growth. But there have been other policy aims. In the UK, the argument has also been framed in social arguments regarding the importance of wages for tackling child poverty, and of early years learning for preventing worklessness in the future. In Germany, reform of parental leave in 2007 was justified additionally as a means to increase the fertility rate. Indeed, it has been all too easy for policy-makers to see policies addressing time to work and time to care as a 'magic bullet' to help solve the new demographic and economic challenges facing welfare states. The nature and balance of the policy instruments chosen depend in large measure on the aims of policy-makers and in turn have implications for the often differing interests of mothers, fathers and children.

It is in any case difficult for policy to meet the interests of all family members. There is first the issue of the unequal contributions to paid and unpaid work made by men and women. Governments are increasingly assuming the existence of an adult worker model family, together with the capacity of all adults to achieve a large measure of economic independence, for example in respect of pension provision. But for this to happen, men must do more to share the unpaid work of care and women must have more access to better paid positions in the labour market. Second, there is the issue of the interests of children, which are not necessarily the same for very young children as for pre-schoolers.

Policies providing time to work are crucial for women to enter the labour market, as most governments have recognised in recent years, but policies to provide time to care have not necessarily targeted fathers. Even in the Nordic countries, the priority accorded to the issue of gender equality has varied. Ellingsaeter and Leira (2006) have shown the extent to which Denmark has focused support on working mothers and provides the least support for fathers; Finland supports mothers who work *and* mothers who care, also with relatively little for fathers; while Sweden alone provides support for working and non-working mothers and for fathers. Furthermore, such policy differences seem to be reflected in family practices. Thus, in Finland, mothers of very young children are much more likely to be at home than working part-time, making use of the long homecare leave (although, as Table 8.1 showed, on an FTE basis women's employment is as high in Finland as in Denmark or Sweden).

In the UK, the Labour governments were anxious to avoid the charge that a 'nanny state' was seeking to interfere in the way in which men and women organise their work and family lives at the level of the household. Thus, despite the fundamentally gendered nature of work and family balance issues and policies, UK policy documents have invariably referred to gender neutral 'parents', insisting, ever more strongly as time passed, that parents must be enabled to make their own 'choices', with no apparent recognition of the very different structural positions of mothers and fathers in most two parent families. In fact, policy-makers have had the behaviour of mothers more firmly in mind than that of fathers, which is problematic given that mothers' choices depend in large part on what fathers are able (and willing) to do. Alone in Western Europe, the UK focused on maternity rather than parental leave as its main policy instrument for providing time to care. Fathers have no individual entitlement to leave. But the cross-national evidence on what parental leave should look like if fathers are to take it is clear: it must be paid at a high rate of compensation, be an individual entitlement, and be flexible (for example, by making possible shorter and longer blocks of leave either full- or part-time) (Deven and Moss 2002; Nyberg 2004). The additional paid paternity leave introduced just before the 2010 election in the UK meets none of these criteria.

All this brings us back to the large issues of norms and values and the role of government in relation to them. In the UK, there is still suspicion of family policy as something that erodes the boundary between public and private. Nevertheless, in the context of family, labour market and welfare state change, there has been a decisive move towards the more continental European position, which has always seen a role for the state in promoting policies to provide time to work and time to care. As we have seen in respect of preferences regarding formal childcare, people tend to express a preference for what exists already. Similarly, if most women work part-time in a particular country, then women tend to report such work as voluntary, while fathers in many countries continue to identify primarily as 'breadwinners' (for example, for the UK, Warin et al. 1999). The issue of how far governments should respect existing norms and values and how far they should seek to change them is central to social policy-making. It is possible for law to legitimise certain forms of behaviour and thus contribute to changing norms.

Nevertheless, it is also a matter of debate as to how far there is any conflict between men and women over the gendered divisions of work and care, and therefore how far there is a case for governments to address the different structural positions of mothers and fathers. Hakim's (2000) application of preference theory to this policy area has centred on the idea that women in affluent, modern societies are now in a position to make real choices about work and care based on their values. In this conceptual-isation, behaviour results from choice, and is thus also construed as being what women want. If this is indeed so, then there is very little for policy-makers legitimately to do beyond respecting, and perhaps further ena-bling, the kind of behaviour that exists. Certainly, many mothers may not want to share childcare leaves with fathers; Ellingsaeter (2006) reported this to be the case for many Norwegian women. In regard to fathers, a Eurobarometer (2004) survey of 5688 men over 18 in EU15 found that only 4 per cent thought that parental leave is for men and women equally. While awareness of parental leave was reasonably high, 84 per cent said that they had not taken leave and were not thinking of taking it in the future. However, if childcare leave policies were designed so as to max-imise fathers' take-up and if a substantial percentage of fathers were to care for small children – 20 or possibly 40 per cent – then it might well become normative behaviour (Brighouse and Olin Wright 2009).

Still, many in the UK would continue to argue that the needs of children are the only proper concern of government, and then only when the child is deemed to be 'at risk'. In regard to the interests of children, there are issues about the extent to which they may conflict with those of adults, but also whether government policies have prioritised children's welfare. Galtry and Callister's (2005) review of the evidence on the impact of taking leave to care on women's employment led them to conclude that short leaves of about six months is best if women are to be able to improve their labour market position, while the OECD has recommended a slightly shorter period of four to six months. However, the World Health Organisation has recommended that infants should be breastfed for six months and that a longer period of one-to-one care is needed to meet the developmental needs of the child. Ekberg (2004) has argued that it is not clear whether it is worthwhile to give fathers incentives to take leave, either in terms of take-up or the child's welfare. He notes that when a month's leave was first reserved for fathers in Sweden, the total number of parental leave days taken fell by five, which is arguably detrimental from the point of view of the child. Kenworthy (2009) has also argued that because fathers tend not to take leave, child welfare must be allowed to trump gender equality, and the entitlement of fathers to leave should be limited. In addition, questions are often raised about how much carework or other domestic work men on leave actually do. If these arguments are accepted, then the focus of many governments on allowing mothers to take childcare leave makes practical sense, but may exacerbate gender inequalities.

In recent years, governments have actually invested more effort in the provision of childcare services, with the main objective of allowing mothers to enter the labour market, albeit often part-time, and, with the emphasis placed on early years learning, of investing in children as the workers of the future. There is general agreement among academic researchers that the over 3s can benefit from high quality formal care, although US data on 3- and 4-year-olds have shown improvement in cognitive behaviour, while raising issues about social behaviour (Belsky et al. 2007; NICHD 2005; Waldfogel 2006). However, the quality of care is particularly variable in the US context, where the market tends to deliver cheap care, often via migrant labour. There is little doubt that the quality of formal childcare in terms of staff/child ratios and, particularly, the qualifications of staff, as well as a considered mix of early years learning and care, is high in some countries, particularly in Scandinavia, but also in France, Belgium and some parts of Italy (notably the Emilia Romagna). The provision of formal childcare in these countries is long-standing and was developed with the welfare of the child as a leading, often *the* leading principle. In the UK accessibility and availability have taken priority over affordability and quality in an effort to promote a rapid increase in mothers' employment in what is a very fragmented childcare market.

Balancing time-to-work and time-to-care policies is a complex task. The UK entered this field in 1998, significantly increasing public expenditure and using a range of policy instruments. The main policy aim has been to increase mothers' employment rate, as a means to greater economic competitiveness, but also to tackling child poverty. The most significant expenditure has been on childcare services. Child welfare, albeit as much or more in respect of the future (in terms of educational achievement and successful integration into the workforce) as the present, has been an explicit priority, but gender equality has not. Rather, the Labour governments of the 2000s in the UK emphasised the importance of 'parents' deciding what balance is best for them, albeit at the same time introducing legislation to enable a degree of choice. The approach of the coalition government in the UK is not yet clear, although demand-side subsidies in the form of tax credits have been reduced. Yet, the context is one of increasing individualisation. There is a sense of increased expectations that adults will become more self-provisioning; welfare is increasingly privatised to the individual's responsibility (Brush 2002; Hacker 2006) as welfare systems tighten the conditionality between paid work and social provision. Given this, government may be argued to have a responsibility to ensure more equal labour market participation, and terms and conditions, which in turn means that fathers need to be encouraged to pick up more of the unpaid work of care. Making some form of 'reconciliation' of work and family possible for women alone, usually via a reduction in working hours and provision for (inadequately compensated) childcare leaves is likely to entail gender inequalities, particularly in old age. A range of policy provisions – such as the vast majority of Western European governments, including the UK, have implemented – is necessary to make work–family balance possible for mothers and fathers, but considerable attention to the policy detail is necessary to maximise the welfare of family members and to minimise the trade-offs.

NOTES

1. An earlier version of this piece was published in the *Child and Family Law Quarterly* (2009), **21** (4), 443–61.
2. The figure for Ireland is also low, but the data are unreliable and are certainly counter-intuitive.
3. For a recent country-based set of studies on care leaves, see Moss (2009).
4. Quality is difficult to measure. Level of qualification of staff is often used and, on this measure, childcare staff in England do particularly badly, especially when compared to a country such as Denmark, where childcare workers usually have degrees. In England the usual qualification is an NVQ2 or NVQ3.
5. The compulsory age for starting school ranges from age 4 in Ireland, to 7 in Finland and Sweden, with the vast majority of children in EU15 starting at age 6. In the USA, the starting age ranges from 5 to 7 between states.

REFERENCES

Ashiagbor, D. (2006), 'Promoting precariousness? The response of EU employment policies to precarious work', in J. Fudge and R. Owens (eds), *Precarious Work, Women, and the New Economy. The Challenge to Legal Norms*. Oxford: Hart.

Belsky, J., M. Burchinal, K. McCartney, D.L. Vandell, K.A. Clarke-Stewart and M. Owen (2007), 'Are there long-term effects of child care?', *Child Development*, **78** (2), 681–701.

Brighouse, H. and E. Olin Wright (2009), 'Strong gender egalitarianism', in J.C. Gornick, M. Meyers and E.O. Wright (eds), *Gender Equality: Transforming Family Divisions of Labor*, London: Verso, pp. 79–92.

Bruning, G. and J. Plantenga (1999), 'Parental leave and equal opportunities: experiences in eight European countries', *Journal of European Social Policy*, **9** (3), 195–209.

Brush, L. (2002), 'Changing the subject: gender and welfare regime studies', *Social Politics*, **9** (2), 161–86.

Commission of the European Communities (CEC) (2000), Communication on the *Social Policy Agenda*, COM (2000) 379 final of 28/6/00.

Commission of the European Communities (CEC) (2007), *Employment in Europe 2007*, Luxembourg: Office for Official Publications of the European Communities.

Cleveland, G. and M. Krashinsky (2003), *Financing ECEC Services in OECD Countries*, Paris: OECD.

Deven, F. and P. Moss (2002), 'Leave arrangements for parents: overview and future outlook', *Community, Work and Family*, **5** (3), 237–55.

Dex, S. (2003), *Families and Work in the Twenty-First Century*, York: Joseph Rowntree Foundation.

Ekberg, J. (2004), 'Sharing responsibility? Short and long-term effects of Sweden's daddy month reform', paper given to the DTI, London, 27 May.

Ellingsaeter, A.-L. (2006), 'The Norwegian childcare regime and its paradoxes', in A.-L. Ellingsaeter and A. Leira (eds), *Politicising Parenthood in Scandinavia*.

Ellingsaeter, A.-L. and A. Leira (2006), *Politicising Parenthood in Scandinavia. Gender Relations in Welfare States*, Bristol: Policy Press.

Eurobarometer (2004), *Europeans' Attitudes to Parental Leave*, Brussels: DG Employment and Social Affairs.

Eurostat (2005), 'Reconciling work and family life in the EU25 in 2003', news release 49/2005, pp. 2–3, Luxembourg: Eurostat.

Galtry, J. and P. Callister (2005), 'Assessing the optimal length of parental leave for child and parental well-being: how can research inform policy?', *Journal of Family Issues*, **26** (2), 219–46.

Hacker, J. (2006), *The Great Risk Shift. The Assault on American Jobs, Families, Health Care, and Retirement*, Oxford: Oxford University Press.

Hakim, C. (2000), *Work-Lifestyle Choices in the Twenty-first Century: Preference Theory*, Oxford University Press, Oxford.

Henninger, A., C. Wimbauer and R. Dombrowski (2008), 'Demography as a push towards gender equality? Current reforms of German family policy', *Social Politics*, **15** (3), 287–314.

Jacobs, J.A. and K. Gerson (2004), *The Time Divide. Work, Family and Gender Inequality*, Cambridge, MA: Harvard University Press.

Kenworthy, L. (2009), 'Who should care for under-threes?', in J. Gornick and M. Meyers (eds), *Gender Equality: Transforming Divisions of Family Labor*, New York: Verso.

Kilpatrick, C. and M. Freedland (2004), 'How is EU governance transformative?', in S. Sciarra, P. Davies and M. Freedland (eds), *Employment Policy and the Regulation of Part-time Work in the European Union*, Cambridge: Cambridge University Press.

Kremer, M. (2007), *How Welfare States Care. Culture, Gender and Parenting in Europe*, Amsterdam: Amsterdam University Press.

Lewis, J., M. Campbell and C. Huerta (2008), 'Patterns of paid and unpaid work in Western Europe: gender, commodification, preferences and the implications for policy', *Journal of European Social Policy*, 18 (1), 21–37.

Manning, A. and B. Petrongolo (2008), 'The part-time pay penalty for women in Britain', *The Economic Journal*, 118 (Feb.), F28–51.

Moss, P. (2009), *International Review of Leave Policies and Related Research*, Employment Relations Research Series no. 102, London: Department for Business, Innovation and Skills.

National Institute of Child Health and Human Development (NICHD) (2005), *Early Child Care Research Network Childcare and Child Development*, New York: Guilford Press.

Nyberg, A. (2004), 'Parental leave, public childcare and the dual earner/dual carer model in Sweden', meeting of the Peer Review Programme of the European Employment Strategy, Stockholm, 19–20 April.

Organisation for Economic Co-operation and Development (OECD) (2007), *Babies and Bosses. Reconciling Work and Family Life. A Synthesis of Findings for OECD Countries*, Paris: OECD.

Strohmeier, K.P. (2002), 'Family policy – how does it work?', in F.-X. Kaufman, A. Kuijsten, H.-J. Schulze and K.P. Strohmeier (eds), *Family Life and Family Policies in Europe*, vol. 2, Oxford: Oxford University Press.

Sylva, K., E. Melhuish, P. Sammons, I. Sirja-Blatchford and B. Taggart (2004), *The Effective Provision of Pre-School Education Project: Final Report Results*, London: DfES.

Visser, J. (2002), 'The first part-time economy in the world: a model to be followed?', *Journal of European Social Policy*, 12 (1), 23–42.

Waldfogel, J. (2006), *What Children Need*, Cambridge: Harvard University Press.

Warin, J., Y. Solomon, C. Lewis and W. Langford (1999), *Fathers, Work and Family Life*, London: Family Policy Studies Centre.

Index

agency employment 127–9, 130–32,
  144
  constructing transnational labour
    force 135–7
  new European labour force at
    hotel 137–41
  older post-colonial labour force at
    hospital 141–3
  data from hotel and hospital in
    London 132–5
agency in relation to household income
  104
Ashiagbor, D. 209
asylum seekers 123
Australia 76, 83
Austria 213, 215
autonomy, *see* financial togetherness
  and autonomy within couples

Belgium 207, 213, 215
Biggs, D. 127
Bjornberg, U. 104
Blossfeld, H.-P. 66
Boye, K. 179, 180, 199
breadwinner model 4
business case for gender equality 14,
  18, 153–4, 158–60, 170–71
  attitudes of investors 161–5
  attitudes of managers 165–70
  research methods 160–61

Callister, P. 220
Canada 76, 77, 78, 83, 155
caring
  childcare 52–3, 212, 215–18
  patterns of work and care in EU15
    countries 208
  time to care 209–14
  time to work 215–18
Castells, M. 127
childlessness 7–8

children
  childbirth 3, 48, 51
    maternity leave 49, 62, 65, 212–14,
      221
    women's careers after childbirth
      62–4
  childcare 52–3, 212, 215–18
  childhood origins of adult socio-
    economic disadvantage 12–13,
    23, 42–4
    analytic strategy 32–8
    control variables 27–32
    data and methods of study 25–38
    gender and cohort interactions
      41–2
    literature review 23–5
    outcome measures 26
    results of study 15–16, 38–42
Coe, N. 129
Colling, T. 169
Confederation of British Industry
  (CBI) 130
Connolly, S. 65
Cornwall, A. 104
corporate social responsibility (CSR)
  18, 153, 161–2, 163–4; *see also*
  business case for gender equality

Denmark 5, 76, 89, 209
  childcare 215, 217
  parental leave 213
  trends in gender division of labour
    83
  trends in paid work time 76, 77,
    212
  work–family balance 218
  well-being and 177, 181, 185, 186,
    188, 196
Dickens, L. 158, 169, 170
Discrimination Law Review (DCLG)
  156

divorce 3, 7
domestic work 3, 5, 182–3
    multinational time-use study of
        gender equality in paid and
        unpaid work 13, 74–5
    data and measures 75–6
    gender segregation within unpaid
        work 83–7
    summary and implications 89–92
    trends in gender division of labour
        82–3
    trends in paid work time 76–80
    trends in total work time (isowork)
        87–9
    trends in unpaid work time 80–82
Dustmann, C. 130

Economic and Social Research Council
    177
education 2, 3
    adult socio-economic disadvantage
        and 24, 38–9, 40, 44
    career trajectories and 55–6, 59
    university education 9
Ekberg, J. 221
Elias, P. 12
Ellingsaeter, A.-L. 219, 220
employment 3, 4, 8, 9–10
    adult socio-economic disadvantage
        and occupational class 42
    changing career trajectories of
        women and men across time 13,
        48–51, 65–6
        birth cohorts' lives and their
            context 51–4
        career progression over the life
            course 57–60
        creating vertical occupational scale
            54
        first occupations 54–7
        part-time pay penalty 64–5
        policy response 66–8
        starting out in low paid
            occupation 61
        women's careers after childbirth
            62–4
    multinational time-use study of
        gender equality in paid and
        unpaid work 13, 74–5
    data and measures 75–6

    gender segregation within unpaid
        work 83–7
    summary and implications 89–92
    trends in gender division of labour
        82–3
    trends in paid work time 76–80
    trends in total work time (isowork)
        87–9
    trends in unpaid work time 80–82
precarious employment and migrant
    workers 14, 123–5
    agency employment and economic
        migration 130–32
    constructing transnational labour
        force 135–43
    data from hotel and hospital in
        London 132–5
    growth of service sector
        employment 125–7
    local jobs, global workers 143–6
    new transnational labour force
        127–30
work–family balance 14–15, 18,
    174–6, 188–98, 206–8, 218–22
    association of work–family
        conflict and well-being
        186–8
    background literature 176–9
    data and measures 181
    hypotheses 179–80
    key variables 181–4
    multivariate regression analysis
        188
    patterns of work and care in
        EU15 countries 208–18
    summary, discussion and
        conclusions 198–201
    work status, family life course and
        gender 184–6
see also wages and salaries
enlightened shareholder value 154
Equal Opportunities Commission
    (EOC) 156, 157
Equal Pay Taskforce (UK) 154, 155
Equalities and Human Rights
    Commission (EHRC) 157
Esping-Andersen, G. 5, 174, 178, 201
European Union (EU) 67, 127, 137,
    178
extramarital births 7

family life
    work–family balance 14–15, 18,
        174–6, 188–98, 206–8, 218–22
        association of work–family
            conflict and well-being 186–8
        background literature 176–9
        data and measures 181
        hypotheses 179–80
        key variables 181–4
        multivariate regression analysis
            188
        patterns of work and care in
            EU15 countries 208–18
        summary, discussion and
            conclusions 198–201
        work status, family life course and
            gender 184–6
financial togetherness and autonomy
    within couples 13, 97–9, 115–17
    concepts and focus of study 99–100
    exploring togetherness and financial
        autonomy through qualitative
        research 101
    access to income to pursue
        personal projects 104–5
    agency in relation to household
        income 104
    financial autonomy 102
    'making a contribution' and
        'money in your own right'
        102–3
    privacy 103
    togetherness 101–2
    quantitative analysis of factors
        influencing 'autonomy' and
        'togetherness' 106–7
    decomposing individual answers
        about satisfaction 108–10
    effects on both partners' average
        satisfaction 110–13
    effects on differences in
        satisfaction 113
    reflections on findings 113–15
    satisfaction with household
        income 107–8
    reflections on findings 16, 105–6
    samples for study 100
Finland 76, 219
    childcare 215
    parental leave 213

trends in gender division of labour
    83
trends in paid work time 77, 79,
    212
trends in unpaid work time 81
Folbre, N. 19
Forde, C. 131
France 76
    childcare 215
    parental leave 213
    trends in gender division of labour
        83
    trends in paid work time 76, 78, 212
    trends in unpaid work time 81
    work–family balance 207
        well-being and 177, 181, 186, 196
Fraser, N. 175
Freedland, M. 128

Gallie, D. 177, 180, 196
Galtry, J. 220
Germany 76
    childcare 215
    parental leave 213
    trends in gender division of labour
        83
    trends in paid work time 76, 77
    trends in unpaid work time 80, 209
    work–family balance 218
        well-being and 178, 181, 185, 186,
            196
Gershuny, J. 74, 199
Glucksmann, M. 18
Goode, J. 104
Gornick, J.C. 175
Greece 213, 215
Greene, A. 158, 161
Gregory, M. 65

Hakim, C. 220
Hawrylyshn, O. 76
Hepple, B. 170
Hobcraft, J. 25, 32
Hobson, B. 178
Hochschild, A. 2, 179, 184

income, *see* wages and salaries
investment
    attitudes of investors to gender
        equality 161–5

socially responsible investment (SRI)
        153, 162, 163, 164–5
    United Nations Principles for
        Responsible Investment 162
Investors in People (IIP) 67
Ireland 213, 215
isowork 75, 87–9, 91
Italy 76, 81–2, 83, 87, 209, 213, 215

Jayatilaka, G. 104
Joshi, H. 4

Kan, M.Y. 74, 89
Kingsmill Review 66–7, 154, 155–6, 161
Kirton, G. 158, 161
Kollind, A.-K. 104
Korpi, W. 179

labour market, *see* employment
Leira, A. 219
Lewis, J. 175, 178
Lichter, M.I. 139
life-course analysis 1–2, 183–4
    changing career trajectories of
        women and men across time 13,
        48–51, 65–6
        birth cohorts' lives and their
            context 51–4
        career progression over the life
            course 57–60
        creating vertical occupational scale
            54
        first occupations 54–7
        part-time pay penalty 64–5
        policy response 66–8
        starting out in low paid
            occupation 61
        women's careers after childbirth
            62–4
    childhood origins of adult socio-
        economic disadvantage 12–13,
        23, 42–4
        analytic strategy 32–8
        control variables 27–32
        data and methods of study 25–38
        gender and cohort interactions
            41–2
        literature review 23–5
        outcome measures 26
        results of study 15–16, 38–42

Lister, R. 116
Luxembourg 213, 215

McGovern, P. 136
management: attitudes of managers to
        business case for gender equality
        165–70
Manning, A. 65, 212
marriage 3, 7; *see also* financial
        togetherness and autonomy within
        couples
maternity leave 49, 62, 65, 212–14, 221
Meyers, M.K. 175
migration
    precarious employment and migrant
        workers 14, 123–5
        agency employment and economic
            migration 130–32
        constructing transnational labour
            force 135–43
        data from hotel and hospital in
            London 132–5
        growth of service sector
            employment 125–7
        local jobs, global workers 143–6
        new transnational labour force
            127–30

Netherlands 76, 89
    childcare 215
    parental leave 213
    trends in gender division of labour
        83
    trends in paid work time 77, 78, 212
    trends in unpaid work time 80, 209
    women's employment 12
    work–family conflict and well-being
        178, 181, 185, 186, 188
Norway 76, 89
    trends in gender division of labour 83
    trends in paid work time 77, 78
    trends in unpaid work time 81
    work–family conflict and well-being
        181, 188

Opportunity Now 157, 161, 166
Organisation for Economic
        Co-operation and Development
        (OECD) 125, 130
Orlof, A.S. 175

parental leave 4, 49, 62, 65, 212–14, 221
Parker, R. 127
part-time employment 68, 209, 212
  pay penalty 64–5
  women's careers after childbirth and 62–4
Peck, J. 129
pension funds 153, 162–3
Peter, F. 104
Petrongolo, B. 65, 212
Poland 123
Portanti, M. 8
Portugal 212, 213
poverty 5
  adult socio-economic disadvantage and child poverty 39
precarious employment and migrant workers 14, 123–5
  agency employment and economic migration 130–32
  constructing transnational labour force 135–7
    new European labour force at hotel 137–41
    older post-colonial labour force at hospital 141–3
  data from hotel and hospital in London 132–5
  growth of service sector employment 125–7
  local jobs, global workers 143–6
  new transnational labour force 127–30
privacy 103
Purcell, K. 12

quality of life
  work–family conflict and well-being 14–15, 174–6, 188–98
    association of work–family conflict and well-being 186–8
    background literature 176–9
    data and measures 181
    hypotheses 179–80
    key variables 181–4
    multivariate regression analysis 188
    summary, discussion and conclusions 198–201

work status, family life course and gender 184–6

Rake, K. 104
refugees 123
regulation 154
reproduction 5
  childbirth 3, 48, 51
    maternity leave 49, 62, 65, 212–14, 221
    women's careers after childbirth 62–4
  fertility control 3
Robeyns, I. 98
Russell, H. 177, 180, 196

Sen, Amartya 106, 107, 175
service sector employment 125–7
Sigle-Rushton, W. 199
Slater, G. 131
Slovenia 82
social class 2, 24, 59
social housing, adult socio-economic disadvantage and 24, 39–40, 41–2, 43–4
socially responsible investment (SRI) 153, 162, 163, 164–5
Sonnenberg, S. 101
Spain 5, 82, 213, 215
Sweden 3, 76, 89
  childcare 217
  parental leave 212, 213, 221
  trends in paid work time 79
  trends in unpaid work time 80, 81
  work–family balance 218
    well-being and 177, 178, 181, 185, 186, 188, 196
Switzerland 12

Taylor, R. 174, 177
time-use studies 174
  gender equality in paid and unpaid work 13, 74–5
  data and measures 75–6
  multinational time-use study of gender equality in paid and unpaid work
    gender segregation within unpaid work 83–7
    summary and implications 89–92

trends in gender division of labour
        82–3
trends in paid work time 76–80
trends in total work time (isowork)
        87–9
trends in unpaid work time 80–82
togetherness, *see* financial togetherness
        and autonomy within couples
total social organisation of labour
        (TSOL) 18–19
trade unions 162–3
Turnbull Report 156

unemployment 53
United Kingdom 3–4, 76, 89
    business case for gender equality 14,
        18, 153–4, 158–60, 170–71
        attitudes of investors 161–5
        attitudes of managers 165–70
        research methods 160–61
    changing career trajectories of
        women and men across time 13,
        48–51, 65–6
        birth cohorts' lives and their
            context 51–4
        career progression over the life
            course 57–60
        creating vertical occupational scale
            54
        first occupations 54–7
        part-time pay penalty 64–5
        policy response 66–8
        starting out in low paid
            occupation 61
        women's careers after childbirth
            62–4
    childcare 215, 217–18
    childhood origins of adult socio-
        economic disadvantage 12–13,
        23, 42–4
        analytic strategy 32–8
        control variables 27–32
        data and methods of study 25–38
        gender and cohort interactions
            41–2
        literature review 23–5
        outcome measures 26
        results of study 15–16, 38–42
    corporate social responsibility (CSR)
        153

financial togetherness and autonomy
        within couples 13, 97–9, 115–17
    concepts and focus of study
        99–100
    exploring togetherness and
        financial autonomy through
        qualitative research 101–5
    quantitative analysis of factors
        influencing 'autonomy' and
        'togetherness' 106–15
    reflections on findings 16, 105–6
    samples for study 100
gender segregation within unpaid
        work 83, 87
parental leave 212, 213, 214
precarious employment and migrant
        workers 14, 123–5
    agency employment and economic
        migration 130–32
    constructing transnational labour
        force 135–43
    data from hotel and hospital in
        London 132–5
    growth of service sector
        employment 125–7
    local jobs, global workers 143–6
    new transnational labour force
        127–30
trends in gender division of labour
        83
trends in paid work time 76, 78, 212
trends in unpaid work time 81, 209
university education 9
wages and salaries 10–12
    legal and policy initiatives for pay
        equality 155–7
women's employment in 8, 9–10, 12,
        74, 78
work–family balance 207, 219,
        221–2
    well-being and 174–5, 177, 178,
        181, 186, 188, 201
United Nations Principles for
        Responsible Investment 162
United States of America 76, 89
    childcare 215
    maternity leave 212
    trends in gender division of labour
        83
    trends in paid work time 76

trends in unpaid work time 81
women's employment in 74, 208
university education 9
unpaid work, *see* domestic work

Vogler, C. 104

wages and salaries
    business case for gender equality 14,
        18, 153–4, 158–60, 170–71
        attitudes of investors 161–5
        attitudes of managers 165–70
        research methods 160–61
    childhood difficulties and 24
    inequalities in 2, 5, 10–12, 48
    legal and policy initiatives 155–7
    Kingsmill Review 66–7
    minimum wages 52
    part-time pay penalty 64–5
    see also financial togetherness and
        autonomy within couples
Waldinger, R. 139

Walker, K.E. 76
welfare systems 97–8
well-being
    work–family conflict and well-being
        14–15, 174–6, 188–98
        association of work–family
            conflict and well-being 186–8
        background literature 176–9
        data and measures 181
        hypotheses 179–80
        key variables 181–4
        multivariate regression analysis
            188
        summary, discussion and
            conclusions 198–201
        work status, family life course and
            gender 184–6
Whitworth, S. 8
Women and Work Commission 67, 68,
    156
Woods, M.E. 76
work, *see* domestic work; employment